By the same author

Theodora: Portrait in a Byzantine Landscape
The Crusades

Antony Bridge

✠ ✠ ✠

Suleiman the Magnificent

Scourge of Heaven

DORSET PRESS

New York

Contents

List of Illustrations

Preface

'I believe that the supreme duty of the historian is to write history, that is to say, to attempt to record in one sweeping sequence the great events and movements that have swayed the destinies of men.' Thus wrote Sir Steven Runciman in the preface to the first volume of his *History of the Crusades*, and it is a definition of the historian's task which even those who make no pretensions to his scholarship and cannot hope to emulate the sweep of his narrative would do well to remember; for in the words of Fernand Braudel, 'history can do more than study walled gardens'. As historians, both Runciman and Braudel are giants, their works monumental in scope and achievement, but it is not everyone who has either the time to embark on works of such magnitude or perhaps the taste for such things. It is, therefore, in the hope and belief that there is a place for shorter works of less magisterial compass than that of the historical *magnum opus* that I have written this book, the theme of which is nevertheless one of the great movements that have swayed the destinies of men.

Indeed, it is concerned with the most fascinating and to my mind the greatest of all the movements of history: the ebb and flow of men and ideas between East and West. It probably started in prehistoric times with the great migratory movements of neolithic tribes of nomadic shepherds and hunters; but historically it began with the westward drive of the Persians under Darius and his son Xerxes, checked first at Marathon and foundering ten years later in the Bay of Salamis, and it was followed 165 years later by the astonishing response of the Greeks under Alexander, who crossed the Bosphorus into Asia in the spring of 334 BC, and took the tide of western arms and ideas as far as Afghanistan and India. Thus the pattern of expansion and recession, ebb and flow, challenge and response and the resulting collision of nations, civilizations and religions was set. It was a pattern which was to determine the course of history for centuries to come, for after the Greeks came the Romans and Byzantines, who were followed by the Arabs and the Seljuk Turks under the banners of Islam, and they in their turn gave way to the Crusaders; and so it has gone on right down to our own day, when a new and precarious point in East–West relations has been reached after fifty years of unprecedentedly rapid western retreat at the end of centuries of equally unprecedented expansion eastwards.

The subject of this book is perhaps the least well-known episode in this continuing saga, namely the counter-Crusade by the Ottoman Turks against western Christendom, which followed the extinction of the Frankish kingdoms in the Middle East, and which culminated in the sixteenth century. The fact that it is so little known is surprising, for not only is it a fascinating period in itself, but its pains and struggles also proved to be the birth pangs of the modern world, which should be of interest to us who live in it. I suspect, too, that a look at it in all its nobility and squalor with its consuming passions and unquestioned certainties, its achievements and brutalities, may even help us to see our own passions and certainties and their crop of wars and brutalities a little more clearly than we might otherwise see them.

Since I have not attempted to produce a comprehensive history of the period but something much less ambitious, I have had to be ruthlessly selective when deciding what to include and what to leave out. I should have liked to have said more on a number of subjects; for instance, Suleiman's most lasting achievement was in the field of Islamic law revision and codification, but since that aspect of his work was not strictly relevant to the story I was telling, I have done no more than mention it. In the same way, I have virtually ignored Turkish social history and economic affairs, and I have mentioned only briefly the desperate financial straits in which both the Emperor Charles V and Francis I of France found themselves as a result of the chronic inflation of their times and the incessant warfare which they waged. These omissions were regrettable, but they left me free to do two things: first, to give an account of the main events in the epic struggle between East and West, Islam and Christendom, Ottoman Turkey and the newly born nation states of western Europe, which culminated during the reign of Sultan Suleiman the Magnificent of Turkey; and, secondly, since history is about people and their experiences, to try to bring that account alive by describing some of the vivid and evocative everyday incidents in the lives and feelings of those people, great and small, who were caught up in the drama of their times. I have done this, not for scholars, but in the hope that it may be of some interest to the intelligent general reader. If there is any virtue in the result, the credit must go to the many historians whose works I have raided, and to whom I am grateful for many things; while its faults and inadequacies are my own.

Chronology

1534   Khaireddin Barbarossa, north African corsair, becomes admiral
       of the Turkish fleet
       Charles V captures Tunis
1536   Charles invades Provence, but is forced to retire
       Ibrahim is executed by order of Suleiman
1537   Suleiman declares war on Venice, raids southern Italy and
       besieges Corfu, but fails to take it
1538   John Zapolya, claimant of Hungarian throne, marries Isabella
       of Poland
       Indecisive naval battle at Preveza
1541   Suleiman marries his Russian concubine, Roxelana, the
       mother of three of his sons
1543   Barbarossa and the Turkish fleet in alliance with France attack
       the coastal towns of Italy; Nice is captured and sacked, and
       Toulon occupied by the Turks to the horror of Christendom
1544   Charles invades France
1545   Barbarossa again attacks the coastal towns of Italy
       Armistice is signed between Suleiman and Ferdinand
1546   Death of Martin Luther, and a little later Barbarossa dies
1547   Death of Henry VIII and accession of Edward VI
       Peace treaty signed between Austria and Turkey
       Francis I dies
1550   Giovanni Maria del Monte crowned Pope Julius III
1553   Suleiman orders the murder of his eldest son, Mustafa
1554   Ogier Ghiselin de Busbecq becomes imperial ambassador to
       the Sultan's court in Constantinople
1556   Thomas Cranmer is burnt at the stake
       The Suleimaniye Mosque in Constantinople is inaugurated
       Charles's son becomes Philip II of Spain
1557   Charles retires to Yuste in Estremadura
1558   Death of Roxelana
       Charles dies at Yuste
1561   Civil war between Suleiman's sons, Selim and Bayezid, flight
       of Bayezid to Persia, and his execution by Suleiman's
       command
1566   The siege of Malta
       Turks besiege Sziget, but Suleiman dies before news of its fall
       reaches him
1570   Selim II the Sot orders the invasion of Cyprus
1571   Formation of a Holy League against the Turks
       Christian fleet under command of Don John of Austria defeats
       the Turks at the battle of Lepanto

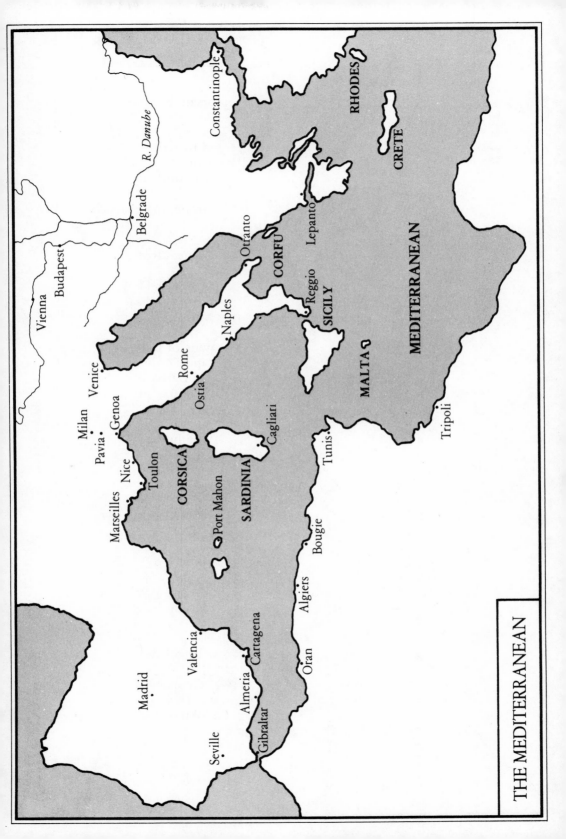

THE MEDITERRANEAN

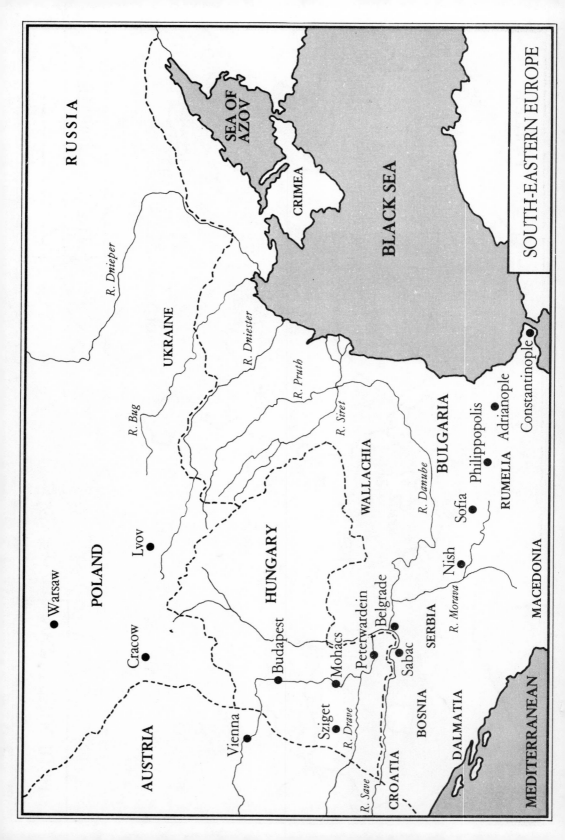

SOUTH-EASTERN EUROPE

RUSSIA

SEA OF AZOV

CRIMEA

BLACK SEA

R. Dnieper

UKRAINE

R. Dniester

R. Pruth

R. Siret

R. Bug

BULGARIA

Philippopolis

Adrianople

Constantinople

RUMELIA

Sofia

R. Danube

WALLACHIA

Nish

MACEDONIA

POLAND

Lvov

HUNGARY

R. Morava

Warsaw

Cracow

Budapest

Peterwardein

Belgrade

SERBIA

Mohacs

Sabac

Vienna

Sziget

R. Drave

BOSNIA

DALMATIA

AUSTRIA

CROATIA

R. Save

MEDITERRANEAN

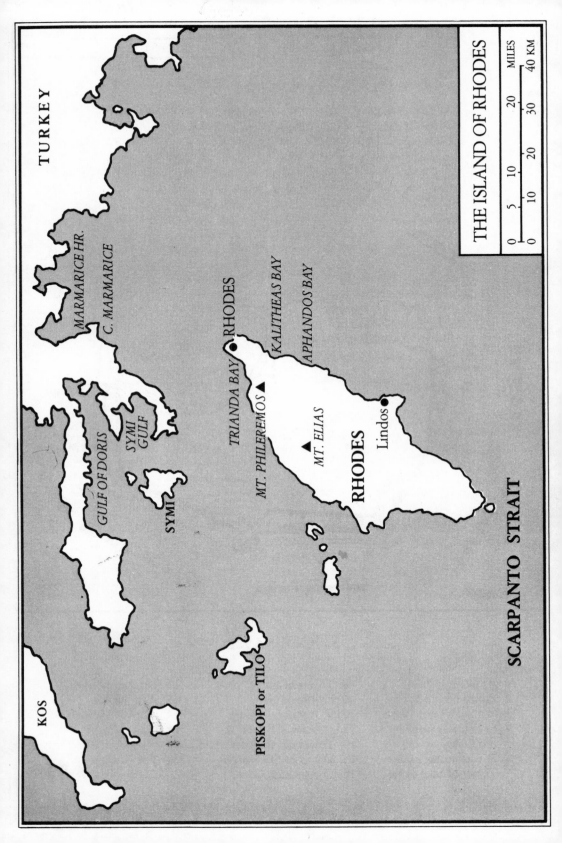

THE ISLAND OF RHODES

TURKEY

MARMARICE HR.
C. MARMARICE

GULF OF DORIS

SYMI GULF

SYMI

KOS

PISKOPI or TILO

TRIANDA BAY
RHODES

KALITHEAS BAY

APHANDOS BAY

MT. PHILEREMOS

MT. ELIAS

RHODES

Lindos

SCARPANTO STRAIT

MILES
0   5   10   20
0   10   20   30   40 KM

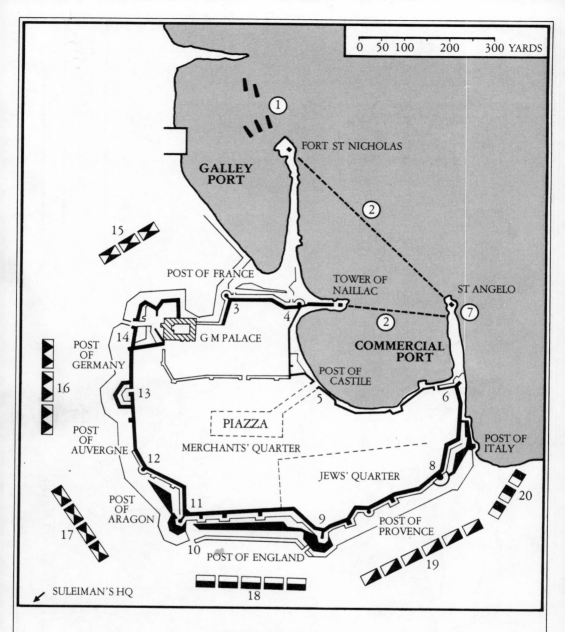

RHODES 1522

1 Blockships	8 Tower of Italy	15 Janissaries
2 Boom Defence	9 St John's Gate	16 Ayas Pasha
3 St Paul's Gate	10 St Anthony's Gate	17 Ahmed Pasha
4 St Peter's Gate	11 St Mary's Tower	18 Qasim Pasha
5 Sea Gate	12 Tower of Aragon (Spain)	19 Mustafa Pasha
6 St Catherine's Gate	13 Tower of St George	20 Piri Pasha
7 Tower of St Angelo	14 D'Amboise Gate	

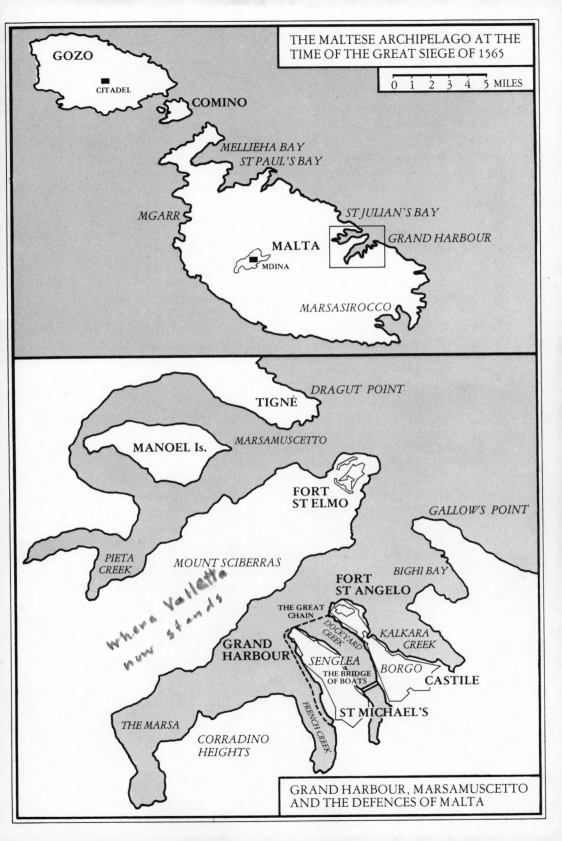

THE MALTESE ARCHIPELAGO AT THE
TIME OF THE GREAT SIEGE OF 1565

0 1 2 3 4 5 MILES

GOZO

CITADEL

COMINO

MELLIEHA BAY
ST PAUL'S BAY

MGARR

ST JULIAN'S BAY

MALTA

GRAND HARBOUR

MDINA

MARSASIROCCO

DRAGUT POINT

TIGNÉ

MANOEL Is.

MARSAMUSCETTO

FORT
ST ELMO

GALLOWS POINT

PIETA
CREEK

MOUNT SCIBERRAS

Where Valletta
now stands

FORT
ST ANGELO

BIGHI BAY

THE GREAT CHAIN

DOCKYARD CREEK

KALKARA
CREEK

GRAND
HARBOUR

SENGLEA

THE BRIDGE
OF BOATS

BORGO

CASTILE

FRENCH CREEK

ST MICHAEL'S

THE MARSA

CORRADINO
HEIGHTS

GRAND HARBOUR, MARSAMUSCETTO
AND THE DEFENCES OF MALTA

Suleiman the Magnificent

I

✠ ✠ ✠

The Womb of Time

There are many events in the womb of time, which will be delivered.

Shakespeare, *Othello*

The Middle Ages died in the year 1500, or so it has been said. If so, no one noticed their passing or the birth of the new world which was about to replace them. Yet some of the men destined to shape and form that world were born between 1475 and 1500 in the final quarter of the last medieval century. In 1475, the wife of an Ipswich butcher, who was churchwarden of St Nicholas's Church in that city, gave birth to a son; his parents named him Thomas, but the world was to know him as Cardinal Wolsey. In March of the same year, the wife of an impoverished gentleman of Florence named Ludovico Buonarotti also gave birth to a son, who was destined to become famous by his baptismal name of Michelangelo; and before the year was out the Medici family was increased by the birth of another boy, Giovanni, who grew up to become Pope Leo X. Two years later (or thereabouts, for the date is uncertain) in the small town of Cadore in the Friuli, Lucia Vecelli presented her husband, Gregorio, with a son; the child was named Tiziano or Titian, and a few years later still, in 1483, Raphael was born in Urbino. In the same year Hans and Margarethe Luther, German peasants of Mansfeld in Thuringia, had a son whom they named Martin. In 1485, Ismail I of Persia, a remarkable man whose name remains undeservedly obscure in the West, was born, while six years later and half a world away Henry VIII of England first saw the light of day on 28 June 1491 at Greenwich. Spanning the world again, the years 1494 and 1495 saw the births of Francis I of

France, head of the house of Valois, and of Suleiman the Magnificent, Sultan of Turkey and head of the house of Osman, the founder of the Ottoman dynasty; while to crown it all Charles Habsburg, who was destined to become King of Spain and Holy Roman Emperor, was born to the purple at more or less the same time as, more humbly and a social world away, a maker of musical instruments in Florence was having his third child baptized Benvenuto. The father's name was Cellini.

The list is far from exhaustive, and some of these people were fated to play more conspicuous parts in the drama of their times than others; but all were going to help fashion the world of the sixteenth century to a greater or lesser extent. One of them, however, was to dominate it for the best part of fifty years. It would be an exaggeration to say of Suleiman, as Cassius said of Julius Caesar, that he did 'bestride the narrow world like a Colossus; and we petty men walk under his huge legs, and peep about to find ourselves dishonourable graves'; for the sixteenth century was rich in men who, far from being petty or dishonourable, were Suleiman's peers and even, in some cases and in some respects, his superiors. But in his influence upon the course of events in his own time he was unique, even the Emperor Charles V being forced during most of his long life to dance to the tune called by the Sultan in Constantinople.

Perhaps the nearest modern analogy to Suleiman's place in the world of his day and his influence upon the lives and fortunes of millions of his contemporaries in countries as far apart as Persia and England on the one hand and Egypt and Poland on the other is provided by Hitler's place in international affairs in the thirties and forties of our own century, when it seemed that the rest of the world was helpless to do anything but react to whatever he chose to do, either by frantic attempts to appease him or by belated and inadequate measures to frustrate him. Fortunately for our own world, Hitler's demonic hegemony lasted for no more than a dozen bloody years. The world of the sixteenth century had to live with the terrifying and ubiquitous political menace of Suleiman the Magnificent for nearly four times as long as that, from the time of his accession in 1520 until he died in 1566, and the experience had such an effect that people still speak about the Turks from time to time as if they were a nation of brutal and bloodthirsty barbarians with a few decadent perverts thrown in. In fact, they are no more brutal than anyone else, nor were they so in Suleiman's day; but this made little difference to the terror and repulsion which they inspired in their Christian opponents, most of whom were convinced by their own propaganda that all Turks were unspeakably evil and Suleiman the Devil himself. In fact, he was a devout Moslem, a just and generous man most of the time, and no more callous or brutal than the majority of his contemporaries; he had his faults, which will become apparent during the course of this story, but there is little doubt that as a statesman he was the greatest of all the Ottoman Sultans and as a man one of the most remarkable products of that perennially remarkable historical phenomenon, the world of the sixteenth century.

Although this is not the place for an exhaustive description of that world, a brief look at it may not be out of place here; for in certain respects, it was a world surprisingly like our own. Social changes were taking place, though on an incomparably smaller scale and much more slowly than has been the case in our own time, and one of the contributory causes of this slow change, then as now, was inflation of the money supply, for the influx of gold and other treasure from the New World increased as the century progressed. As in our own day, too, western Europe was under constant threat by a large, autocratic superpower in the East with a radically different ideology from her own, namely Ottoman Turkey; and then as now the various peoples and countries of eastern Europe and the Balkans were largely impotent to affect the course of events, for they were either occupied by the armed forces of their eastern neighbour or governed by one of its puppets.

But if there are political and military similarities between the world of the sixteenth century and that of today, the differences are much greater, and some of these are easily overlooked or forgotten. For instance, histories of the time speak of Spain, France, England, Germany, Poland, Hungary, Russia and the rest, and it is only too easy to imagine that they are speaking of the countries with which we are familiar, as they appear today on modern maps; but this is not so. To give a few examples only, in the territorial area which we think of as Spain – that is to say, the Iberian peninsula apart from Portugal – a number of small kingdoms had come together over the years to form the kingdoms of Castile and Leon, on the one hand, and the quite separate kingdom of Aragon, on the other, and these were not united until as late as 1479, when the marriage of Ferdinand of Aragon to Isabella of Castile brought the two together. Meanwhile, the Moorish kingdom of Granada did not succumb to Christian arms until thirteen years later in 1492, when at last the map of Spain assumed the political shape which it has retained ever since. France, too, was very different then from what it is today; although it had perhaps made slightly more progress towards unity than any other European state, in the closing years of the fifteenth century much of her territory was subject more to the nominal jurisdiction of the kings of France than to any real authority exercised by them. The dukes of Burgundy, who also owned the counties of Charolais, Mâcon, Auxerre, Bar-sur-Seine,

Ponthieu, the Somme towns, Artois and Flanders together with extensive possessions in the Netherlands, had taken the English side in the Hundred Years War, and were accustomed to act as independent sovereigns in their own right when it suited them to do so, largely regardless of the kings of France, whose subjects technically they were. Similarly, the heads of the great feudal houses of Bourbon, Orleans, Anjou, Dreux, Armagnac and Foix, *de facto* if not *de jure*, had always enjoyed an independence, which they guarded jealously. Germany consisted of a number of small principalities, which were united more by a common language than by anything else, though they owed a vague allegiance to the Holy Roman Emperors, who were chosen by various Electors to sit on the throne of Charlemagne. At the same time, after the exhaustion of the disastrous Hundred Years War, England had been torn apart by the Wars of the Roses, to emerge weary of the viciousness and brutality of war and determined to preserve her fragile unity under the Tudors; and this meant ensuring that the king should have an heir around whom everyone could rally at his death rather than plunging back into the horrors of civil war. It is no wonder that, when he eventually came to the throne, Henry VIII was determined to find someone to bear him a son. What was the fate of a few wives when weighed in the balance against another war? Hungary, geographically very similar to what it is today, was so divided socially by hatred between the rulers and the ruled as to be virtually two nations living within the same borders; while Russia as we know it came into being only in the latter half of the fifteenth century, when the long period of Mongol domination was finally brought to an end, and the various petty principalities ruled by virtually independent grand princes were brought under the autocratic rule of the Tsars of Muscovy during the reign of Ivan III.

If the political face of western Europe began to take on a new look as the fifteenth century gave way to the sixteenth, gradually becoming more like the Europe of today with which we are all familiar, it was also having to face a new challenge, which medieval Europe had not known. For over a thousand years, the Byzantine Empire had stood between the people of western Europe and wave after wave of barbarian invaders from Asia; Huns, Goths, Avars, Pechenegs, Arabs and Seljuk Turks had all fought their way westwards in search of new lands in which to settle with their wives and children and their flocks, but all of them had broken on the rock of Byzantium. Many of these Asiatic nomads had actually washed up around the walls of Constantinople itself, but as long as the Byzantine army was still intact behind its formidable battlements, and its navy was safely at anchor in the Golden Horn, the Empire had not been beaten, and in the end the waves of nomadic invaders had always been forced to retreat, receding again in a great tide of men and tents and horses into the wastes of Asia. In much the same way, after the rise of Islam and its militant expansion in the eighth century, Moslem armies had swarmed across Asia Minor on several occasions, reaching the Asiatic shore of the Bosphorus in a fine fury of fundamentalist faith and homicidal anti-Christian intent, only to be halted by the sight of the forbidding towers and frowning walls of Constantinople across the narrow water. All this had changed, however, on Wednesday, 29 May 1453, when 'the city defended by God', as the Byzantines described their capital, had fallen to the men of the Turkish Sultan Mehmed II, and the shield behind which the people of western Europe had been given a thousand years' grace to bicker and fight each other had been shattered once and for all. From that day, the invasion of Europe by the Ottoman Turks had become inevitable; indeed, it had already begun, for they had already spread out over some of the eastern Balkans.

Western Europe was ill-prepared to meet their assault. It had known little but war for centuries, though there had been a few breathing spaces of peace during which the various nations recovered sufficiently to embark on the next conflict, which as often as not was the result of dynastic disputes with their claims and counter-claims by the ruling families of Europe. The worst of these medieval wars had been the Hundred Years War in France, which had left the country desolate and ravaged. It had ended in 1453, the year in which Constantinople had fallen to Mehmed the Conqueror, and so devastating had it been that as long as thirty years later the vast majority of Frenchmen were living in conditions of misery, and the population of the country was probably about half what it had been a century and a half earlier. Foreign armies had spared no one, and bands of French soldiers had been almost as bad, plundering the country unmercifully, burning, pillaging, raping and murdering wherever they went, until life had been made almost impossible for everyone else. A sober English statesman, Sir John Fortescue, who knew the country well, was appalled by what he saw when travelling through France after the war. He found peasants trying to keep alive on a diet of brown bread and water unvaried by a taste of meat unless it was the sodden refuse from the kitchens of the rich; their clothes were made of coarse canvas, their legs were bare, and their feet unshod. So difficult was their struggle to keep alive that 'they have gone crokyd and ar feble, not able to fyght, nor to defend the Realme; nor have they wepon, nor monye to buy them wepon withall; but verily they lyvin in the most extreme Povertie and Miserye, and they dwellyn in one of the most fertile Realmes in the Worlde'.

But even in countries not suffering from the immediate after-effects of war, life was far from secure. Those who managed to run the gauntlet of deadly diseases in infancy and childhood were well aware how lucky they were. They lived with the ever-present possibility of death, and the effect of this radical insecurity on the way in which they lived their lives was far-reaching. Since they could never count with certainty on being alive next year, next month, or even next week, they lived from day to day with a gusto and a kind of decisiveness which, in historical retrospect, looks both enviably vigorous and yet also terrifyingly volatile. At their best, they dared, they ventured, they took every flood-tide which fortune offered them, and were carried along on the turbulent waters of their time, until they either triumphed or drowned; often they lived with a selfless dedication to the things in which they believed and with a sublime courage which was magnificent; while at their worst they were selfish, brutal, cruel and utterly callous of the sufferings of others. Husbands beat their wives; parents thrashed their children; village fought with village; street brawls broke out everywhere, and men killed, as a savage kills, with enjoyment and without a qualm. Public executions were enormously popular and conducted only too often with great barbarity. Johan Huizinga, the Dutch historian, has recorded the fact that the citizens of Mons actually bought a criminal for a large sum of money in order to enjoy the spectacle of him being quartered, 'at which the people rejoiced more than if a holy body had been raised from the dead'. In 1488, the citizens of Bruges so much enjoyed the sight of a number of traitors being publicly tortured on a high platform in the middle of the market place that they threatened to injure the executioner if he should give his victims the *coup de grâce* a moment before every last drop of pleasure had been wrung from the sight of their sufferings. Etienne Ponchier, Bishop of Paris, had to issue a decree in 1500 insisting that condemned criminals should have the right to make a last confession before their execution, and not be denied it by people who wanted them to die unshriven so that they might go straight to hell with its eternal pains. There had been a case a few years earlier of an impoverished nobleman who had been hanged for turning brigand, but not before a high official of the French Court, who hated him for some reason, had mounted the scaffold, shouting insults and beating him with his stick before thrashing the executioner for exhorting the condemned man to think of his eternal salvation; the hangman had become so nervous that he had bungled his task, the rope had broken, the wretched criminal had fallen to the ground where he had broken a leg and some ribs, and in this condition he had been forced to climb the ladder again before a crowd of cheering spectators to suffer at last a lingering and painful death at the rope's end.

But if some people of the time were callous and brutal, while others were magnificent in their courage and nobility of spirit, most of them were a mixture of the two; and it was not only in the manner in which they alternated between kindness and cruelty, selfless generosity and murderous violence that they showed their volatility, for their moods of despair during times of disaster, pestilence or famine would change into outbursts of bubbling gaiety and rejoicing at the smallest sign of relief. At one minute people might be weeping and bewailing the misery of being alive, and at the next they would break out singing, dancing and revelling as though the whole of existence was a pageant. Johan Huizinga was right when he said that life was so motley at the end of the Middle Ages that 'it bore the mixed smell of blood and roses'. People oscillated between hatred and love, harsh asceticism and passionate attachment to the delights of this world, the fear of hell and a childish enjoyment of forbidden fruit precisely because it was forbidden; and their attitude towards religion, too, was a curious compound of apparently irreconcilable attitudes and practices. To someone brought up in a Protestant or neo-Protestant country, the religious scene at the beginning of the sixteenth century does not inspire much enthusiasm. As J. S. C. Bridge has remarked in his *History of France*, 'though dominant to outward appearance, religion was a matter of forms and ceremonies; in the empty ritual of prescribed observances there was nothing to elevate conduct or ennoble belief; and the laity found no incentive to godly living in the example of worldly prelates and of ignorant and licentious priests. Superstition flourished, and there was widespread belief in sorcery and witchcraft and the efficacy of charms, amulets and spells. Blasphemy, immorality, drunkenness and gluttony were prevailing sins. Public opinion did not condemn the illicit amour; bastards were openly acknowledged and brought up as younger sons; there were brothels everywhere; and the terms "housekeeper" and "servant-maid" were habitually used with a signification which leaves little doubt about the moral standard of the age.' Even those who were supposed to be the guardians of public morals sometimes behaved in ways which still have the power to astonish. In 1535, Pope Paul III sent his son, Pierluigi Farnese, as ambassador to the court of the Emperor Charles V with a threefold brief: he was to try to fathom the Emperor's political intentions, to make a good impression, and to abstain from sodomy while staying with the Emperor.

But if much of what has been adduced in evidence against the religion and morals of the time is true, it is not the whole truth; for behind the so-called empty forms and rituals, despite the worldliness of most prelates and the debauchery of many priests, side by side with the superstition and the credulity and notwithstanding the widespread enjoyment of fornication and adultery, there was a solid and enduring structure of belief in God, in the redemptive work of Christ, in the divine mission of the Church, however corrupt it might be, and in man's eternal destiny as a member of the Church, which few people doubted. It was a faith which might not moderate men's appetites or make much difference to their ability to control their passions, but it gave purpose and point to their lives, it offered them a way to cope with their sins and guilts, and while threatening them with damnation if they did not tread that way in the time available to them in this mortal life, to those who did so it held out the hope of glory beyond death: a hope without which it would have been even more difficult than it already was to live their lives, overshadowed by death as they were, in anything like a fully human manner. It was a faith, too, which drove some men and women to lead lives of extraordinary self-sacrifice and heroic sanctity; many more were prepared to fight and, if needs be, to die in its defence, while others risked their lives in order to reform its abuses. Indeed, many people felt so strongly about the Christian faith that the sixteenth century gave rise to the great reformers – the Dutchman Erasmus (born in the previous century), Luther the German monk, Zwingli of Switzerland, and Calvin, who was born in Picardy and studied theology in Paris – whose various teachings split every western European country down the middle, giving rise to endless religious strife. Thus the faith of the day, though it expressed itself in forms and ceremonies which may seem trivial and perfunctory to a later age, was far from being a mere matter of empty ritual to the people who practised it, and who believed what they believed with a good deal more passion than is often evinced by their latter-day critics: a passion, indeed, which was one of the major causes of their disunity.

The other was dynastic. The ambition of their rulers, most of whom were at bitter odds with each other much of the time in a bloody contest for pre-eminence, deeply divided them and diverted their attention from the common danger of Turkish invasion. But although their behaviour was sometimes peacock-like to the point of absurdity, nearly always devious, often brutal and usually unedifying, it is difficult not to find them fascinating as men; for they were the principal actors in one of the great dramas of history, and as they played their parts in the events of their day, they did so with such verve and style that, in retrospect, there is a magnificence about them which makes them appear to be a little larger than life. In fact, whatever else may be said of the Emperor Charles V, his brother Ferdinand, Francis I of France, Henry VIII of England and many of the men who surrounded them, they were princes of the Renaissance on the grand scale, and even if they had most of the faults typical of their time they also embodied much of its splendour. Unlike the succession of dreary if ruthless dictators, stereotyped generals and pre-packaged politicians who follow each other in the seats of power in our world, the men who ruled the world of the sixteenth century were seldom mediocre or boring. It is time to look at some of them.

II

✠ ✠ ✠

The Thrust of Greatness

Be not afraid of greatness; some men are born great, some achieve greatness, and some have greatness thrust upon them.

Shakespeare, *Twelfth Night*

In the drama of the Ottoman assault upon Europe at the height of Islam's counter-Crusade against Christendom in the sixteenth century, the principal player on the Christian side was Charles of the house of Habsburg, the elder son of Philip the Fair of Austria and Joanna the Mad of Aragon and Castile. He was born at Ghent on 24 February 1500, and while he was still a babe-in-arms his parents departed for Spain, leaving him behind in Flanders. Three years later, their younger son Ferdinand was born at Alcalá-de-Henares, and Joanna began to show signs of the madness which was to plague her for the rest of her life; by the time Philip died two years later, she was completely insane.

It was not an auspicious beginning for the infant Charles, but fortunately he was too young to be consciously affected by the disasters which befell his family at this time. As a result of them, however, he was still a mere child when he was thrust precipitately into his inheritance, which was a remarkable one even by the standards of the day. Dynastically, he was so desirable that, even before the death of his parents, when Charles himself was not quite two years old, he was engaged to be married to the little Princess Claude of France, Louis XII's daughter, who was not quite three, though as things turned out their engagement did not last long. At the age of seven, as soon as his father was safely in his tomb, he was crowned Duke of Burgundy and acknowledged as Count of Flanders and heir to his father's possessions in the Netherlands; at the same time, in Brussels he was proclaimed King of Castile, though his Spanish subjects were slower to pay him the same compliment, waiting until 1518, when they finally recognized him conjointly with his hopelessly deranged mother. Then, when his grandfather, the Emperor Maximilian, died, Charles entered into his Habsburg inheritance at the age of twenty; the duchy of Württemberg was soon added to it, and after an enormous expenditure in bribes and a hasty visit to Henry VIII of England and his then wife, Catherine of Aragon, Charles's aunt, despite the opposition of Pope Leo X and the bitter rivalry of Francis I of France, on 23 October 1520, when he was just twenty years old, he was crowned King of the Romans – a euphemism for German King – at Aix-la-Chappelle. Three days later, he received the Pope's somewhat grudging permission to use the style of Emperor Elect of the Holy Roman Empire pending his coronation.

As inheritances go, that which descended upon Charles sounds formidable, and so it was; indeed, it was even more formidable than it sounds, for each element in it brought further titles and possessions. The crown of Castile brought with it the two recently conquered kingdoms of Navarre and Granada together with the new colonies in America and a handful of scattered possessions in North Africa; that of Aragon comprised the three states of Aragon, Valencia and Catalonia, and in addition the kingdoms of Naples, Sicily and Sardinia, which were to cause Charles endless trouble in the future; and then there were the Netherlands, which were rich enough to tempt him to impose extra taxes on them, when he desperately needed more money, and independent enough to revolt against him when he did so. His inheritance of the duchy of Burgundy, which had been lost in all but name by his great-grandfather, Charles the Bold, to the kings of France, who had incorporated it into their realm and had no intention of allowing anyone to take it away again, set him permanently at odds with the French; while his Habsburg inheritance set him against the Turks, who had threatened the whole of eastern Europe with invasion and domination ever since the fall of Constantinople half a century earlier, and who continued to do so. The task of governing such an enormous, scattered and precarious domain was not made any easier by the rise of Protestantism during Charles's reign, nor by the fact that his finances never recovered from the enormous expenditure which he incurred during the massive campaign of bribery which had secured his election as Emperor. But Charles was equal to the challenge, for in an age famous for the splendour of its princes, despite the circumstances of his childhood, he turned out to be the most splendid of them all: not the most ostentatious, nor the most concerned with his own magnificence –

'Monsieur François' of France, Henry of England, several Popes and Suleiman of Turkey all outdid him in their ebullient exhibitionism and in their almost child-like vanity – but the most able, the most humane, and the most modest of the Renaissance princes and thus, in some people's judgement, the greatest of them all.

His remarkable inheritance was the result of his equally remarkable ancestry; the blood of Byzantine Emperors of the house of Paleologus mingled in his veins with that of almost every ruling family in Europe. Some of his forebears had been Castilian, some Portuguese, three French, two Plantagenets, an Italian, a Pole, a Lithuanian, and a number of German Habsburgs. If rumour is to be believed, there may have been a drop or two of Moorish blood in him and a trace of never-to-be-mentioned Jewish blood too, the legacy of a *mésalliance* between one of his remote ancestors and the daughter of a rich Jewish tax collector, who had bettered herself by marrying into the Spanish aristocracy. But eminent as was his actual ancestry, notwithstanding its Moorish and Jewish elements, it was nothing to that which he was taught to believe in. According to family legend, Charles was descended from a prince of the royal house of Troy, Priam, who had travelled to Austria and become king there, while yet another Trojan prince, Paris, had founded the city of that name, while his son, Francio, had given his name to France. In the time of Christ, the descendants of these founders of the family had renounced their crowns in deference to his divine kingship, but had nevertheless continued to breed a noble line of chivalrous Christian knights. Many of these had married into the royal houses of Christendom, while others had distinguished themselves in battle against the enemies of Christ, especially during the time of the Crusades. The Dukes of Burgundy shone with great lustre in these lengendary family annals as champions of Christendom who would have won back Constantinople and the lost lands of Byzantium from the Turks if they had had their way; but the meanness and avarice of the kings of France had always prevented them from achieving their noble aims, thus amply justifying the hostility of the house of Burgundy to the French monarchy.

Suckled on such romantic tales of family greatness, Charles grew up at Malines in the Low Countries in the care of Margaret of York, the childless and by this time elderly widow of Charles the Bold, lately Duke of Burgundy. Known as 'Madame la Grande' and much loved by all, she was the surviving sister of Edward IV of England, and it is perhaps not too fanciful to suppose that the earliest stories heard by the boy Charles were of the Wars of the Roses and of the vanished splendours of the Burgundian court: stories which would have reinforced the francophobe tradition of the family. But however this may have been, Margaret of York died when Charles was four, and her place was taken by another staunch Burgundian, Margaret of Austria, who liked to describe herself as *bonne Englese*, making no secret of the fact that she regarded England as the ally of her country, Burgundy, and France as the enemy of both. With such people around him in childhood, it is not surprising that Charles grew up to be obsessed with his Burgundian inheritance and wary of the king of France.

The greatness of his inheritance was not matched by a princely or imposing appearance. On the contrary, Charles was a rather insignificant, ill-favoured little man with a face made almost grotesque by a protruding lower jaw – the famous Habsburg lip – which ran in the family but was even more pronounced in him than it had been in his father or his grandfather. As a child he was shy, awkward and slow to learn, preferring to spend his time playing the spinet or the flute rather than learning Latin or some other academic subject; for he had a lifelong love of music, as indeed he had of painting too. Later in life, he was so delighted with the portrait which Titian painted of him, when he was in Bologna in 1532, that he issued letters patent creating the artist a Count Palatine and a Knight of the Golden Spur; these were unheard-of honours to be heaped upon a mere court painter, but Charles was not bothered by considerations of precedent, and formed a friendship with Titian which lasted for the rest of his life. As he grew to manhood, he lost the gaucherie of his earlier years, and it soon became apparent that, even if he was lacking in good looks, he had a natural charm and magnetism which were acknowledged by friends and enemies alike. As a man, too, he threw off his early aversion to academic work, and over the years he became the hardest-working monarch of his time and perhaps one of the hardest-working sovereigns of any time; he was conscientious almost to a fault, and determined to make good the omissions of his childhood. When he first arrived in Spain at the age of seventeen, his subjects there were horrified to find that he could not speak a word of Spanish; but they were no more dismayed than Charles, who set about learning the language, and succeeded so well that it became his native tongue. Indeed, it has been said that Charles 'was born in French and died in Spanish'. In addition, he spoke Flemish, German, and enough Italian and Latin to understand ambassadors when they addressed him in those languages, and there may be some truth in the celebrated story that he once said that French was the language he spoke to diplomats, Italian to women, German to stable-boys, and Spanish to God.

At the time of his birth, a Neapolitan astrologer, Lorenzo Miniate, predicted that Charles would become the greatest captain of his age.

Claims to overall supremacy in any field are always difficult to substantiate, but if he did not become the greatest commander of his time – and there are many who would claim that he did – he certainly became a soldier of distinction, whose greatest military ambition was to win battles with the least possible loss of life: an ambition for which his soldiers, not surprisingly, loved him. They loved him, too, for his courage and for his willingness to share the hardships and dangers of the battlefield with them. In a crisis he was always at his best, remaining cool and unflustered while others panicked, and demonstrating again and again his ability to pluck victory from the jaws of defeat; when violently attacked in the scorching heat of the desert just outside Tunis, when his men were stampeded outside Algiers, when he forded the Elbe at Muhlberg even though he was ill at the time, and when he came under the murderous fire of the vastly superior Lutheran artillery under the walls of Ingolstadt, it was his firmness and resolution which rallied his men and saved the day. It is no wonder that they admired him; tired as they often were, the sight of Charles sitting on his horse in the midst of a battle hour after hour, even though his leg had to be held in a sling because of the excruciating gout from which he was a chronic sufferer, was enough to give them the courage to endure almost any hardship as long as he was their leader, for they recognized a great soldier when they saw one.

But if anyone tried to flatter Charles by telling him how great his military achievements were, he was likely to receive the coldest of cold receptions; he disliked flattery. When he was told by someone who had commissioned some paintings of battles, in one of which French troops were to be shown running away from his own imperial soldiers after a conflict in 1554, Charles objected; there had been no rout, he said – the French had retreated in good order, and the artist should be told not to falsify facts or slander an honourable foe in the moment of his adversity. Magnanimity was natural to him, a by-product perhaps of two other virtues of which he showed ample evidence: honesty and modesty. There is a well-known story of Charles losing his way when out hunting and falling in with an old Spanish peasant, with whom he exchanged greetings and began to pass the time of day. The conversation came round to the subject of politics, and the old man said that he had seen the reigns of five kings, of whom the best, he reckoned, had been Ferdinand, and the worst 'this one we have now, always gadding about abroad, instead of staying in Spain, where he belongs'. While Charles was attempting to justify himself, the other members of his hunting party came up and revealed his identity. The old man then said bluntly that had he known he was speaking to the King, he would have spoken even more plainly; and far from being offended, Charles was so delighted that he insisted upon giving the old man's daughter a dowry as a souvenir of their meeting.

Of course, he also had his faults; it would be absurd to pretend that he was that mythical creature a *chevalier sans peur et sans reproche*. After long and patient efforts to reconcile the opposing religious factions of his day, when at last he was forced by the rigidity of the Protestants and the intransigence of the more bigoted Catholics to recognize that compromise was impossible, he resorted to draconian measures in an attempt to restore unity to the Church, and he has been blamed for the severity of his treatment of those whom he considered to be irredeemable heretics; but it would be unfair to condemn him too harshly for this. No one was more patient than Charles in his attempts to bring the two sides together before resorting to rougher measures, and when at last he did act, he was no more brutal than anyone else involved in the bitter religious struggles of the day; indeed, he was less brutal than many. Moreover, it was an age in which appalling cruelty was commonplace and condemned by few; for certain crimes a man might be hanged by the neck, cut down while still alive, disembowelled, dismembered limb by limb, and finally beheaded, and almost no one raised his voice in protest. No doubt, too, Charles had heard stories of the excesses of people like the Anabaptists – stories which lost nothing in the telling – and as a result had reluctantly come to the conclusion that anything was better than that the Christian world should be allowed to slide down a slippery heretical slope into religious chaos and anarchy. Compared with such a disaster, the burning of a few contentious heretics was a lesser evil. The Catholic Church might be corrupt and desperately in need of reform; indeed, it was, and no one knew better than Charles how far short of perfection some of the Popes had fallen (on one occasion, Charles referred to one of them contemptuously as 'that poltroon'), but neither the corruption of the Church nor the inadequacy of the Popes seemed to him to be a good reason for abandoning the fight to preserve the truth once delivered to the saints or the unity of Christ's holy Catholic and apostolic Church. Fidelity to such aims seemed supreme to Charles, and on the whole he pursued them with more moderation and less brutality than most of his contemporaries.

Perhaps more serious is the accusation that, on two occasions, he was accessory to political murder, the assassination of two French ambassadors to the court of the Sultan in Constantinople, who were travelling through Italy in July 1541 on their way to take up their posts there, and the murder of Pierluigi Farnese in Piacenza in September 1547 six years later. The deaths of these men certainly came at opportune moments for Charles, and when he was told of them, he does not seem to have been unduly distressed or angry; but neither the fact that they died conveniently for him nor his calm reception of the news proves that he himself was involved. Political assassination was a fact of life, however, in sixteenth-century Europe – especially in Machiavelli's Italy – and Charles may have been implicated; if so, no one at the time would have blamed him. Indeed, no contemporary statesman with any pretensions to realism would have shown much astonishment or wasted much indignation over the murder of Francis I's ambassadors to the infidel Suleiman, especially since one of them was a notorious Spanish renegade, and few people would have shed many tears over the death of Pope Paul III's somewhat unsavoury son. In any case, whether Charles knew of the plans to murder them or not, he should be judged by the standards of his own time, not by those of a later age, which likes to think that, give or take an American president or two, it has banished murder as a political weapon.

Whatever his political sins of commission and omission may have been, like most men Charles also had his personal faults and weaknesses. He was a glutton, and even though he knew that over-indulgence at the table would inevitably bring on another of his painful attacks of gout, to which he became increasingly a victim as the years went by, he was never able to resist the temptation to eat too much. His sexual morals were not above reproach either, though by the standards of the day they were less open to criticism than those of most men in positions like his. He married the delicate and lovely Isabel of Portugal when he was twenty-six years old, and despite the fact that he had never seen her before in his life the marriage was a great success, and Charles loved her dearly until the day she died thirteen years later. Before he married he had fathered two illegitimate daughters, and eight years after Isabel's death he had a fleeting affair with a certain German lady, Barbara Blomberg of Ratisbon, who was notoriously prodigal with her favours, and who presented him with a son. The child grew up to become Don John of Austria, who distinguished himself as a soldier, and who was believed by everyone to be the Emperor's bastard, although he may have been nothing of the sort; for apparently on one occasion, when his mother was in a rage, she told Charles that the child was probably the son of a common soldier. Perhaps she herself did not know whose child Don John really was, but there is no doubt that Charles believed himself to be the father. The lady lived on until nearly the end of the century without mending her ways, while succeeding in making the maximum nuisance of herself to a large number of eminent men in the process. She died at Laredo, requesting that a really enormous number of masses should be said for her soul and that Philip II should pay her almost equally enormous debts.

★

Francis I of France – '*Monsieur François qui est tout françois*', as he has been called – was as different from Charles as he could have been. Physically, where Charles was small and insignificant, Francis was a giant of a man; where Charles was frail, gouty and ungainly, Francis was strong, athletic and graceful. In contrast, too, to Charles with his ponderous Habsburg lip and lower jaw, which made it difficult for him to close his mouth and gave him a permanently adenoidal appearance, Francis was described by Louis XII as *un beau gentilhomme*, a verdict with which most French historians have agreed. 'Was there ever a more beautiful prince than the King Francis?' asked Charles Terasse rhetorically in 1945 in his biography of him, and the context makes it quite clear that the reader is expected to answer, 'Never!' As a young man, like Charles he wore his hair in the medieval fashion, long to the nape of his neck, but by the time that Titian painted him later in life he had cut it short in the new Italian style; his beard was scanty, his face long, and his nose longer still, while above its truly remarkable extension he possessed a pair of small, smiling eyes, and below it a fine, well-formed, humorous mouth. Not everyone would adjudge him to be beautiful, for the length of his nose might not appeal to everyone; but beautiful or not, there is no doubt that Francis was and is a hero to his countrymen – a Frenchman's idea of the perfect prince – as another French historian, Pierre Mesnard, has made abundantly clear recently, when he put him alongside Richelieu, Louis XIV, Napoleon and Clemenceau as one of those 'heroes particularly dear to the French heart', partly at least for having pursued the struggle with the house of Habsburg and by implication with the Germans, which has been such a feature of French history for centuries. However this may be, there is no doubt of Francis's immense popularity in his own country.

He was born at Cognac at about ten in the evening of 12 September 1494, six years before his Habsburg rival. His father, Charles of Valois, Count of Angoulême and great-grandson of the French King Charles V, died two years later, leaving his wife, Louise of Savoy, to rear Francis and his four-year-old sister Marguerite on her own. She had been married at the age of eleven; the match had been purely political, and neither she nor her husband had had any say in arranging it, having been betrothed to each other by command of Louis XI when Louise was still only two years old. Her future husband, Charles, who was sixteen years older than her and by no means insensible to the charms of the opposite sex, did not feel obliged to remain celibate while waiting for Louise to attain marriageable age. He had three illegitimate daughters by three different mistresses, with one of whom, Antoinette of Polignac, he continued to live quite openly even after his marriage. She moved with the newly wed couple into the castle at Cognac, where she looked after Charles's three bastard daughters and shared Charles's bed when his wife was not in it. The arrangement does not seem greatly to have surprised or distressed Louise, who made friends with her instead of quarrelling, and thereafter shared with her the care of her own legitimate children, bringing them up in company with their illegitimate half-sisters.

It was not an age in which children were much indulged, even royal children being no strangers to the birch and the rod; but such severity was not for Francis. Louise doted on him. She was not quite twenty years old when her husband died and she did not marry again, though she had many opportunities to do so, and was urged to choose another husband. Instead, she preferred to devote herself to her children and especially to Francis, who became a substitute for a husband and almost indeed a substitute for God. Other children might be bent to the will of their elders by being subjected to corporal punishment in the accepted manner of the day, but no one was allowed to raise a hand against Francis – though this did not mean that he was left without education. On the contrary, great care was taken to educate him, and even though he showed no great taste for academic work he proved to be a willing enough pupil. At the age of six, he began to receive instruction from a chaplain named Ytier Bouvereau in the rudiments of the Catholic faith, while the abbot of a neighbouring monastery, Saint-Mesmin de Micy near Orleans, taught him to read and write. It was not long before the abbot added Latin and history to the curriculum, while Louise herself undertook to teach him Italian and Spanish.

But it was the riding lessons, which he received from an equerry, that Francis enjoyed above all; for despite the adoration of his mother, which might easily have turned him into a mollycoddle, he was no such thing. On the contrary, he grew up to be a boisterous, physically tough, wild and rumbustious boy with a taste for violent sport, which often terrified his mother. There was a fearful occasion, when he was seven, when his pony bolted; Louise, who was watching from a distance, recalled that moment twenty years after the event with horror, even though, as it turned out, Francis came to no harm. Such incidents did not frighten him or deter him from continuing to play rough games with his contemporaries. Throughout his life, when he was depressed or frustrated, he would throw himself into some violent pastime in order to forget his worries, rather as another man might indulge in a violent drinking bout to achieve the same end. In January 1520, when he was twenty-six and in a black mood, he nearly killed himself three times in a single day: the morning was bitterly cold, and the ground hard with ice, but this did not prevent Francis from taking his horse out galloping over the frozen fields, until at last the beast slipped, and he was thrown. As luck would have it, he was not hurt. He did not suffer injury later in the day either, when in the course of a silly game he hid in a hamper, which was set on fire by mistake. But then his luck ran out. In the afternoon, he organized yet another game, and this time it was a mock battle; one side was to defend a castle, while the other was to attack it. Francis led the attackers and all went well until one of the defenders in a momentary access of over-enthusiastic realism threw a large log down upon the attackers; it hit Francis on the head, and he was carried unconscious into the house, where for a time it was feared that he was dead. To everyone's relief, however, he recovered slowly, though his convalescence lasted for two months. His mother wanted to punish the man who had thrown the log, but Francis would have none of it. If he wanted to play the fool, he had to take the consequences.

But if he loved the rough and tumble of games and sport of all kinds, hunting was his true passion. 'No matter how old or ill I may be,' he is said to have remarked later in life, 'I will have myself carried to the hunt; and when I die, I shall want to go there in my coffin.' He revelled in the excitement of the chase, and being a brilliant rider he threw himself into the sport with immense dash and courage, seeming to be oblivious of the dangers and the risks he ran. As a horseman and a member of the hunt, he outdid all his contemporaries – no mean feat, for most members of the European ruling class, whatever their nationality, were almost equally passionate in their addiction to the chase in one form or another. Henry VIII of England was following the hounds at the age of ten; Charles V, despite his physical defects, loved hunting; and throughout the length and breadth of Europe forests and moors and huge tracts of land were strictly preserved from the vulgar and ruinous attention of peasants and farmers so that the birds and animals might multiply in peace and provide the nobility with worthy quarry. Even such a man as Pope Leo X, fat and ungainly as he was, mounted a large and docile horse from time to time and trotted out dressed in green leather with a feathered hat on his head to hunt any animal which might be infirm or stupid enough to await his coming.

Much as Francis loved the hunt, it was not his only nor his most consuming passion, unless women be included in the list of animals he was to spend a lifetime chasing. It would perhaps be unfair to say that, if legend traced Charles V's ancestors back to the Trojan King Priam, it might with greater plausibility have made Francis the descendant of the Greek god Priapus, but it would not be far from the truth; for he was, as one of his biographers has put it, *amoureux comme un chat* – as randy as a cat. Women fascinated him, and he was nothing if not catholic in his tastes; it has even been suggested that he made incestuous advances to his sister Marguerite, who doted on him, but this may not be true. Certainly he made some sort of suggestion to her, which horrified and greatly distressed her, but it may not have been an amorous proposal, as many people have believed. The mere fact, however, that so many people have indeed believed such a thing of him is witness to his reputation as a sexual athlete with little or no discrimination. Yet despite the fact that he was attracted by so many women, he does not seem to have loved any of them with much depth or permanence, although he may have been a little fonder of Anne of Heilly than of most of his other mistresses. For the most part, he fell in love with them, was kind to them, and fell out of love with them as soon as his current mistress began to pall and someone else appeared who attracted his attention. Perhaps the only woman he ever really loved was his mother, and perhaps her passion for him was so stifling that unconsciously he determined never again to be so completely possessed by a woman. It is significant that on his death-bed he warned his son Henry never to be dominated by a woman, knowing full well that Henry was already completely dominated by the formidable forty-seven-year-old mother-figure of Diana of Poitiers, who had managed to come between him and his young wife, Catherine de Medici, almost from the day of their wedding. Leaving his own mother out of account, Francis had never allowed a woman to dominate him in such a way, and he was appalled by the thraldom of his sober and rather dull son. Women were marvellous as objects of the chase, and lovely as playthings when captured, but the roles of the sexes should never be reversed; to Francis such an idea was abhorrent.

If Francis was a lover of women and of the chase, he was also a great lover of the arts. In this he was typical of other great princes of the Renaissance, and like them he surrounded himself with artists and architects and jewellers, musicians, poets, book-binders and gold-smiths, commissioning them to work for him, partly because he was a genuine lover of the things they produced, and partly because their works redounded to his glory. When, as a young man, he descended upon Italy with an army of Bretons and Basques and men from Picardy together with over 20,000 mercenaries from Lorraine and Guise in the first of his campaigns in that hapless and much fought-over land, he was enormously impressed and excited by the splendour and elegance of towns like Milan and Bologna. He bought the *Mona Lisa*, and returned home in triumph after his victory in the battle of Marignano with that great picture as a prize; but not content with the masterpiece itself, somehow he also managed to persuade its painter to leave the land of his birth and travel northwards with him, and on reaching France he installed the aged Leonardo in a splendid apartment at Amboise, where the old man lived and worked until he died three years later. No one could replace Leonardo, and Francis knew it; but Andrea del Sarto was better than nothing, and he was duly brought from Italy with as many other artists, architects, craftsmen, master masons and sculptors as could be persuaded to come to France where, despite the King's chronic lack of money, they eventually built and decorated the Château at Chambord. Far from satisfying his appetite for building suitably magnificent buildings in which to emphasize his own magnificence and his obvious superiority to his two great rivals, the Emperor Charles and Henry VIII of England, the building of Chambord merely whetted it, and his own glorification and that of his country became passions almost as absorbing as his delight in the chase and his desire for women. His own countryman, François Clouet, painted him again and again; Titian did his portrait; he welcomed a host of minor artists to his court from Italy and gave them work, and when Benvenuto Cellini came to France he treated him almost as a brother. For five years the Florentine worked in Paris and at Fontainebleau, producing some splendid things, but he was not an easy man and after a time he was stupidly rude to Anne of Heilly, the reigning mistress at the time, and antagonized a number of other court favourites by his hot temper. He was a quarrelsome man, and in Italy he had settled many of his disputes with the sword; but since he could hardly do the same in France he returned to his native Florence, where he died twenty-five years later. Had he not behaved so aggressively, there is little doubt that he would have been given work in France for the rest of his life, for the King's delight in his work, as in all Renaissance art, never faltered. He was a compulsive and extravagant patron all his life.

Francis did everything with Rabelaisian gusto, and in fact he may have been that writer's model for Pantagruel; he was Rabelais' contemporary, his patron, and his admirer, and there seems to have been a natural affinity between the two men. Perhaps one of the reasons why Francis brought such zest to the task of kingship was that he had not been born to the throne; this had been reserved for the son of Louis XII as dauphin, and it was only when he died that Francis became the King's heir. Thus the trappings and riches of royalty came to him with all the excitement of an unexpected birthday present to a child. Curiously enough, much the same was true of Henry VIII of England, whom no one at first expected to see on the throne, for he had an elder brother, Arthur. As a result, throughout his childhood Henry took second place to the heir to the throne, and it was only after Arthur's sudden death at the age of fifteen that Henry found himself in direct line of succession to his father. He ascended the throne in the early summer of 1509 at the age of eighteen and, like the French King, he brought great zest and gusto to the task of ruling the country, which had become his so unexpectedly. In almost every other way, however, he was a very different man from the Frenchman.

The popular picture of Henry as a rollicking royal Falstaff, gnawing legs of mutton in his bare hands and ordering one of his minions to go and cut off someone's head – preferably that of one of his wives or of a saintly Catholic like Thomas More – is a travesty. Henry was a talented man with gifts which would have made him outstanding at any time and in any company, but he was also a very complex one set in a highly complex situation. As a youth, people had the highest hopes of him; he was so different from his cunning and avaricious old father that they looked forward to his reign as the beginning of a golden age. William Blount who, as Lord Mountjoy, was made chamberlain to Catherine of Aragon, and who had been a pupil of Erasmus as a young man, wrote to his old master at about the time of Henry's marriage to the Spanish princess in the most glowing terms. 'O! My Erasmus,' he wrote, 'if you could see how all the world here is rejoicing in the possession of so great a prince, how his life is all their desire, you could not contain your tears for joy. The heavens laugh, the earth exults, all things are full of milk, of honey and nectar! Avarice is expelled from the country. Liberality scatters wealth with bounteous hand. Our King does not desire gold or gems or precious metals, but virtue, glory, immortality . . .'

This was strong stuff, but most people at the time would have agreed with Mountjoy that Henry promised to be a great improvement on his father. As a scholar, he outdid most men born in a similar position; he was genuinely interested in and fascinated by theology; he spoke French fluently, had enough Latin to converse with foreign ambassadors in that language when necessary, and learned a little Spanish from Catherine. In addition to these academic accomplishments, he had a real love and understanding of music; he wrote the settings for various hymns and romantic songs, sang them himself, composed two masses, was a skilful player on the lute, and tried his hand rather less successfully as a poet and a playwright. Above all, he was deeply and sincerely religious. As a youth, he headed his letters to friends with the words 'Jesus is my hope', and to one of them he confided that his aims in life were 'piety, valour, courtesy, prowess, the gift of poetry and eloquence, and dexterity in the management of the horse, the sword, the lance and the bow'. As a young man, too, he was accustomed to hear mass at least three times a day and sometimes as many as five times, and after their marriage he and Catherine heard vespers and compline together in her apartments every evening. Even allowing for the fact that he lived in an age in which nearly everyone was as interested in spiritual matters as people today are in politics, an age in which princes were expected to set an example of active piety to their subjects, the sincerity and depth of Henry's religion cannot be denied. Indeed, many of his later troubles might have been avoided if he had not been a man of such deep religious convictions; the fact that he also fancied himself as something of a theologian was also destined to make matters worse than they might have been.

But if men like Mountjoy welcomed Henry for the promise he held out of becoming a great and civilized prince, the people of England welcomed him for less elevated reasons. He was everyone's idea of a prince, six feet four inches tall, handsome and golden-haired, and as he rode in state from the Tower of London to Westminster Abbey for his coronation on 28 June 1509, the people of London rose to him in delight. Like Francis, he was a magnificent horseman, and as he made his way down Eastcheap, Cannon Street and Ludgate Hill dressed in a coat embroidered with gold and studded with pearls and precious stones, a scarlet velvet cloak trimmed with ermine falling from his shoulders over his horse's crupper, the crowds of people who turned out to see him recalled the stories they had heard of his prowess at fencing, pole-jumping, wrestling, jousting and hunting, and gave him a rapturous welcome. Of course, there were more solid grounds for their rejoicing than Henry's appearance, splendid as that was; the people knew that they were greeting the first English King in whose veins the blood of the House of Lancaster flowed together with that of York, and that he thus represented a better hope of peace and political stability than the country had had for years. Even in Henry VII's time there had been frequent plots and rebellions, each of which had threatened to plunge the realm back into the horrors of the Wars of the Roses. Henry VII had managed to defeat the various Perkin Warbecks and Lambert Simnels who had troubled his reign, without civil war breaking out again, but he had done so only by the skin of his teeth; for although he had married Elizabeth of York he had been a Lancastrian, and his enemies had not ceased to hate him. Others had learned to dislike him for his avarice; but in this, as in much else, his son had proved himself to be very different from his father, and to everyone's delight one of the first things he had done on ascending the throne was to arrest or dismiss the most extortionate of his father's ministers, and thus by implication to promise a less grasping administration in the future. It is no wonder that everyone greeted his reign with such high hopes, but the fact that they did so also poses this question: Why did they become so disillusioned and disappointed with Henry as time went by?

The answer is that in many ways they were not disappointed. The idea that he was a brutal despot detested by his people is not true; he could be extremely brutal, but so could most people at the time, and his cruelties did not shock his contemporaries as they shock us, though the execution of Thomas More sent a ripple of disgust through the courts of Europe. Anne Boleyn had never been popular, and her downfall and execution worried very few people; whether the charges against her of adultery and treason were true or not is a matter of opinion, but it seems as certain as anything very well can be that Catherine Howard was guilty of some promiscuity before her marriage to the King and infidelity to him afterwards, and no one wasted many tears on her either. As for his divorces, everyone understood only too well his need for a male heir, for only if he had a son before he died could the land be sure of maintaining peace after his death. Since the Pope refused to grant him a divorce on grounds which everyone recognized to be almost purely political, few people blamed him for taking matters into his own hands. Similarly, although he was indeed a despot, his autocratic ways were not resented at the time as fiercely as they would be today. In the sixteenth century, princes were admired the closer they approximated to Machiavelli's prescription for princeliness, and Henry came as near as anyone to being an incarnation of that strange political ideal. Moreover, there was a very real sense in which, although he bitterly antagonized the Church and many of the old aristocratic families, his interests and those of the great majority of ordinary common people were very similar; and so, if he was ruthless and brutally autocratic from time to time in order to achieve his own ends, on the whole the people supported him, for their ends were well served in the process and England gained in both power and influence during his reign. But while Henry's contemporaries did not regard him as the kind of tyrannical monster envisaged by later generations, they were well aware that he was no paragon of virtue. His greatest defect seems to have been an almost pathological intolerance of being thwarted; usually he was cheerful, boisterous and amiable, but the moment that he was crossed he became a different man, implacable and dangerous. It was in such moods of frustrated megalomania that he was liable to act with callous brutality, apparently without a qualm of conscience, and upon such actions his reputation as a monster has been built.

Henry's importance in the story of the great Turkish onslaught upon western Europe, which is the subject of this book, is only peripheral, for England was too far away to be directly menaced by the Turks; but he nevertheless influenced the course of events by the way in which he was able to alter the balance of power between the Emperor Charles V and Francis I of France by bestowing his favours first on one and then on the other, as they struggled for pre-eminence and fought endlessly over the disputed territory of Italy. This is not the place to describe in detail the origin of these Italian conflicts between the Emperor and the French King, but since they intimately affected the conduct of the war against the invading Turks, something must be said on the subject here.

The root cause of the conflict was the political map of the Italian peninsula. Italy was divided into a number of small states, most of which had had their day, and were now reduced to a state of chronic weakness. This inevitably tempted her stronger neighbours into casting covetous looks at one or more of these little kingdoms and principalities. Venice, which had been a world power in her heyday after the fall of Constantinople to the men of the Fourth Crusade, was past her prime. Milan, which had been rich and comparatively powerful under Sforza rule in the fifteenth century, had tempted the French into a military adventure against it in the time of Charles VIII, and a little later Louis XII had laid claim to the kingdom of Naples, although Ferdinand of Aragon also claimed it as his own, and a war had followed. Thus, by the time Francis I came to the throne, there were precedents for war between France and Spain for the mastery of Italy, and it was not long after his accession that fighting broke out there once again. It was precipitated by Pope Leo X, who was feeling aggrieved by the insolence of the French and decided to change sides and enlist the help of the Emperor Charles in chastising the men who had been rude to him. He offered to give Charles the investiture of the disputed kingdom of Naples, if he would come and drive the French out of Italy. Persuaded by an Italian-born minister named Gattinara to grasp such a golden opportunity to attack his enemy in a place where Francis was least expecting to be assaulted, Charles sent an army to Lombardy, where at first his men carried all before them. No one, least of all Charles, knew at the time how long, costly and distracting the ensuing war was destined to be, or how much comfort it would provide to the greatest of Charles's enemies, the Sultan Suleiman the Magnificent.

III

✠ ✠ ✠

The Scourge of Heaven

A scourge sent against us by the anger of Heaven, such as was Attila in the olden time, Tamerlane within the recollection of our grandfathers, and such as the Ottoman Sultans are in our own days.

Ogier Ghiselin de Busbecq, *Turkish Letters*

Suleiman the Magnificent was born in 1494 or 1495. His early years were so obscure that even the date and place of his birth are not known for certain; but if we know little or nothing of his childhood, we know a great deal about his father who must have been a dominant influence on his early years, and is thus worth looking at for a moment. His name was Selim, and he was an extremely vigorous, able and dangerous man, who could not have been an easy parent. He had been the youngest of five brothers born to Sultan Bâyezid II, any of whom might have inherited the throne, for the succession did not necessarily go to the eldest son in Turkey but to the son chosen by God, or so the Turks believed. In effect, this meant that it went either to the one considered by his father to be best fitted to be Sultan or to the one who proved his fitness to rule by seizing power when the time came. Selim did not even wait for his father to die before making his bid for the throne. In 1511, when the Sultan was busy trying to suppress a revolt in eastern Anatolia, he rebelled against him and attacked Adrianople; a battle was fought between father and son, and Selim was soundly beaten. Because of the speed of his horse, romantically named Black Cloud, he escaped with his life, and fled to the Crimea where his father-in-law was Khan of the Crimean Tatars. There, undismayed by his defeat, he set about raising another army.

While rebellion against one's father was regarded by all Moslems as impious, Selim's savage determination to seize power and the ferocious courage he had shown during the battle in which he had been defeated, had impressed those with whom he had fought, and especially had it won the admiration of that Turkish *corps d'élite*, the Janissaries, of whom much will be heard during the course of this story. Of the Sultan's various sons, two were already dead and, of the remaining three, Selim, though the youngest, was much the most powerful as a personality; the other two were peaceful individuals, who did not appeal to the Janissaries, whereas it was obvious that Selim enjoyed nothing more than homicide. The soldiers in the capital, Constantinople, therefore determined that at all costs they must ensure Selim's succession, and they brought such pressure upon the old Sultan Bâyezid that a few months after Selim's defeat he sent an invitation to his son to return from his self-imposed exile in the Crimea.

Selim received his father's letter in the dead of winter, and immediately assembled a small army of about 3,000 horsemen, setting out for Constantinople. The cold was intense, but he was determined to reach the capital before his father changed his mind, and he forced the pace. The men rose each morning before dawn, and then marched all day with hardly a break until after dark; men and horses died of exhaustion and exposure on the way, but Selim would allow no respite. Rather than making a detour to cross the Dniester by bridge, they crossed on the ice, and reached their destination in early April. A few days later, the old Sultan yielded to the clamour of the army and the people, and abdicated in favour of Selim.

In a touching show of filial piety and affection, Selim escorted his father to the gate of the city, walking on foot by the old man's litter and parting from him outside the city wall with tears in his eyes. Bâyezid had expressed a wish to end his days at Demotika, the small town south of Adrianople where he had been born, but he was not destined to do so; he died at a little village on the road three days after saying goodbye to his son. He was an old man, and he may have died a natural death; if so, it was very sudden, and at the time many people whispered to one another that he had been poisoned on his son's orders. It may not have been true, but it is easy to understand why such a rumour was widely believed; for the old man was hardly in his grave before Selim decided to forestall any possible objections by his two elder brothers to his seizure of power, and there was only one way to do that effectively. He ordered a small gang of deaf mutes to murder them, and they were duly strangled with a bowstring. While this made his position as Sultan much safer, there were still five potential rebels, for the murdered men had had five children between them, and Selim decided to deal with them too. While he listened to their cries from an adjoining room, his five orphaned nephews, the youngest of whom was five years old, were also strangled by the mutes. By the standards of his fellow countrymen, none of this was particularly unusual; indeed, it had become customary for a new Sultan to sacrifice inconvenient members of his own family to his own security and that of the State. So, on the whole, Selim's ruthless elimination of his brothers and nephews was greeted as proof of his fitness to become Sultan, and when he followed it up by launching a savage attack on some Moslem heretics in eastern Anatolia and slaughtering 40,000 of them, everyone was so delighted that he was dubbed Selim the Just. It is only in the West that he became known as Selim the Terrible, though even in Turkey, as time went by, he also became known as Selim Yavuz or Selim the Grim.

Suleiman's childhood could hardly have been an easy or untroubled one with such a father, but at least he survived, and stories that Selim hated him and tried to have him killed, though often repeated, are no more than stories; they are unlikely to be true for if his father had wanted to kill him, he could have done so easily enough. In fact, it is unlikely that he saw much of his father, for Selim spent so much of his time in the field with the army that he had little left for his family, and Suleiman must have been brought up by his mother. Her name was Hafssa or Hafiza Khatoun, and apparently she was a woman of great charm and intelligence, who was destined to be a powerful influence in his life for many years, but of his life with her in childhood there is no record. He begins to emerge from obscurity into the limelight of history after his father became Sultan, and then only for brief moments do we get glimpses of him. At some time during his adolescent years, while Selim was triumphantly waging war against the Persians and conquering the Mameluks of Egypt, Suleiman was made governor of Adrianople, and on Selim's return from the wars father and son met and spent a day or two together in Constantinople. After this meeting, Suleiman departed to take up another governorship, this time of Manisa – the ancient Magnesia – a few miles from Smyrna in Asia Minor, where he disappears once again from the historian's view. But this retirement was not destined to last long. As Selim began to make plans and preparations for an attack on the island of Rhodes, which had long been a nuisance to Turkey, he began to show signs of increasing illness, and late in the evening of 21 September 1520 he died of cancer at the age of fifty-four.

The reign of Selim the Terrible had lasted less than nine years, during which time he had vastly extended the Turkish empire by his conquests in Syria and Egypt, and had proved himself to be the most murderous of all the Ottoman Sultans, few of whom showed much reluctance to kill those who got in their way. Apart from the men who were killed during the course of his various wars, and the Shi'ite heretics whom he slaughtered whenever opportunity arose, those who served him as officials in the palace or as generals in the army went in constant fear for their lives; so many army officers were executed for real or imaginary faults or failures in the field that no one felt safe, and no fewer than seven Grand Viziers were beheaded on his orders. Indeed, the phrase, 'May you become Selim's Vizier!' came to mean, 'Drop dead!' in common Turkish usage. At one time, too, he even contemplated massacring every Greek Christian in Turkey on the grounds that such a sacrifice would be well pleasing to God; fortunately for his intended victims he was induced to spare them by a remarkable man named Ali Djemali, who was the head of the College of Islamic canon law and about the only person with the courage to stand up to the Sultan and contradict him to his face when he considered him to be in the wrong.

Selim's death was kept secret, as was customary when a Sultan died, until his successor could reach the capital and forestall any trouble which might break out there. Suleiman arrived in Constantinople on Sunday, 30 September 1520, only eight days after his father's death, and was acclaimed by both people and army. It is not surprising that he was welcomed so warmly, for he was a great improvement upon his savage father. A few weeks after his accession, a Venetian living in Constantinople, Bartholomeo Contarini, described him in a letter: 'He is twenty-five years of age, tall but wiry and of a delicate complexion. His neck is a little too long, his face thin, and his nose aquiline. He has a light moustache and a small beard; nevertheless he has a pleasant expression, though his skin tends to pallor. He is said to be a wise Lord, fond of study, and all men hope for good from his rule.' His first actions seemed to bear out this optimism. After rising early on the day after his arrival in the capital and receiving the homage of the palace officials, with proper piety he went in procession to the gate of the city, dressed in black, to meet the funeral cortège which was bearing his father's body back to Constantinople to be buried there. In the days which followed, he distributed the customary and expected gifts of money to the Janissaries and other household troops, he set 600 Egyptian prisoners free, and he redressed a wrong done to some merchants by his father in a fit of pique. This display of generosity delighted his subjects, and so did his treatment of several senior officers in the armed forces, including the admiral of the fleet, who were accused of cruelty and corruption, brought to trial, convicted, and executed. This combination of fairness and firmness was what everyone looked for in a Sultan. In a work entitled *Kutadgu Bilig* written in 1069 for the Turkish ruler of the Karakhanids in Asia, the ideal principle of government was described: 'To control the State requires a large army. To support the troops requires great wealth. To obtain this wealth the people must be prosperous. For the people to be prosperous the laws must be just. If any one of these is neglected, the State will collapse.' Suleiman promised to rule the empire on just such principles, and that boded well for everyone.

But if such principles regulated the internal life of the Turkish State, its foreign policy was governed by the concept of *gaza* or Holy War. The State existed above all to make war on its infidel neighbours, not in order to destroy them, but to win them for Islam. It was the prime religious duty of everyone from the Sultan down to his humblest subject to do everything in his power to further this warfare. To wage war against non-Moslems was not evil but entirely godly, and the Ottoman Turks cannot be understood unless this is remembered. Their country and empire had been won by war, and the cultural patterns of their life, both religious and secular, were dictated by the demands of continuous Holy War. The fact that the endless wars waged against their various neighbours had been vastly enriching was regarded as a proof of God's approval, for plainly he would not have rewarded his servants so lavishly if he had not been pleased with their martial efforts on his behalf; but the acquisition of wealth was only a by-product of war and not its principal objective. But although the Turks went into battle for higher motives than mere loot, they expected to be allowed to pillage the places they captured and take their share of prisoners as slaves. This was a way of life which they greatly enjoyed, and which had lasted for centuries.

In origin, the Turks were nomadic shepherds from central Asia, appearing first in Mongolia in the sixth century AD, and quickly spreading across the semi-desert steppe south and west past the Altai mountains as far as Lake Aral. They led a life of extreme hardness, living in tents and moving north in summer and south in winter with their flocks and herds to their traditional feeding grounds. As long as no one interfered with these annual migrations, they were peaceful people; but if other tribes encroached upon their pastures, or if they themselves were forced by drought or some other disaster to trespass on the territory of others, they fought with the tenacity and ferocity of those who knew that their survival depended upon victory. At such times, they were as formidable as the Huns – to whom they were closely related – had been before them and for much the same reasons. First, they were immensely tough, for their way of life tended to eliminate all but the hardiest; secondly, they were used to living without any comforts of any kind, subsisting even in good times on a minimal diet and in bad on almost nothing; and thirdly they were superb horsemen and expert archers, who could shoot a running hare while galloping at breakneck speed on one of their wiry little horses, which were as tough as they were themselves. But it was not until the various tribes into which the Turkish people were divided stopped bickering among themselves and joined together in the tenth century under a single leader that they began to become formidable enough for the major powers like China, Persia and the Byzantine Empire to take them seriously; and the name of the leader who succeeded in uniting them was Seljuk.

Up to this time, the religion of the Turks had been shamanism, an extremely primitive form of belief in a multitude of spirits, both good and evil, which could be magically manipulated by shamans or witch doctors; but as the tribes spread westwards and came into contact more and more frequently with Arabs, Jews and Byzantines, the superiority of the Moslem faith, of Judaism, and of Christianity became obvious to them, and many were converted to one or other of these great monotheistic religions. If this process of piecemeal conversion had been allowed to continue indefinitely, the Turkish nation might in the end have given their allegiance to any one of them, but the Seljuk family, which united it, were converts to Islam and their influence tipped the scales. The empire which they founded became Moslem.

This is not the place to describe the rise and fall of the Seljuk Turks; it must suffice to say that they conquered most of Anatolia from the declining Byzantine Empire, and at one time towards the close of the eleventh century ruled an empire of their own which stretched from the Dardanelles to the borders of India, and took in almost the whole of Arabia and the Moslem lands of Asia. Their control of this enormous domain was wrested from them by the Mongols under Jenghiz Khan and his successors, and the day of Turkish greatness seemed to have passed. But in the early fourteenth century internal political upheavals shook the great empires between the Danube and the Oxus – the Byzantine Empire in the west, that of the Ilkhanids in Persia, and that of the Golden Horde in what is now southern Russia – and Osman, leader of a small tribe of Turks, made the most of the disorder of the times and the weakness of the Byzantines to carve out a small kingdom for himself. By the end of the same century, his descendants, the Osmanli or Ottoman Turks as they came to be called, had established a new Turkish empire which stretched from the Euphrates in the east to the Danube in the west, though they did not capture Constantinople until half-way through the following century, when it fell to Mehmed the Conqueror on 29 May 1453. Theirs was an astonishing achievement.

In the course of their journey from the wastes of central Asia to eventual dominion in Constantinople, the Turks, while remaining as tough as they had ever been, had inevitably been changed by their conversion to Islam and by their contacts with the Persians, the Arabs and the Byzantines, and the conquest of Constantinople was the cause of even greater changes. For a thousand years the city had been the seat of the Roman Emperors, and when Mehmed the Conqueror captured it, he considered himself to be their successor, announcing that henceforth his throne would be Constantinople, and ordering the immediate construction of a palace in the centre of the city, in which he might dwell in a manner fitting to his new station as heir of the Caesars. In fact he disliked the first palace to be built for him and in 1549, six years after the conquest, he ordered another one to be built on a promontory overlooking the Bosphorus, where the Topkapi Palace stands today. Once installed in this new and splendid abode, Mehmed, not content simply to live in a palace similar to the Sacred Palace in which the Byzantine Emperors had lived, also adopted many of the features of Byzantine life, and his successors furthered the process. The result was that by Suleiman's time the Sultan lived in almost oriental seclusion, and the complexity of the etiquette which surrounded him was truly Byzantine in its elaboration; indeed, much of the ceremonial of his court was taken over directly from Byzantine days and had been described by the Emperor Constantine VII Porphyrogenitus in his great work on court ritual, *De Caerimoniis Imperio*.

But there was one crucial difference between the palace which Suleiman inherited and that in which the Byzantine Emperors had lived: Suleiman's palace was peopled exclusively by slaves. To European ears the word 'slavery' is immediately associated with humiliation and the most offensive form of injustice; to enslave fellow human beings is to deny them their most fundamental human rights. But to be a slave in the Sultan's service in Ottoman Turkey was regarded by no one as shameful; on the contrary, his slaves were proud of their privileged position close to the source of all power: a position which gave them and them alone chances of advancement to the highest and most powerful posts in the land, which were open to no one else. They could and did become Grand Viziers, governors of provinces, admirals, commanders-in-chief of the Turkish army and holders of any of the highest offices of state, where they acted as extensions of the Sultan himself, whose power was absolute and unquestioned.

Originally, the Sultan's supply of slaves had been provided by prisoners of war; he had always had the right to claim one out of every five people captured in battle or after the taking of a city, and wars had been so continuous that they had usually sufficed to supply him with all the slaves he needed. On the few occasions when he had had to supplement this source of supply by seeking slaves elsewhere, he had resorted to the slave markets of Constantinople, where it has been reckoned that at one time about 20,000 people were bought and sold every year. But as time went by another system of supplying the Sultan with slaves was developed; it was known as the *devshirme,* and it consisted of a levy upon the children of his Christian subjects. When more slaves were needed – and this might be about once every three years – a commissioner appointed by the Sultan was sent to each governmental district where, accompanied by a local government official, they toured the villages. Christian families were warned in advance of their coming, and it was the duty of every father to wait upon the commissioner with all his male children between the ages of eight and twenty; those who appeared to be the fittest and most intelligent were then chosen, their names were entered in a register, and they were packed off in groups of about a hundred to Constantinople. It was a brutal business, though parents with only one child were exempted for humanitarian reasons, and people went to great lengths to cheat the *devshirme*; but there is some evidence that in the very poorest districts in the Taurus mountains and elsewhere, where life was particularly hard, some parents were happy enough to offer their children to the commissioner when he arrived in the village.

When the boys arrived in Constantinople, they were then taken to places of special training, where the aim was to turn them first and foremost into convinced Moslems and secondly to give them the best possible education. The temperament and ability of each individual boy were carefully studied in the process, and those who showed an aptitude for a particular subject were encouraged to specialize in it, but all of them were taught to ride, to use the bow, to fence and to wrestle. Discipline was strictly enforced, and the boys' lives were regulated down to the smallest detail: they got up in the morning, ate their meals, worked, played, rested and went to bed at night according to a fixed timetable; they were not allowed to talk except at certain times, and all access to the outside world was forbidden. Their tutors were the palace eunuchs, who treated them with much the same severity as was meted out to English public schoolboys in the nineteenth century by Victorian housemasters at such establishments as Eton, Winchester or Marlborough and for much the same reasons: namely, in England to produce tough and reliable rulers for the outposts of the British Empire, and in Ottoman Turkey to produce 'warrior statesmen and loyal Moslems', as one who was trained in the palace in Constantinople described the aim of his education, 'who at the same time should be men of letters and polished speech, profound courtesy and honest morals'. To achieve so desirable an end, the eunuchs of Turkey were prepared, as Dr Arnold and his colleagues were ready at a later date, to reprimand their pupils for the smallest faults, to beat them unmercifully for graver misdemeanours, and to expel them if a beating was considered inadequate to fit the seriousness of their offence. In one respect, the powers exercised by the Sultan's eunuchs actually exceeded those of their nineteenth-century English successors in the art of corporal punishment, for as a last resort they were allowed to inflict the death penalty.

When their education was complete, the most talented of these specially trained slaves entered the Sultan's service in the palace itself, while most of the others joined the Janissaries. The name 'Janissary' is a corruption of the Turkish words *yeni tscheri* meaning 'new troops', and the corps of Janissaries played such a vitally important part in shaping the fortunes of the Ottoman empire, not least in Suleiman's time when it consisted of about 12,000 men, that its nature and the place it filled in the world of the day must be understood; for the Janissary corps performed much the same function in Islam as that played by the great military Orders, the Knights of St John and the Teutonic Knights, in Christendom. The Janissaries, like the Knights, were regular, professional soldiers, whose whole life was devoted to soldiering, and who were not disbanded in peacetime. They were dedicated infantrymen, expert with the bow, fanatically loyal to the Sultan as long as he rewarded them adequately and led them to victory often enough, brave to the point of fearlessness, and immensely proud to be the terror of all non-Moslem countries and the pride of Islam. Like the praetorian guard in Roman days, as time went by and the character of the Ottoman Sultans deteriorated, the Janissaries became a public menace, demanding and receiving huge bribes from the reigning Sultan before they would behave themselves, rebelling whenever it suited them to do so, and making and unmaking Sultans almost at will; but in Suleiman's day they were both loyal and formidable. The English historian, Sir Edward Creasy, writing in 1878, described them in these words:

Cut off from all ties of country, kith and kin, but with high pay and privileges, with ample opportunities for military advancement and for gratification of the violent, the sensual and the sordid passions of their animal natures amid the customary atrocities of successful warfare, this military brotherhood grew up to be the strongest and fiercest instrument of imperial ambition, which remorseless fanaticism, prompted by the most subtle statecraft, ever devised upon earth.

The only footnote which should perhaps be added to that judgement upon the Janissaries is that they were by no means the only people who gratified their baser passions during the wars of the day; many of their Christian enemies proved themselves to be at least as expert as the

Janissaries at indulging their nastier desires when given a chance to do so.

But the widespread use of slaves by the Ottoman Sultans did more than provide them with a ruthless and fanatically loyal labour force which they could use as they liked, drafting some men into the fighting forces and others into governmental posts; it also freed Turkey from the worst effects of a powerful and deeply entrenched hereditary class of people who could and often did make the government of countries still wedded to the feudal system extremely difficult. Writing towards the end of Suleiman's reign, Ogier Ghiselin de Busbecq, who was imperial ambassador in Constantinople for eight years, did not disguise his admiration of the Turkish system of government:

The Sultan's headquarters were crowded by numerous attendants, including many high officials. All the cavalry of the guard were there, the Spahis, Ghourebas, Ouloufedjis, and a large number of Janissaries. In all that great assembly no single man owed his dignity to anything but his personal merits and bravery; no one is distinguished from the rest by his birth, and honour is paid to each man according to the nature of the duty and office which he discharges. Thus there is no struggle for precedence, every man having his place assigned to him in virtue of the function he performs. The Sultan himself assigns to all their duties and offices, and in doing so pays no attention to wealth or empty claims of rank, and takes no account of any influence or popularity which a candidate may possess; he only considers merit . . . Those who hold the highest posts under the Sultan are very often the sons of shepherds and herdsmen, and, so far from being ashamed of their birth, they make it a subject of boasting, and the less they owe to their forefathers and to the accident of birth, the greater is the pride they feel. They do not consider that good qualities can be conferred by birth or handed down by inheritance . . . Our method is very different; there is no room for merit, but everything depends on birth, considerations of which alone open the way to high official position.

It is worth quoting de Busbecq at a little greater length, for he goes on to describe Suleiman's court in all its splendour, and once again he cannot withhold his admiration; he plainly considers Turkish ways superior to those of his own country in many respects, and this is a refreshing change from the usual anti-Turkish prejudices of the day. This is what he has to say:

Now come with me and cast your eye over the immense crowd of turbaned heads, wrapped in countless folds of the whitest silk, and bright raiment of every kind and hue, and everywhere the brilliance of gold, silver, purple, silk and satin. A detailed description would be a lengthy task, and no mere words could give an adequate idea of the novelty of the sight. A more beautiful spectacle was never presented to my gaze. Yet amid all this luxury there was a great simplicity and economy. The dress of all has the same form whatever the wearer's rank; and no edgings or trimmings are sewn on, as is the custom with us, costing a large sum of money and worn out in three days. Their most beautiful garments of silk or satin, even if they are embroidered, as they usually are, cost only a ducat to make . . . What struck me as particularly praiseworthy in that great multitude was the silence and good discipline. There was none of the cries and murmurs which usually proceed from such a motley concourse, and there was no crowding. Each man kept his appointed place in the quietest manner possible. The officers, namely generals, colonels, captains and lieutenants – to all of whom the Turks themselves give the name of Aga – were seated; the common soldiers stood up. The most remarkable body of men were the several thousand Janissaries, who stood in a long line apart from the rest and so motionless that, as they were at some distance from me, I was for a while doubtful whether they were living men or statues, until, being advised to follow the usual custom of saluting them, I saw them all bow their heads in answer to my salutation.

A few other western observers shared de Busbecq's admiration for the Turks and the way in which the Sultan ruled his people. An Italian, Paolo Giovio, wrote in 1539, when Suleiman had been on the throne for nineteen years, that 'their military discipline is so just and strict as easily to outdo the ancient Greeks and Romans', and the French ambassador to Constantinople just after Suleiman's time was greatly impressed by the way in which the country was governed. 'The Sultan,' he wrote, 'governs many different peoples, speaking different languages, practising different religions, and having different customs in such a way that his empire seems to be but one great city, so great is the peace and civil obedience everywhere.' Another Frenchman, Jean Bodin, writing a few years later was full of admiration for the way in which the Sultan tolerated the various religious minorities in his realm:

The King of the Turks, who rules over a great part of Europe, safeguards the rites of religion as well as any prince in the world. He constrains no one, but permits everyone to live according as his conscience dictates. What is more, even in his seraglio at Pera he permits the practice of four different religions, that of the Jews, the Christians according to the Roman rite, and according to the Greek rite, and that of Islam.

There were times when the Turks were far from tolerant of people of other religions, but on the whole it is true that they treated the large population of Greek Christians and the smaller communities of Jews inherited from Byzantine days with much greater justice than some Protestants received from Catholics and *vice versa*, and indeed with greater toleration than they often showed towards the Shi'ite sect of

ABOVE LEFT: The Emperor Charles V by Titian, who painted him on several occasions. As a young man Charles shaved his chin and wore his hair long in medieval fashion, but later in life he adopted the short hair which was fashionable in Italy. Perhaps he hoped that his beard would disguise his prognathous jaw – the celebrated Habsburg lip – but it hardly did so. After the death of his wife, Isabel, in May 1539 he always wore black.

ABOVE RIGHT: Isabel of Portugal, Charles's Empress, whom he married in 1526 to the fury of Henry VIII of England, to whose daughter, Mary, Charles had been betrothed since 1521, when Mary was five years old. Titian never saw Isabel in the flesh; he must have based this portrait on pictures by other painters. It was probably painted after her death at Charles's express command, for he loved her dearly and took this portrait of her with him to Yuste when he retired there.

LEFT: Francis I of France by François Clouet. The contrast between the magnificent physique of the French King with his passion for sport and his even more absorbing passion for the opposite sex and the Emperor Charles with his hunched, gouty body and undershot jaw comes out clearly in these two portraits, as does Francis's taste for personal magnificence against Charles's modest – and sometimes even shabby – black clothing.

The Hall of the Sultan in the harem in the Topkapi Palace in Constantinople. When visiting his harem, the Sultan sat at ease under the baldequin, but some of the furniture seen here is of more recent date than Suleiman's time.

A contemporary 16th-century Turkish miniature of Sulieman with his Grand Vizier in a pavilion in the gardens of the Topkapi Palace. The boys in tall conical hats are pages, and there are two court dwarfs in the centre foreground.

Istanbul at sunset looking up the Golden Horn. Not even the smog or the smoke from the multitude of ferries, which carry most of the city's commuters to and from work, can destroy the romance of the city's skyline with its minarets and domes or make the visitor forget the greatness of Constantinople's past.

In Suleiman's time Dubrovnik was a small independent republic named Ragusa, which had been 'protected' by Venice for centuries, but when Suleiman overran Hungary the city prudently changed protectors and paid the Turks an annual tribute. By a mixture of political opportunism and the maintenance of the kind of formidable fortifications seen here, it retained its independence until the time of the Napoleonic wars. The fortress on the right overlooks the harbour and dates from the 16th century, while that on the left is two centuries older.

Islam. Christians were subject to certain legal disabilities, and they were taxed rather more heavily than Moslems, but they were allowed to practise their own religion, and the large numbers of Christian peasants in Anatolia and elsewhere were protected by the Sultan's government from the kind of exploitation by a wealthy land-owning aristocracy which had been common in Byzantine days, while those in the countries conquered by the Turks in the Balkans were often so much better treated by their new masters than they had been by their feudal overlords, who had been their fellow Christians, that they positively welcomed the change.

As to the everyday lives of the ordinary Turkish working men and women, materially they did not differ very much from those of the common people in Europe: their existence was precarious, they worked hard, and they were poor. The rights of the urban poor were to some extent protected by trade guilds, which all working men joined, and whose existence was guaranteed by law; even so, some members of the guilds were very poor indeed. In the great city of Bursa, where records were kept during the second half of the fifteenth century of the wealth of those who died, twenty-six per cent owned fewer than twenty ducats at the time of their deaths, while only sixteen per cent owned 200 ducats or more. In the country, most peasants were Greek Christians, and only a few Turks worked on the land; these too were poor, but whatever their religion might be, their rights were safeguarded by Islamic law, and although they were far from well off they were not exploited as badly as many of the poorest country folk in Christian countries further west. Meanwhile, a large number of poor Turks still led a nomadic life, following their flocks and herds to their traditional pastures in the huge empty spaces of Anatolia, co-existing with the little settled communities of Christian peasants, trading with them, and as the years went by intermarrying with them more and more frequently. Their lives were hard, but they were no harder than they had been in their fathers' days or those of their grandfathers.

In fact, all the evidence, such as it is, goes to show that by nature the Turkish people were easy-going, friendly human beings, contented with their lot, averse to change, deeply faithful to the ways of Islam, and happy enough with the political structure of their country under the absolute autocracy of the reigning Sultan. At times, they were capable of outbreaks of mass brutality, and these have been more frequently recalled than their more amiable achievements. Yet they had some endearing characteristics which have seldom been mentioned by western historians, whose accounts, understandably, have been coloured by the prejudices and propaganda born of the centuries of bitter warfare waged between their own countries and 'the unspeakable Turk', to quote Mr Gladstone. For instance, de Busbecq remarked on their love of flowers. 'The Turks are very fond of flowers,' he wrote in 1555, 'and though they are otherwise anything but extravagant, they do not hesitate to pay several *aspres* for a fine blossom.' Tulips were favourites, and they loved roses so much that they believed that they had sprung from the sweat of Mohammed. Similarly, they were extremely fond of animals, treating them with great consideration and becoming furious with anyone who dared to ill-treat them. A Venetian living in Constantinople in Suleiman's time had to be rescued from an angry mob which had attacked him for subjecting a bird (it seems to have been a nightjar) to a form of captivity which the people regarded as cruel; and the invaluable de Busbecq noticed how well the country people treated their horses. 'On my journey to Cappadocia through the region of Pontus and the part of Bithynia which is called from its condition Axylus (woodless), I noticed what care the peasants bestowed on their colts while they were young and tender, how they petted them and admitted them to their houses and almost to their tables, and stroked and caressed them; you might say that they almost counted them among their children.' In fact, when taxed with treating their animals better than the human beings they captured in war, the Turks admitted to de Busbecq that they did so, arguing that since animals were dumb creatures of mere instinct and impulse, they deserved to be treated with more forbearance and kindness than Christian captives, who, in their view, had failed to use their God-given human freedom to choose rightly by rejecting the one true God and Mohammed his prophet.

It was over such people and such a realm that Suleiman assumed absolute power in September 1520, at the age of twenty-six. His youthfulness was not considered to be at all unusual at the time, even if it tends to astonish those of us who live in a later and incurably gerontocratic age. Henry VIII of England had come to the throne at the age of eighteen, and was still only thirty years old; Francis I of France was the same age as Suleiman, the Emperor Charles V was twenty, and King Louis of Hungary, of whom more will be heard later, was only fourteen. Indeed, far from being alarmed at the youthfulness of their new Sultan, Suleiman's accession raised great hopes in Turkey, and Christians in the western European countries were so thankful to hear that Selim the Terrible was dead that they welcomed his successor almost as warmly as the new Sultan's own subjects. In Turkey people noted with delight the auspicious signs which clustered round their new sovereign: the number ten, being that of the fingers and toes, the Commandments in the Pentateuch, the disciples of the Prophet Mohammed, the parts of the Koran, and the astronomical heavens of Islam, was considered perfect, and Suleiman had been born in the first year of the tenth century of the Moslem era; on top of that, he was the tenth Sultan of the Ottoman dynasty, and had been named Suleiman like the wisest of kings in biblical days, Solomon, the son of King David. It all augured miraculously well for the future.

On a more mundane level, the rulers of western Europe were delighted by the first reports which they received of the new Sultan's apparent fitness to reign, his fairness, nobility and strength of character; high hopes were raised that perhaps a golden age of peace and co-existence with their traditional enemies over the eastern horizon was at last dawning, and this was all the more exciting after the savage wars of Selim's short but terrifying reign. No one had yet told them that Suleiman had another side to his character – that he was more than a little narcissistic, fiercely determined to be 'Lord of the Age' and to allow no other prince the pre-eminence, and both willing and eager to prove his superiority by force of arms. It was not long, however, before the princes of the West found out.

IV

✠ ✠ ✠

The King of Hungary's Peace

Heaven grant us its peace, but not the King of Hungary's.

Shakespeare, *Measure for Measure*

When Suleiman came to the throne, his empire was at peace. This did not last long, however, for a man named Ghazali, who was the governor of Syria, took the opportunity provided by the death of Selim to rebel against the new young Sultan, and to make a bid for independence. In origin he was a Mameluk who had already played the traitor once in his life by betraying his Egyptian masters by changing sides at the time of Selim's conquest of Egypt, for which Selim had rewarded him with the governorship of Syria; now he compounded his treachery by staging a full-scale military revolt against Selim's son. He had no difficulty in establishing himself as master of Damascus, Beirut and Tripoli, where he met little opposition; most of the Turkish garrisons acknowledged his authority at once rather than cause trouble, and those who did not do so were slaughtered. But when he reached Aleppo, the local governor refused to open the gates of the city to him, and Ghazali was forced to besiege it.

Meanwhile, news of his insurrection was not long in reaching Constantinople, and in early November 1520 Suleiman dispatched an army eastwards under the command of a certain Ferhad Pasha with orders to crush the rebels. News of Ferhad's coming was brought to Ghazali, who was forced to raise the siege of Aleppo and retire hastily to Damascus. On arrival there, he massacred 5,000 Janissaries, upon whose loyalty he felt that he could not count, and sat down to wait for

Ferhad and his army. He did not have to wait long, for Ferhad arrived before the walls of the city on 22 December and promptly laid siege to it. Damascus was not prepared for a siege, and Ghazali had no alternative but to stake everything upon the outcome of a battle. He led his men out of the city early on the morning of 27 January 1521 and attacked Ferhad's army, which was drawn up to meet him. The issue was never in doubt. Ghazali's motley force of Mameluks, mercenaries and renegade Turks was no match for Ferhad's trained and disciplined troops, who slew their opponents with very little difficulty and considerable enjoyment. Ghazali, who tried to escape, did not get very far; betrayed to Ferhad by one of his own principal lieutenants, he was decapitated and his head was sent to Constantinople as a present to Suleiman. It arrived on 6 February in an advanced and malodorous state of putrefaction, a grisly proof of the foolishness of rebelling against the new Sultan, but Suleiman was delighted with it: so delighted, indeed, that he decided to send it to the Doge of Venice as a proof of his esteem, and it took all the diplomatic skill of the Venetian representative in Constantinople to dissuade him.

Having dealt satisfactorily with Ghazali, Suleiman turned his attention to the Hungarians. Nominally, Turkey was at peace with Hungary, but that did not stop people living on the border between the two countries fighting each other. There were raids and counter-raids, villages and country houses were burnt, and at times pitched battles were fought in which lives were lost on both sides. Six years before Suleiman's accession, the governor of the Hungarian province of Transylvania, John Zapolya – of whom more will be heard – had led an army of 10,000 men across the Turkish frontier into Serbia in a great predatory raid, and had been engaged by the local Turkish Pasha, who had soundly beaten him; the surviving Christians had made their way back to their own country as best they could, while the triumphant Turks had sold their prisoners in the slave markets of Constantinople. War, however, had not broken out as a result, for Selim had been too busy elsewhere to chastise the Hungarians for their aggression; but relations between the two countries had not been improved.

Having inherited this tangled and tense situation, Suleiman's first move was to send an envoy named Behram to the court of King Louis of Hungary with orders to offer him a lasting peace on condition that he paid the Sultan a large sum of money annually as tribute. It is impossible to say whether Suleiman expected the Hungarians to agree tamely to his proposal or not; he may have done so, but on the whole it is more likely that he both expected them to refuse and hoped that they would do so, thus providing him with a ready-made excuse for declaring war. But whatever his motives may have been, the

Hungarians made the outbreak of war virtually inevitable by their treatment of the Turkish envoy. All reports agree that they treated Suleiman's offer with contempt, heaping insults upon the unfortunate Behram and throwing him into prison, while some go even further and allege that they cut off his ears and nose, and sent them back to Suleiman; others again assert that they put the wretched man to death. The anger of the Hungarians was understandable, for they were a proud people and they loathed the Turks; but their behaviour was also foolish, for they were in no position to fight a war. After a period of national greatness, when they had been led from strength to strength by two great national heroes, John Hunyadi and his son Matthias, the country had suffered a catastrophic collapse. Indeed, seldom has such a rapid and disastrous decline been recorded in the history of any other European country as that which reduced Hungary from great strength to near-impotence just before Suleiman's time, and it is important to understand its causes.

Where Hunyadi and Matthias had enriched and united the country, bringing the best out of men of all sections of society and inspiring them again and again to feats of heroism, their successors squandered the country's resources, squabbled endlessly among themselves, split the land into warring factions and treated the common people so badly that in the summer of 1514 the peasants staged an open revolt against their oppressors. At first they had some success; they were so numerous that in their first encounter with a small force of nobles and their retainers they won an easy victory despite their complete lack of training and the inferiority of their weapons. Elated by success, they overran the country, burning castle after castle, massacring the noblemen and their families who were unfortunate enough to fall into their hands, after torturing them and raping the women. But their triumph was short-lived; the various factions on the opposing side, realizing that unless they forgot their differences and united against the common enemy they would all be destroyed, joined forces and marched out to meet the over-confident and disorganized peasants. The result was a foregone conclusion; the rebels were completely defeated, their leader was captured, and their brief moment of self-assertion and hope for the future was soon turned into despair, as the savage work of retaliation began.

John Zapolya, who had played a leading part in suppressing the rebellion, was made president of a tribunal which was set up to judge the rebels and mete out whatever punishment seemed appropriate to their crimes. Mercy was shown to none of them. The brother of the chief rebel was beheaded, while much less pleasant fates were invented for all the other principal rebels. First, they were thrown into prison, where they were starved for a fortnight, during which time one of them died; the survivors were then paraded in front of a large assembly of nobles with their families and supporters, who had gathered for the occasion, and after a good deal of brutal by-play and sadistic ill-treatment, the ringleader of the rebels was singled out to be the first to suffer. He was forced to sit on a mock throne of iron, which had been heated until it was red hot, while a red hot iron crown was rammed savagely down on his head, and a red hot sceptre was thrust into his hand. It is said that the smell of his roasting flesh was too much for his famished companions, who rushed upon him with cannibalistic intent and began to tear him to pieces; but like many wartime atrocity stories this sounds a little too bad to be true. What is certainly true, however, is that all the leading rebels were tortured to death publicly, and their defeated followers returned to an existence of virtual slavery on the estates of their former masters, where they were even worse treated than before.

The cost of this miniature civil war was appalling. It was bad enough that 50,000 lives had been lost, but the legacy of bitterness between the peasants and their masters was even worse, and despite the ever-present threat of Turkish invasion, which could only be countered by a united country, the ruling class seemed to have learned nothing from the uprising. Instead of trying to repair the damage done by the war they made matters worse by passing a severely repressive and unjust law, which could only result in exacerbating their relations with the common people. On 19 November 1514 the ruling party in the Diet passed an act which exempted the nobility from all taxes, while stating that 'the recent rebellion . . . against the whole nobility, led by a robber chief, has for all days to come put the stain of faithlessness on the peasants, and they have thereby utterly forfeited their liberty and become subjects to their landlords in unconditional and perpetual servitude. The peasant has no sort of right over his master's land save bare compensation for his labour and such other rewards as he may obtain. Every species of property belongs to the landlords, and the peasant has no right to invoke justice against a noble.' Having thus settled the fate of the serfs to their own satisfaction, the land-owning nobles returned to their own quarrels, while their young King, unable to do anything to control them and uninterested in doing so in any case, continued to enjoy himself in his own carefree and careless way.

King Louis was an amiable youth. He had been born prematurely, and it had taken all the medical skill of the doctors available at the time to keep him alive. For weeks he had been laid in the warm carcasses of animals slaughtered and cut open especially to receive him, and by this means saved from death. He had inherited the throne from his father when he was only fourteen, and had ruled the country with the help of a triumvirate of guardians: a cardinal, the governor of Buda, and the Margrave of Anspach. The Margrave was fond of the boy, but he was also fond of riotous living, and probably without meaning to do so he had imparted his own taste for intemperance to the child in his care; his studies under a tutor named Jacob Piso had been progressively neglected in favour of riding, hunting, playing games of various kinds and feasting as often as possible. As he grew up, the young King had surrounded himself with playboys and empty-headed courtiers with little claim to sobriety and less to intelligence, with whom he had amused himself all day long and during most of the night; among them was a man named Peter Korogi, whose talents were not untypical of those of the King's other companions, even if they were somewhat more idiosyncratic. He had an apparently indestructible stomach and a nature without a trace of squeamishness, and this happy combination enabled him to keep the court in fits of laughter as he ate live mice, dead cats' tails, carrion found in the streets, and even inkstands with the ink in them. Louis was twenty-four when Suleiman came to the throne, and it would be interesting to know what the young Sultan thought of Louis, but we have no information on the subject. What we do know, however, is that when his envoy to Louis's court was insulted and maltreated, he began to make immediate preparations for war.

Since no attempt was made to hide the progress of this Turkish mobilization, the news soon reached Hungary that military preparations on a large scale were being made to invade her. It was obvious to everyone that the country did not have much time to make her own counter-preparations, and that in her divided and weakened state she desperately needed help to withstand the coming assault; but help proved difficult to find. The rest of Europe was too preoccupied with its own troubles to worry much about Hungary's affairs, though everyone was sympathetic. Giovanni de' Medici, Pope Leo X, listened with real concern as the Hungarian ambassador described his country's plight and the growing Turkish menace to the Christian lands of eastern Europe, but when asked for money he begged to be excused; he had none to spare at the moment. The Doge of Venice was equally sympathetic and promised to help in any way he could, if the other European princes would do so too, but refused to act alone. Great things were expected of Sigismund I of Poland, for he was uncle to King Louis of Hungary, but once again all that the Hungarian ambassador received was sympathy; Poland's southern frontier with Turkey was long and uncomfortably vulnerable, and fond as Sigismund was of his nephew he was not prepared to go to war for his sake. Moreover, he suspected that if he became involved in a war with the Turks the Muscovites might take the opportunity to attack Poland from the north and east, and his apprehension was not lessened by the news that a Muscovite embassy had recently arrived in Spain, whence his own ambassador – a remarkable man named John Dantiscus – wrote to him to warn him that the Emperor Charles was encouraging the Russians to attack him. As it happened this was quite untrue, and the only thing that these Russian ambassadors succeeded in doing during their stay in Spain was to astonish their hosts by their extraordinary behaviour; for despite the heat of a Spanish summer they invariably appeared clad in heavy furs and bathed in sweat to the huge, if politely disguised, amusement of the Spanish court. Most of the time, however, they sedulously avoided meeting their diplomatic colleagues and stayed in their lodgings, blind drunk.

Having been turned away by the Pope, the Doge and the King of Poland, the Hungarians sought the help of the Emperor Charles, whose realm had most to fear from a Turkish victory in Hungary. On 3 April 1521 their ambassador, Hieronymus Balbus, appealed to the Diet at Worms for immediate and substantial help in a long and passionate speech. He warned them that if Hungary were to succumb the whole of Europe would lie open to the horrors of invasion: horrors which Hungary herself had suffered again and again in the past without complaint, knowing that she was defending, not only her own country, but the whole of Christendom from the terrible ravages of the Turks. 'For who prevented their ungoverned frenzy from spreading further?' he asked, according to the *Deutsche Reichstagsaken unter Karl V.* 'The Hungarians. Who shielded the throat of Christendom from the Turkish arrows? The Hungarians. Who chose to meet the whole power and might of these barbarians, rather than let them pass into other people's countries? The Hungarians. Long, long before now, a terrible hurricane would have swept into the heart-lands of Germany and Italy, if the Hungarians had not prevented it from spreading farther than the borders of Pannonia. But now the Hungarian kingdom is in such straits, and its people have been so frequently massacred by the Turks, that it is not only too weak to conquer them, but unless it is given help, it will no longer be able to stop them in their tracks.' It was magnificent, and Balbus's appeal moved his audience deeply, but it could scarcely have come at a more awkward or inconvenient moment for the Emperor.

Charles, who had been Emperor for less than two years, was surrounded by a sea of troubles: he was at odds with the Diet over membership of the Council of Regency; there was a revolt in Castile; he was on the brink of war with Francis I; and William of Croy, the Lord of Chièvres, who had been both his Grand Chamberlain and a virtual father to him since the death of his own father when he was seven, had just died. As if all this was not enough for him to bear upon his twenty-one-year-old shoulders, on 18 April Martin Luther had made his celebrated speech to the Diet, where pandemonium had been let loose as a result. Charles, who was deeply conservative in religious matters and respectful of the traditions of his ancestors, was appalled. On the morning of the next day he read a statement to the Diet in which he proposed to put Luther under the ban of the Empire; but the Germans would have none of it, shouting and waving their arms in anger, while the Spaniards applauded the Emperor, and tried to silence the Germans. It was not an edifying scene and it upset Charles. It was in the evening of the same day that he met Balbus and the other Hungarian envoys, and handed them his reply. Although they must have been aware of the difficulties confronting Charles, nevertheless they were bitterly disappointed. Nothing could be done at the moment to help their country, he told them, though he held out hope of help in the future. In the meanwhile, if King Louis could not withstand the coming onslaught of the Turks, he, Charles, would not object if he made a truce with them, as long as its terms 'did nothing to damage the interests or the security of the Empire, the Catholic Church, or the Commonwealth of Christian nations'. Angry and frustrated, Balbus and his fellow countrymen went home.

They were made no happier by what they found on arrival, for the imminence of the Turkish invasion had not united the country but had rather exacerbated its divisions. The peasants were surly, unco-operative and frankly hostile to the authorities, who, having deprived them of their human rights and oppressed them for years, were now encouraging them to fight to preserve the *status quo*. They reckoned that they had nothing to gain by exposing themselves to the hazards of battle, while if they refused to fight and the country was conquered by the Turks, they could hardly turn out to be worse than their present task-masters. Meanwhile the nobles, who had returned to their eternal bickering and jockeying for position, were behaving like spoilt children, standing on their dignity and refusing to accept any orders from the central government, if those orders did not happen to be to their liking.

The Council of State met on 24 April to discuss the emergency, and addressed itself first to the defence of the two great frontier fortresses of Sabać and Belgrade, which stood across the path of the invader, thirty-five miles apart. They were vital to the security of the country, but they were commanded by two typical Hungarian noblemen, who flatly refused to take orders from the Council; instead they angrily asserted that they were quite capable of holding the Turks at bay without any interference from any jack-in-office in Buda. When charged with insubordination they packed their bags and went home to their estates, where they nursed their injured pride and sulked in morose silence. In their place command of Sabać was given to two men of courage and integrity, Simon Logody and Andrew Torma, while in marked contrast the more important fortress of Belgrade was entrusted to a pair of young aristocrats, Francis Hedervari and Valentine Torok, who had nothing to commend them but the nobility of their birth and who were soon to prove themselves to be incompetent, faithless and cowardly; but at least they were willing to come to the aid of their country in its hour of extreme need, and this was more than most of their fellow nobles were prepared to do. Instead most of them were preparing to travel to Pressburg, where King Louis was about to marry the Habsburg princess Mary of Austria, and there to enjoy the festivities which had been specially arranged to mark the occasion. No one seems to have suggested to the young King that some of the money spent on his nuptials might have been better used to pay the sailors of the Danube fleet, who had received no pay for three years, and who were presently seeking justice in the capital; but apparently it occurred to no one to do so, and when the sailors received nothing once again but vague promises of payment in the future, many of them went home and left the river unguarded, Turks or no Turks.

Meanwhile on 16 February Suleiman had marched out of Constantinople at the head of his army. Some idea of its size may be gained from the fact that it was accompanied by a train of 33,000 camels and 10,000 wagons carrying powder, shot and other provisions for the troops; a hundred pieces of artillery followed the army, and forty ships of the Turkish Black Sea fleet were ordered up the Danube towards Belgrade. Although the weather was still cold it was not unusually wet, and the roads were in a better condition than was often the case at this time of year; nevertheless the progress of the army was slow for it halted frequently, partly to rest the men and partly to allow Suleiman to hold court and receive local dignitaries in his tent. It did not reach Adrianople (the modern Edirne) until 27 May, and Philippopolis a fortnight later on 9 June. At Nish the army was divided into two parts, half being put under the command of a certain Ahmed Pasha, the governor of Rumelia (as the eastern part of European Turkey adjoining Constantinople was called), while the other half was entrusted to the Grand Vizier Piri Pasha. Ahmed was sent westwards against Sabać on the River Save with Suleiman himself following a few days behind the main body, and Piri Pasha made straight for Belgrade while a large force of irregular cavalry, the *akinji*, was ordered to spread out all over Transylvania to the east of the city and lay it waste.

As they poured down from the foothills of Serbia on to the great Hungarian plain the Turks met little resistance. The weather was perfect without a cloud in the sky, the fields were ripening to harvest, and the young grapes were hanging in clusters from the vines. The terrified peasants had deserted their homes several days earlier, and the villages were abandoned and empty. The Turks burnt them as they passed, and the garrisons in Sabać and Belgrade were given warning of the coming of the enemy, as a forest of columns of smoke from burning hamlets and farmsteads rose lazily into the blue sky to mark their passage. Sabać was the first to be attacked. It was defended by no more than 500 men, who were so vastly outnumbered that there could be only one conclusion to the siege; but they fought with magnificent if futile heroism until only sixty were left alive after sixteen days of siege and constant bombardment by Turkish cannon. When they could no longer man the walls, rather than surrender they waited for the invaders in the main square of the city, where they fought until the last man was killed.

During the whole of the campaign, Suleiman kept a diary, in which he recorded the events of each day, referring to himself always in the third person as 'the Sultan' or simply as 'Suleiman':

On July 7 came news of the capture of Sabać; a hundred heads of the soldiers of the garrison, who had been unable to escape across the Save, were brought to the camp. The next day these heads were stuck on pikes alongside the road to the camp, and Ahmed Pasha was granted an audience to kiss the Sultan's hand. Suleiman visited the city and ordered the building of a new bastion and a surrounding moat; he also commanded that a bridge should be thrown across the river so that the army might cross to the northern bank . . . He sat in a shed nearby to encourage the men working on the bridge by his presence. The pashas, armed with rods, also encouraged them to work hard.

But despite this mixture of encouragement and chastisement, the bridge was not finished until 18 July, by which time the fine weather had given way to rain and the river had begun to rise ominously high. As soon as it was complete as many men as possible crossed the river, but by the morning of the next day it was unusable; those who had not already crossed to the northern bank had to be ferried across before the army could set out to join Piri Pasha before the walls of Belgrade. However, they reached the city on the last day of the month, and Suleiman's arrival was greeted by cheers from the besiegers, while the gloom of the Hungarians trapped inside the city deepened. They had already been deserted by their two aristocratic commanders, and the garrison of 7,000 men had been much reduced during the month of fighting since Piri Pasha's arrival; the city was cut off from the south and west from any hope of reinforcements or supplies, and the first thing Suleiman did on arrival was to place some of his heaviest cannons – heavier than anything which had been bombarding the city before – on an island in the Danube, from which point they began to subject the city to a terrible pounding. It was known that a large army under John Zapolya was not far away, and rumour had it that another force under the command of a nobleman named Bathory, the Palatine, was also approaching; and everyone's hopes were pinned to the coming of these two contingents of friendly troops. Perhaps it was as well that no one in the city knew that Zapolya and Bathory hated each other, and so strong was the personal rivalry between them that they were more intent upon destroying each other than upon coming to the relief of their countrymen in Belgrade.

On 2 August, the Janissaries were ordered to assault the place, which they did with their usual dash and fanatical courage, but in the event they were thrown back by the defenders with heavy losses. Suleiman mentioned this reverse in his diary, writing laconically, 'Assault; moat is filled with corpses; five or six hundred men are lost.' A week later the attack was renewed, and this time the Hungarians, who had been reduced to a few hundred in number, were forced to abandon the walls of the city and retire to the citadel. There they held out for another three weeks, when the Serbian mercenaries among them refused to fight any more and forced the Hungarian commander to ask for terms of surrender. He was told that the lives of his men would be spared. As further resistance was virtually impossible he had no alternative but to agree; the survivors marched out and gave themselves up to the Turks, who promptly massacred all but the Serbians despite their promises. It seems, however, that this was done without Suleiman's knowledge or authority, though it is not known whether those who committed this crime were punished or not.

The fall of Belgrade was a blow to the whole of Christendom. The city had withstood a siege by Mehmed the Conqueror, and despite the lack of preparations by the Hungarians no one had expected it to fall to this young Sultan on his first campaign. It was a disaster of the first magnitude, and as the news spread throughout Europe people trembled for the future. Meanwhile, it was a triumph for Suleiman, who celebrated his victory on Friday, 18 August 1521, by going to the cathedral in Belgrade to say his Friday prayers and to consecrate it as a mosque. Most of the able-bodied citizens, both men and women, were packed off to Turkey to be sold as slaves, while the Serbians were rewarded for their help during the siege by being allowed to retain their freedom; some of them accompanied the Turks when they returned home, and founded a village near Constantinople which they named Belgrade, where some Serbian monks built a monastery to house the deeply revered corpse of the Serbian saint, Svata Patniza. This act of piety by the monks was destined to prove useful to them in a rather unexpected way, for when they fell on hard times they sold the saint's mortal remains to the Greek patriarch for 12,000 ducats.

Meanwhile Suleiman returned to his capital, where he was greeted rapturously by the people of the city. It was a moment of glory for him, but unfortunately it was overshadowed by the news that while he had been away two of his infant children had died, and ten days after his arrival in the capital his nine-year-old son, Mahmoud, also died of smallpox. He was not a callous man, and as he received ambassadors from Russia, Ragusa and Venice, bringing congratulations from their governments upon his Hungarian victory, he was noticeably depressed by this series of family tragedies, each little death coming hard on the heels of the last. It was an age of such high infant mortality, however, that while parents mourned the loss of their children, they were not surprised by their deaths; so mourning, though deep and genuine, was usually short, and it was not long before Suleiman was planning his next campaign. Contrary to everyone's expectation, he did not decide to follow up his capture of Sabać and Belgrade with another drive into Hungary; that could wait. Instead, he cast his eye upon quite another target: a target which his father Selim had planned to attack, had he not died before he could do so, the island of Rhodes.

V

✠ ✠ ✠

A Strong Town

Fifteen mile the sea brode is
From Turkey to the Ile of Rodez . . .
And on a hill there all alonen,
Is a Castell stiff and strong.
The Castell hight men saie so
Sancta Maria de Philerimo . . .
A strong town Rodez hit is
The Castell is strong and fair I wis.

Matthew Paris, Purchas His Pilgrimes

When Suleiman came to the throne, the island of Rhodes had been in the hands of the Knights of St John of Jerusalem for over 200 years, as had a number of the smaller islands nearby and a very strong castle dedicated to St Peter on the Turkish mainland at Bodrum, the ancient Halicarnassus. The Knights were members of a religious Order, which traced its origins back to the time of the First Crusade, when it had come into being after the capture of Jerusalem. There had been hospitals in that city for the care of pilgrims to the holy places of the Christian faith from very early days; one had been set up on the orders of Gregory the Great in AD 600, and 200 years later Charlemagne had been encouraged by the Caliph Haroun al-Raschid of *Arabian Nights* fame to enlarge and improve it. It had survived until the reign of the mad Caliph Hakim, who had destroyed it together with the Church of the Holy Sepulchre and many other Christian buildings in 1009; shortly afterwards, however, he had announced that he was divine and had given orders that his name should be substituted for that of God in all the prayers said in mosques throughout the Moslem world; this had so shocked his fellow Moslems that it had not been long before he had disappeared from the scene, probably murdered by his sister, an ambitious woman named Sitt al-Mulk. With toleration restored to the Christians, some Italian merchants from Amalfi had built another hospital on the site of the old one, dedicating it to St John the Almsgiver, a seventh-century patriarch of Alexandria, and it was this hospital which the Crusaders had found in active use, caring for the sick and wounded of all creeds, when they captured the city in 1099.

At the time, it was run by a French monk named Gerard. He had been in the city while the Crusaders were besieging it, and it was said of him that when they were half starving for lack of food, he had done his best to help them by throwing loaves of bread to them from the walls, while telling the Moslem defenders that he was bombarding them with stones. His trick had been discovered, however, and he had been dragged before the Moslem governor accused of treachery; but when the incriminating loaves were produced they had been miraculously turned into stone, and Gerard had been acquitted. The story had won him immense fame and popularity after the capture of the city, and he had taken the opportunity to enlarge the hospital and recruit more monks to serve in it. The fame of the Order had spread far and wide, and while gifts and endowments of land had poured in from all the crowned heads of Europe, the duties of its members had been enlarged and subtly changed. Their primary task continued to be the care of the sick, but to this was added the defence of pilgrims to the Holy Land; and from this time they had been speedily transformed, as the emphasis upon their military duties had grown, into a *corps d'élite* unique in the world of the day save for the other great religious Order, the Templars, which had had its origin in the same place, Jerusalem, at about the same time, and which became the great rival of the Hospitallers. Thereafter during the whole course of the history of the Crusader kingdoms, there had not been a battle in which the Knights Hospitaller had not taken a leading and usually an illustrious part. When, on Friday, 18 May 1291, the city of Acre had fallen to a greatly superior Moslem army after a siege lasting six weeks and a culminating battle of great ferocity, in which the Hospitallers had fought with sublime courage, only seven had survived.

But the Order had not died. Such was its immense prestige that its ranks had soon been replenished by new recruits. It had taken temporary refuge in Cyprus after the fall of Acre, but by the beginning of the fourteenth century it had become strong enough to seek a permanent home of its own, where it could adapt itself to the new situation and play a new part in the continuing struggle between the religions of the Cross and the Crescent for domination of the known world. At that time the island of Rhodes was under the control of a Byzantine governor, who had repudiated his allegiance to the Emperor in Constantinople, and had established himself as head of what was in effect a pirate state. Since an attack upon the place could therefore in no way be construed as an attack upon the territory of another legitimate Christian sovereign, the consciences of the Knights had been perfectly clear when they had decided to attack it and make it both their home and their base for military operations against the Turks; and this they had succeeded in doing in 1307.

Once installed on the island, they were splendidly placed for the task of harassing their enemies. The Order was composed of three classes of men, all of whom took religious vows and then trained as soldiers: first there were the Knights, who, as time went by, were recruited solely from aristocratic families in Europe; they were followed by the Sergeants, and then there were the Chaplains. Vowed to poverty, chastity and obedience, they elected one of their number to be their Grand Master, who was subject to the authority of no one but the Pope. The Knights were organized in *langues*, which were not strictly national groups, as their name might imply, but cut across nationality; by the end of the fifteenth century there were nine of these *langues*; Provence was the senior, followed by Auvergne, France, Italy, Aragon, England, Germany, Castile and Portugal. Each had its own *auberge,* and there the younger Knights lived a strictly disciplined life under the authority of an official known as the Conventual Pilier; they ate together in the same mess, took turns on watch and on duty in the hospital, attended mass and the other daily monastic offices prescribed by their rule of life, and learned to be expert seamen and trained fighters. As such they were the terror of every Moslem sailor who put to sea in the eastern Mediterranean. The Turkish writer, Mustafa Gelal-Zada, described his countrymen's hatred and fear of the Knights in his account of Suleiman's attack upon the island and his reasons for making it his next target after the fall of Belgrade:

It was the resolve of the Sultan, Father of the World and Conqueror of the whole Earth, to launch an attack upon Buda, capital of the unhappy country of Hungary; but one sect of the accursed Franks, worst of the sons of error, sent by Satan and well-known for their cunning and falsity, outcasts, damnable workers of wickedness, expert seamen and outstanding navigators, owned great fortresses everywhere along the Mediterranean coasts . . . These infidels were the lords of much territory, and their Corsairs, famous for their initiative and courage, attacked and cut the sea lanes, inflicting great loss and suffering on peaceful merchants, capturing or destroying their ships and carrying their crews off into slavery. Above all, the fortified city of Rhodes was a sanctuary for these execrable Franks. Its fortresses were without peer and its defences unrivalled in the whole world, and here these damned souls had a secure base from which to send out their swift galleys to the hurt and loss of Islam, allowing no merchant or pilgrim ship to pass towards Egypt undamaged by their cannon, enslaving and imprisoning innocent people . . . How many sons of the Prophet are captured by these children of lies? How many chains are put about their necks and fetters on their ankles? How many thousands of the faithful are forced to deny their faith? How many virgins and young women? How many wives and children? Their wickedness knows no end.

Rhodes had been a nuisance to Turkey for too long, and Suleiman decided to do what Mehmed had tried and failed to do: to cast the Knights out of the island once and for all.

The Grand Master at the time of Suleiman's accession was a man named Fabrizio del Caretto, but he died in 1521. In his place the Knights elected Philip Villiers de L'Isle Adam, who was on a visit to Paris when he heard of his election. He was fifty-seven years old, a member of the illustrious Villiers family, born at Beauvais in the Ile de France and a descendant of another Grand Master of the Order who had commanded the Knights during the last battle for Acre before they were expelled from Outremer. He had joined the Order before he was twenty and thereafter his promotion had been rapid. By the time he became Grand Master he was, according to one account, 'tall, lithe, graceful, alert, with a delicate, sensitive face, high cheek bones and aristocratic, aquiline nose, soft, flowing white beard and hair . . . a stern ruler, tactful diplomat and sincere Christian'. On receiving the news of his elevation, he set out at once to return to the island.

He had an eventful journey. Having embarked at Marseilles on a large armed vessel belonging to the Order, the *Sancta Maria*, which had been sent to fetch him accompanied by four smaller vessels as an escort, de L'Isle Adam set sail for Rhodes. He had not travelled far, however, when one of the escorting vessels, the brigantine *Reine des Mers*, caught fire off Nice; the crew were about to abandon ship when de L'Isle Adam intervened, threatening to hang anyone who did so, and eventually the fire was brought under control and the ship was saved. A few days later during a storm off Malta, the *Sancta Maria* was struck by lightning, and nine of the crew were killed; but although the Grand Master's sword was reduced to a twisted splinter of useless metal, he himself was unhurt: a miraculous delivery in which some saw the manifest hand of God. The five ships put in to Syracuse to repair the damage done during the last few days, but no sooner had they anchored than a local fishing vessel followed them into the harbour with the news that a celebrated Turkish corsair, Cortoglu by name, was cruising just off shore with a powerful flotilla which was cleared and ready for action. It was a dangerous situation, but one for which years of war at sea had prepared de L'Isle Adam. While waiting for the sun to set he prepared to put to sea, and for the second time in a few days God showed his hand by delivering the little Christian fleet from its enemies; aided by his superior seamanship and a favourable wind, de L'Isle Adam outmanoeuvred and outpaced the Turkish ships in the night, sailing on without further adventure or mishap to reach Rhodes on 19 September 1521. He landed one month and one day after the fall of Belgrade, and as their new Grand Master stepped ashore neither the Knights nor de L'Isle Adam were in much doubt that they and their island must be high on Suleiman's list of military objectives.

It was not long before whatever doubts they may have entertained were dispelled. Shortly after his arrival, de L'Isle Adam received a letter from the Sultan which had been dispatched by Suleiman on 10 September. A few historians have suggested that this letter is a later forgery, but they have been in the minority and most people have regarded it as genuine; it is worth quoting:

Suleiman the Sultan, by the grace of God, King of Kings, sovereign of sovereigns, most high Emperor of Byzantium and Trebizond, all powerful King of Persia, Arabia, Syria and Egypt, Supreme Lord of Europe and Asia, Prince of Mecca and Aleppo, Master of Jerusalem, and Ruler of the Universal Sea to Philip Villiers de L'Isle Adam, Grand Master of Rhodes, greeting and health: I congratulate you on your new dignity and upon your safe arrival in your estate. I hope that you will rule there in prosperity and even more gloriously than your predecessors. It rests with you to share in our favour; accept therefore our friendship, and as a friend congratulate me that, emulating my father who conquered Persia, Jerusalem, Arabia and Egypt, I have made myself master of that most important city Belgrade . . . I took many other strong and beautiful cities, destroying most of their inhabitants either by the sword or fire, and selling the rest into slavery. Now, after sending my large and victorious army home for the winter, I myself am able to return in triumph to my court in Constantinople. Farewell.

De L'Isle Adam rightly interpreted this letter as a thinly disguised threat, and as a result he replied in blunter language than was usual in such diplomatic exchanges:

Brother Philip Villiers de L'Isle Adam, Grand Master of Rhodes, to Suleiman, Sultan of the Turks, I have well understood the purport of your letter, which has been delivered by your ambassador. Your proposals of peace between us are as agreeable to me as they will be unwelcome to Cortoglu. That pirate omitted no efforts to surprise me on my passage from France; but having failed to stop me, as I sailed past him by night into the Rhodian sea, he tried to carry off two merchantmen, but the galleys of my fleet drove him off and forced him to flee. Farewell.

There could be no mistaking either the tenor or the intention of this letter. If Suleiman had expected the Knights to be intimidated by the immensely superior force at his disposal he had now been served notice that they were not accustomed to trembling before any man, and the 'Sultan of the Turks', as de L'Isle Adam somewhat contemptuously addressed him, was no exception. But war did not follow at once; the two men continued to exchange letters, while each prepared for the coming conflict. Suleiman assembled one of the largest armadas ever seen by the citizens of Constantinople, while at the same time he set about collecting troops from all over his empire. Even more important, he had spies on Rhodes who sent him detailed reports of the progress being made on the island in building up forces, repairing and strengthening the defence works and gathering supplies for the coming siege. One of these informers was a Jewish doctor named Apella Renato, who had been planted on the island by Suleiman's father, Selim, and who had successfully deceived everyone for years by masquerading as a Christian convert; while a senior member of the Order itself, a man named D'Amaral, who both hated de L'Isle Adam and disagreed with his decision to defend the island, was also a traitor – or so it was later believed, though his guilt was never proved beyond all possible doubt. Similarly, the Grand Master had his own spies in the enemy camp, who had little difficulty in passing their messages to him by way of the Castle of St Peter at Bodrum on the Turkish mainland or through the island of Kos, where the Knights also had a fortress. So each side knew pretty well what the other was doing, and neither doubted that war was imminent.

Meanwhile, emissaries were sent all over Europe to ask for help in the coming battle, but the Knights fared no better than the Hungarians had done a few months previously. They were welcomed wherever they went with warmth and sympathy, but the Emperor was still at war with the French King, and both of them were too distracted by their own affairs to spare much time, let alone men or money, for the Rhodians, though they assured the Knights of their prayers. More was expected of the new Pope Adrian VI, a Dutchman who had been tutor to the Emperor Charles in his boyhood, for Cardinal Giulio de' Medici, who was himself a member of the Order, had promised to plead the Knights' cause with the Pope; but although Adrian protested that he could not speak of the plight of the heroic Christians on Rhodes without tears, he refused to send troops to their assistance, preferring to keep them in Italy to fight the French.

Since help was not forthcoming from Europe, it became all the more important for the Knights to help themselves in every way possible, and one such way was to ensure that the enemy should have the bleakest of welcomes when eventually he landed on the island; so the Rhodians were set to the thankless task of destroying everything which could be of comfort to him. Houses, gardens and orchards

were destroyed; wells were poisoned or filled with muck; crops, such
as there were so early in the year, were harvested or burnt; and the
Rhodians themselves, together with their domestic animals, were
brought into the city, 'the women with their hair dishevelled,
scratching their cheeks, as is the custom of the place, weeping and
imploring God's help, with their tiny children lifting up their clasped
hands to heaven and praying him to have pity on them', as a
contemporary described the scene. The men were armed and
organized, and the sailors and harbour-men enrolled and charged with
the defence of the port; the peasants were set to work as pioneers, and
the slaves captured in previous encounters with the Turks were
employed digging trenches and strengthening the already formidable
fortifications and city walls.

By the end of April all was ready, and de L'Isle Adam staged a grand
review of his forces; they were small enough. Each *langue* was drawn
up in front of its own *auberge*, the Knights in full armour with their
scarlet surcoats displaying a white cross on each side, worn only in
time of war. There were 500 of them with about another hundred
Chaplains, and they were supported by a thousand mercenaries and
possibly another thousand Rhodian militiamen; that was all. In a
welcome if rare show of unity the Greek bishop of Rhodes, Bishop
Clement, appeared with his opposite number in the Catholic Church,
a Genoese named Balestrieri, and both men addressed the troops,
calling on them to put their trust in God and in the Mother of God.
Then, as a climax to the day's proceedings, a much revered image of
Our Lady of Philerimos was carried in solemn procession through the
streets of the city and placed in the Church of St Martin.

At the beginning of June the island of Kos was attacked by the
Turkish vanguard; it was more of a raid than a full-scale attack, and
most of the invading Turks were killed by the Knights of the small
garrison stationed there. Then on the eighth day of the month the men
on duty on the walls of Rhodes during the evening watch saw signal
flares to the north in the direction of the Turkish coast, and a ship was
sent to investigate. It returned with a formal ultimatum from
Suleiman:

The Sultan Suleiman to Villiers de L'Isle Adam, Grand Master of Rhodes, to
his Knights, and to the people at large. Your monstrous piracies, which you
continue to exercise against my faithful subjects, and the insult you offer to
my imperial majesty, oblige me to command you to surrender your island
and fortress immediately into my hands. If you do this, I swear by the God
who made heaven and earth, by the four thousand prophets which came
down from heaven, by the four sacred books, and by our great Prophet
Mohammed that you shall be free to leave the island, while the inhabitants who

remain there shall not be harmed. But if you do not obey my order at once, you shall all pass under the edge of my invincible sword, and the walls and fortifications of Rhodes shall be reduced to the level of the grass that grows at their feet.

De L'Isle Adam did not reply. Instead, martial law was declared on the island and last-minute preparations for its defence were put in hand.

These included the recruitment of a splendid individual named Gabriel Tadini of Martinengo. With a face which looked as if it had been hewn out of rock and with a great prow of a nose, he was a professional soldier and engineer, and probably the greatest expert of the day on the use of artillery and on military architecture, mining and counter-mining. At the age of twenty-six, he had been employed by the Venetians, and thereafter he had served them in the various wars in which the republic had been involved; at the time of Suleiman's threat to Rhodes he was in Crete, where he had been made supreme commander of artillery and charged with the task of strengthening the fortifications of the island which, like Cyprus, was a Venetian possession. When the governor of Candia, the island's capital, heard that the Grand Master had invited Tadini to join him in Rhodes, he forbade him to leave Crete lest his departure be construed by the Turks as a breach of Venetian neutrality; but such bureaucratic interference was not to Tadini's taste and with the help of a certain Antonio Bosio, a member of the Order who was on the island at the time, he made his escape and reached Rhodes a few days after the first Turkish ships had been sighted. His presence was an invaluable addition to the island's defences, and so grateful was de L'Isle Adam that he admitted him into the Order as a Knight of Grace in the *langue* of Italy.

According to Ottoman accounts, the Turkish fleet of 700 vessels manned by 40,000 sailors and carrying 20,000 irregular troops had sailed from Constantinople on 5 June 1522, to be joined at Gallipoli by more ships and by the corsair Cortoglu. Suleiman had left the city two days previously at the head of an army 140,000 strong, marching south along the coast of Asia Minor towards the small port of Marmaris (the ancient Physcus) on the coast immediately north of Rhodes. Almost certainly, neither his fleet nor his army was as large as this; contemporary observers nearly always exaggerated the strength of the forces involved in the battles of the day, but nevertheless the Turkish invasion force was undoubtedly a very large one indeed, hugely outnumbering the Knights with their Rhodian auxiliaries and handful of mercenaries. It seems to be generally accepted by historians that the Turkish fleet consisted of at least 200 vessels, and that the army probably numbered over 100,000 men.

On 26 June, the Feast of Corpus Domini, the first Turkish ships sailed past the city to anchor in Kalitheas Bay six miles down the coast to the south. A Victorian lady named Drane, who wrote a history of the Knights of St John which was published in 1858, described the scene in a splendidly purple passage, thus:

The palace gates were thrown open, and there rode out a brilliant and gallant train. Many Knights in armour and scarlet surcoats, the three standards floating over their heads, each borne by chosen men, to whom they had been solemnly delivered in charge . . . De L'Isle Adam in golden armour was at their head; and as the procession came along, and the trumpets sounded with a loud triumphant flourish, such a thrill of glad and glorious enthusiasm stirred through the crowd as banished fear; and they rushed to window and terraced roof to watch the coming of the Turkish fleet, and almost to welcome its advance. What a magnificent spectacle! In the streets below that glorious chivalric procession, the finest steeds and the brightest armour and the gallantest hearts in Christendom! Suddenly, and as though by some preconcerted signal on every rampart and battlemented wall, from the inns of the various languages and all the posts of separate command, there wave a thousand flags. Each nation has its own proud ensign and its own representative among the Knights of Rhodes. There you may see the golden lilies of France floating not far from the royal lions of England; there is the plain cross of Savoy, first borne in honour of the Order; there are the white flag of Portugal, and the time-honoured banners of Castile and Auvergne; and you know that beneath the silken folds of each are posted brave and gallant hearts, who will add fresh honour to their old renown. Look out over the port to the tower of St Nicholas, the key to Rhodes; twenty Provençal Knights are there, claiming, as Provence ever would, the post of danger and glory. The rest of the French you may distinguish drawn up with admirable regularity from the tower of France to the Ambrosian Gate; and thence to the Gate of St George stand the Germans . . . Spain and England stand together; the banner of the Turcopolier, Sir John Buck, waves out over their ranks; only nineteen English are there, but every man a hero, and ready for a hero's death . . . Lastly, those venerable unwarlike forms, bearded and saint-like, at whose approach Knights and sentinels and glittering ranks kneel as for a father's blessing, are not the least defenders of Rhodes. Leonard Balestrieri is the Latin metropolitan, reckoned the most eloquent preacher of the day; Clement, the Greek archbishop . . . and they love one another like brothers, so that, as they go from post to post, they are seldom to be met apart.

All this you may see as you look down upon the city. But glance over the ocean, and another spectacle awaits you. The blue line of the Levant, sparkling in the summer sunshine, and kissed into life and motion by a northern breeze, and on its bright expanse three hundred Turkish sail, gathered from every coast that owns the Ottoman rule, from Egypt, Syria, and every part of Asia . . . whilst a hundred thousand men under Suleiman himself are advancing along the western coast of Asia Minor. Alas for Rhodes and her six thousand defenders!

Regrettably, the reality must have been less colourful. Even in their heyday in crusading times the Knights had not worn ornate ceremonial armour in time of war, and on receiving news of the Turkish approach it is unlikely that they would have sallied forth from the Grand Master's palace on horseback in the cramped and narrow streets of the city of Rhodes. Moreover, although no doubt the blue line of the Levant did indeed sparkle across the sea towards Turkey, for the climate of Rhodes is superb in June, it is doubtful whether the city would have appealed to the modern tourist on that fateful summer morning; its drains were inadequate at the best of times, and with the place crammed to capacity with Knights, mercenaries and thousands of refugees from the country together with their flocks of domestic animals, the stench must have been appalling: bad enough perhaps even to reach the nostrils of the Turks as they sailed past with colours flying and bands playing just near enough to the harbour to tempt the gunners in Fort St Nicholas to open fire on them. It seems probable, too, that as the noise of the cannon rumbled and echoed across the town, however gallant the hearts which beat beneath armour or padded jacket or peasant's smock, there must have been some people to whom the thought occurred that the morning air would soon be made even more malodorous as human bodies rotted in the sun, and the smell of death began to vie for predominance with the stink of excrement. Distance may lend enchantment to the view of medieval warriors and their battles, as it does to other things, but at close quarters war was no more romantic then than it is now.

It took some time for the whole Turkish armada to forgather in Kalitheas Bay, and once assembled the process of disembarking the troops was slow; but by mid-July most of Suleiman's men and equipment were ashore, and a battery of heavy guns had been installed on a hill to the south of the city opposite the Post of England, while two more were soon sited in front of the Tower of Aragon and the Post of Provence respectively; but so fierce and accurate was the counter-battery fire of the defenders under the direction of Gabriel Tadini from the city walls that the Turkish guns were destroyed before they could do any damage, while the gunners fled out of range of the Knights' artillery. Even there, however, they were not safe, for during this early part of the siege the defenders made a number of highly successful sorties from the city, cutting off and destroying small parties of Turks and generally harassing the enemy to such an extent that his siege works were seriously hindered, and some of his troops were badly demoralized. There was even talk on the Christian side of a mutiny in the Turkish ranks, which was suppressed only by the arrival of Suleiman himself, who reached the island and took command on 28 July; but Turkish historians mention no such mutiny, and it may not have taken place. Despite the fact that it was the beginning of Ramadan, the Sultan's arrival on the island was greeted with salvoes of salutes, and the noise of brass bands gave notice to the men in the besieged city that someone out of the usual was being welcomed; it was not difficult to divine his identity.

With the coming of Suleiman the siege began in earnest. The city was completely invested by land, the artillery was in place, and the corsair Cortoglu was placed in command of a naval task force blockading the two harbours. On the morning of 29 July, as the Turkish engineers began to dig a maze of trenches leading up to the city wall and others carted away the debris to build a huge earthwork opposite the Tower of Aragon, their artillery began a fierce bombardment of the city. The Turkish cannon varied greatly in size; some were enormous, firing huge stone balls seven or eight feet in circumference, many of which can still be seen lying about round the city of Rhodes; others were smaller, and some were made of brass or iron. They also used some primitive incendiary shells, which they lobbed into the city from mortars and which burst into flames on landing. When the bombardment began, the Turks probably had between sixty and eighty heavy guns, supported by many more smaller pieces, and the noise must have been deafening; the older Knights were used to the din of battle, but as the thunder of the heavy guns, the sharper explosions of the lighter weapons, the high-pitched whine of the cannonballs, the crashing of masonry, the screams of frightened women and children, the squeals of stray animals hit by flying stone splinters and the howling of terrified dogs filled the morning air, as they must have done, it would have been surprising if some of the younger Knights had not felt tremors of fear, as they took what cover they could, crouching behind parapet or bastion and wondering where the next cannonball was going to land. As for the islanders themselves, crowded together with their women and children in cellars and basements and little back rooms, they must have been scared out of their wits by the cannonade. But although Suleiman's gunners kept up their bombardment for the whole of August, it did not do much damage and, as people became accustomed to it, they learned to ignore it most of the time. This lack of success was in part the result of the accuracy of the counter-battery fire by the Knights, which reduced the Turkish artillery to about half its original strength by knocking out a large number of guns and killing their crews; but it was also due to the fact that the artillery of the day was incapable of doing much damage to a target as large as a city. Some houses were damaged; the tower of the Church of St John, which was used by the Knights as an observation post, was destroyed;

and as the weeks passed some of the city's fortifications were battered into rubble, although an open breach was not made; but after a month's bombardment only twenty-five people had been killed, and the Turks themselves realized that they were wasting both their time and their ammunition.

More serious was the war of mines and counter-mines over which Gabriel Tadini presided with unflagging energy and vigilance. The comparatively recent discovery of gunpowder had revolutionized the art of mining, although it had always been one of the ways of trying to gain entry into a besieged city. In the past men had laboriously undermined the walls of a city under attack, propping them up with timber as they worked, until they were saved from collapse only by an infra-structure of posts and beams; when all was ready a fire was lit under the timber, the engineers ran for their lives and as the wood burned everyone waited in great excitement for the wall to come crashing down in a great mountain of smoking rubble, over which a dense mass of infantrymen would try to stumble into the city as soon as the dust settled. With the coming of gunpowder, however, tunnels were driven under the enemy's fortifications, charges were placed, the sappers were withdrawn, and the mine was then blown with greater or lesser effect according to the accuracy with which the tunnel had been dug and the position of the mine determined. Mining was by no means an exact science; sometimes the shaft was too deep, sometimes off target, and sometimes the charge was too small to do much damage. Meanwhile, as the besiegers burrowed like moles under a city's defences, they knew that the defenders would be lying with their ears to the ground, straining every nerve to detect the tap-tap-tapping of their picks, so that they themselves could undermine their enemies and blow them up before they had had time to reach their objective and plant a charge. Gabriel Tadini invented a number of new and sophisticated techniques in the art of counter-mining the enemy and defeating his efforts; he discovered how to dig ventilator shafts, which would help to dispel harmlessly the force of an enemy mine when it exploded, and he also invented a device which could detect the Turkish miners at work much more sensitively than even the most acute of human ears. It was very simple; he stretched a piece of fine parchment on a diaphragm, and attached to it a number of small delicately suspended bells; when this primitive seismograph was properly placed in contact with the fortifications or the ground beneath them, the bells tinkled as they picked up the tiny vibrations made by the burrowing Turks, whose whereabouts were thus betrayed to Tadini who began to counter-mine them immediately. It must have been a nightmare for the miners on both sides; they had to work in the narrow and stifling confines of dark, cramped shafts with little or no ventilation, choked by dust and in constant danger of being buried alive by the collapse of the tunnel's roof or as a result of the springing of a counter-mine. Often enough each side could hear the other working close by in the grim race to kill or be killed in the increasingly complicated maze of dark and fetid tunnels beneath the city, and casualties on both sides were indeed heavy; but this did not deter them. The Christians knew that they were fighting for their lives, and the Turks knew that if they showed any sign of faltering or weakness the least they could expect was to be bastinadoed, while they might well be beheaded if their overseers were minded to make an example of them.

The worst damage to the city's fortifications and the most numerous casualties suffered by its defenders were inflicted by some batteries of Turkish guns installed on a huge earthwork opposite the Tower of Aragon, which had eventually been finished by Suleiman's pioneers; but they had suffered terribly in the process for de L'Isle Adam had found out early in the siege the purpose for which the great mound was being constructed, and had given orders that the men working on it should be killed by every means possible in order to delay its completion. When it was first begun, one of the islanders who spoke fluent Turkish had volunteered to try to discover what it was the Turks were building, and why they were pressing ahead with it despite the casualties inflicted on them by the defenders' guns. With some other Turkish-speaking Rhodians, he had sailed quietly out of the harbour at night in a fishing vessel, easily evading Cortoglu's blockade, and having spent the night fishing he had sailed round behind the Turkish lines and had landed on the coast at a spot where an open-air market of a sort had been established for the use of the Turkish army. Here he had sold his fish, mingling with the crowd and chatting with some of the Turkish soldiers until evening, when he had somehow managed to inveigle three of them into his boat, where he had promptly knocked them on the head. When one of them had proved more pugnacious than the others, he had been beheaded, and the Rhodians had then sailed back to the city with one Turkish head and two terrified prisoners, who were easily persuaded to tell de L'Isle Adam all they knew of the earthwork which their countrymen were building so busily; it was to be piled up until it overtopped the city walls, when as many batteries of Turkish guns as possible would be mounted on it to fire down upon the defences and into the city itself. It was as a result of this information that orders had been given to harass the pioneers at work on the great mound, and they had been killed in their scores; but Suleiman and his commanders were prepared to be prodigal with the lives of their men when occasion demanded, and despite the carnage the work was finished by the middle of August, and heavy batteries sited on it. From then on, the Turkish artillery bombardment became highly effective and extremely dangerous.

Casualties were heavy on both sides, for neither side could take cover from the fire of the other; the Turkish gunners on the top of their mound were exposed to the fire of the Knights' guns, while the Knights themselves found it virtually impossible to hide from the Turkish cannon as they pointed down on them. Mehmed Pasha, the chief of Suleiman's artillery and one of his favourite commanders, lost both his legs to a cannonball; the Spanish master gunner and the Knight commanding the Post of Aragon were both killed, and so were most of the English, while the damage done to the city's fortifications became more and more serious as the days went by. As the walls and bastions crumbled under the ceaseless pounding of the Turkish heavy guns, so the rubble from their collapse filled the ditch at their feet. The walls were repaired at night, but inevitably they were battered down again the next day, and as the Turks drove their trenches closer and closer to the counter-scarp in readiness for an assault, it became obvious that a crisis was approaching. Hugely outnumbered as they were, the Knights could ill afford more casualties than they were already suffering, but something had to be done and it was decided that a number of sorties should be made in an attempt to destroy the Turkish guns which were doing so much damage. The first was led by Gabriel Tadini; at the head of 200 mounted Knights and Sergeants he rode out from the Post of Italy on 19 August, urging his horse forwards over no-man's-land towards the Turkish cannon. The ground was criss-crossed by shallow trenches filled with terrified Turkish infantrymen, who stumbled over each other in the confined space of their ditches in a frantic attempt to escape from the Knights, who impaled them on their lances as they passed like so many stuck pigs. On reaching their objective, some of them set fire to the heavy guns on their wooden carriages while others dealt with those of their crews who had not already fled in terror at their approach. It was a fierce little action while it lasted, giving the Turks little time to recover from their initial panic, but as their enemies retreated again towards the city they rallied and pursued them, only to be mown down by musket fire from the men on the walls of Rhodes. Further sorties were made from other sectors of the city perimeter on the day after Tadini's highly successful action and again on the 22nd and 24th of the month, and on each occasion, while the Christian casualties were light, Turks were killed and others were brought back to the city captive, while the Knights rode in with turbaned heads stuck grotesquely on the end of their pikes.

But despite the success of these raids and the damage done to the enemy artillery, the bombardment went on and the defences were beginning to suffer so badly that a number of breaches were made in them, and a general assault on the city could not be much longer delayed. De L'Isle Adam sent messengers to the courts of Europe begging for immediate assistance, and the fact that they had no difficulty in defeating Cortoglu's blockade so infuriated Suleiman, when he heard of their escape, that he gave orders for the old pirate to be publicly bastinadoed on the deck of his own ship; but the Sultan need not have worried unduly about de L'Isle Adam's messengers, for the crowned heads of Europe were no more ready in late August to help their embattled fellow Christians on Rhodes than they had been earlier in the year, so busy were they fighting each other. The men on the island realized that they would have to continue to look after themselves. Gabriel Tadini was already doing everything he could; he was mounting batteries of every kind of gun on specially constructed traverses on either side of the breaches in the walls, and posting trained marksmen on the roofs of the houses overlooking the danger points, while at the same time he was directing such a massive programme of counter-mining that by the beginning of September it was reckoned that four-fifths of the walls and ramparts had been undermined by tunnels of one kind or another.

On the afternoon of 4 September, the long-awaited attack came. De L'Isle Adam was attending vespers in the Church of Our Lady of Victories when the whole city was shaken by an enormous explosion; a mine had been detonated beneath the bastion of England, reducing a great mass of its masonry to rubble and making a gap in the wall twelve yards wide, through which Turkish soldiers began to rush as soon as the huge cloud of choking dust and fumes from the explosion had settled enough to allow them to do so. As the Grand Master ran to the scene accompanied by his standard bearer, Henry Mansell, bearing aloft a great banner of the Crucifixion, the English met the oncoming Turks with swords and pikes, while Frenchmen from the Post of Provence on their left flank and Spaniards from that of Aragon on their right fiercely attacked the invaders with muskets, arquebuses and bows, pouring a deadly fire into their ranks from the walls on either side of the breach, as they stumbled and scrambled over the debris in the gap. It was a murderous business. The Turks were as brave as the men of any other race and indeed braver than most, but the carnage was too much for them, and they began to fall back. Mustafa Pasha, their commander, who had led the first wave into the attack with a bravery so typical of him that it was acknowledged even by his enemies, was carried back with the rest despite all his efforts to stop them; forced into the ditch below the shattered walls, somehow he rallied his men and drove them back into the attack again, but having lost the momentum of the initial onslaught, their task was a hopeless one, and after two hours of bloody hand-to-hand fighting even Mustafa admitted defeat. As he drew the survivors back into the comparative safety of their own trenches the ground was piled high with the bodies of those who had been killed, and the evening air was filled with the cries and groans of the wounded. It would be gratifying to report that their Christian adversaries had mercy on these unfortunates, but the truth is that the men of Europe had no intention of allowing the Turks to rescue their wounded comrades, and when darkness fell they sent patrols into the wilderness of no-man's-land to finish off anyone with breath still left in him. Their own casualties had been nothing like as heavy as those of their enemies, who had lost over 2,000 men, but nevertheless their losses were greater than they could afford: one Grand Commander of the Order had been killed; so had Henry Mansell, the Grand Master's standard bearer, and other senior Knights had either been killed or were to die of wounds later, while the number of rank and file capable of bearing arms – already brought dangerously low as a result of previous casualties and of sickness – was further reduced. It was not a process which de L'Isle Adam's little garrison could endure for long, and he knew it. So, of course, did Suleiman.

It is difficult to discover the Sultan's reaction to the events of the siege, for his diary is more than usually laconic at this time. The entries for the first few days of September are terse to the point of distortion. 'September 1st, divan; Ahmed Pasha begins to bombard and breach the walls near St Mary's Tower. September 2nd, news received of the death of Mahmoud-Reis in the attack on Tilos, but the island surrenders nevertheless. September 3rd, the ditch below the city wall in Ahmed Pasha's sector is filled in by his troops. September 4th, explosion of a mine in front of Mustafa Pasha's sector; general bombardment by all batteries.' That is all; no mention of the attack, the Turkish losses, or the eventual retreat of Mustafa's men. Perhaps Suleiman's silence was the result of his unwillingness to record for posterity anything but Turkish victories. It is impossible to be sure, but certainly, as the years passed, he became more and more averse to admitting failure; other men might fail, but he was Lord of the Age and did not fail. But whether or not he was already subject to this kind of self-deluding megalomania, even though he was still in his twenties, he certainly did not mention in his diary the defeat suffered by his men on 4 September, and despite the casualties they had suffered, he allowed them little rest.

The month of September was a nightmare for the defenders of the city. Mine after mine was blown, though many of them were rendered ineffective by Tadini's skill in digging the ventilator shafts that dispelled the force of the explosions. Attacks were launched by the Turks on the 9th against the Post of Provence, on the 11th against England, on the 13th and 14th against Aragon and Provence again, where on the 18th another mine was exploded, which, either in error by the Turkish engineers or by one of Tadini's counter-mines, killed some hundreds of Turkish soldiers. The next day the Jewish spy, Apella Renato, was caught in the act of preparing to fire a bolt from a crossbow towards the enemy lines with a message attached to it, informing them that the garrison was almost at its last gasp. He was dragged before de L'Isle Adam where, after torture, he confessed to having been in the Turkish service for years, and to having passed a number of other messages to them during the course of the siege. He was hanged, drawn and quartered, but not, according to one source, before confessing his sins and dying 'a good Christian'.

For the next week fighting was incessant, and the Turks managed at last to effect a lodgement on what was left of the city's fortifications in the Post of Aragon; they were counter-attacked with dogged ferocity by the Knights, who used every weapon they could to dislodge them, shooting them, cutting them down, crushing them with stones, burning them to death with streams of Greek fire and pouring boiling oil and pitch on them, as they screamed and the smell of their roasting flesh filled the air. The Christians lost 200 men and the Turks at least ten times that number and perhaps more, before they were forced to abandon their foothold on the city walls. But despite the Turkish losses the exhausted defenders were allowed no respite, for on the next day two more mines were exploded, one of them harmlessly thanks to Tadini, while the other blew a great hole in the sector held by the *langue* of Auvergne, killing several hundred Janissaries who were incautious enough to stand too close to the mine when it was detonated, and although neither explosion was followed by an immediate attack, it was obvious from the flurry of activity behind the enemy lines that a large-scale operation was being prepared.

At daybreak on the morning of 24 September the Turkish guns opened fire along the entire front in a great barrage which shook the city and deafened the men of both sides; from the Post of France around the entire perimeter of the battered and half-ruined city to the Post of Italy a great pall of smoke from the guns covered the no-man's-land between the Turkish assembly points and what was left of the city walls, as the massed cannon hurled a continuous stream of stone and iron projectiles at the bastions and towers and ramparts which had defied them for so long. For a time the Knights could not tell where the attack was going to come, so furious was the bombardment along the whole length of the front, and it was only when wave upon wave of Janissaries led by their Aga in person emerged out of the smoke to storm the Post of Aragon and plant their banners on the ruins of the ramparts there that they knew where the main weight of Suleiman's attack was destined to fall; but as soon as the point of maximum danger was identified, reinforcements were rushed to the scene and the enemy advance was checked. The Knights had many faults, but throughout their history they had always displayed one great virtue: a sublime and selfless courage which blossomed most splendidly in times of crisis; and so it was now. From the Post of Aragon to that of Italy down by the sea to the south-west of the city, Suleiman's men came on in such huge numbers that to lesser men their advance might have seemed as inexorable as that of a flood tide or a flow of molten lava from an erupting volcano; but it did not daunt the Knights, who fought back like the steel-clad demons incarnate which the Turks had always believed them to be. They were magnificently supported by the Rhodians, who seem to have been so inspired by the example of these aristocratic fighting monks that they fought shoulder to shoulder with them with a courage as magnificent as that of the Knights themselves; their women also played their part, keeping the men supplied with ammunition, food and water, and tending the wounded. One of them achieved immortal fame. She was, it is said, the mistress of an English Knight who was killed during the course of the battle. When she stumbled upon the corpse of her lover she was so appalled by the prospect of a Turkish victory that she rushed off and killed her children rather than allow them to fall into the hands of Suleiman's men, and then, strapping on her dead lover's steel corselet and grasping his sword, she threw herself at the Janissaries with her hair streaming out behind her like one of the Greek Furies, killing several of them before they recovered sufficiently from the shock of her appearance to cut her down and send her after her dead lover.

The battle lasted most of the day. No one had much idea of the overall progress of events. Even Suleiman, who had caused a large wooden platform to be erected from which he could watch the onslaught upon the city as from a grandstand, could not guess the outcome. Most of the bastions and towers fell to the Turks at one time or another, only to be recaptured by the Knights in desperate counter-attacks. One such was led by the French Knight, Jacques de Bourbon, whose personal account of the siege was published in Paris four years after the event; the Tower of Aragon had fallen, and he was ordered to regain it. With a chosen band of men he led the way through one of Tadini's counter-mining tunnels; crouching low, stumbling forward in the dark and covered in sweat and dust, he and his men emerged breathless just below the Tower and prepared to rush the enemy on the summit. But the Turkish banners were flying over piles of Turkish dead, killed by the gunners of Auvergne less than

200 yards away, and the handful of exhausted men who were still alive were far too tired even to speak, let alone to fight. Silently and wearily they gave themselves up to Bourbon and his men.

There comes a time when men can do no more, and after six hours of continuous hand-to-hand fighting the Turks had reached that point. However loudly their commanders shouted at them, threatened them and beat them with the flat side of their scimitars, nothing would drive them back on to the ruins of the city wall again. As Eric Brockman has said in his history of the siege of Rhodes, 'At length the roar of the cannon and the crack of the hand-guns, the screams and groans of the dying, the shouted war-cries, the hissing of the seething pitch, the ring of steel on steel, diminished. No more threats, or promises, no visions of paradise could induce the Moslem to return to the broken walls over tumbled rubble slippery with blood.' It was finished. As an English Knight wrote to the Earl of Surrey after the event, 'although, after that the wall of the towne was downe, they gave us battall often tymes upon even ground, that we had no manner of advantage apone them; yet thankid be God and Saint John, at euvry battall they returned without their purpose.'

Suleiman was enraged. He had been told that victory was assured, and he was so angry that he condemned Mustafa Pasha to death for his failure; when one of the other senior commanders, Piri Pasha, dared to plead for him the Sultan condemned him to death too, and threw yet another of his most trusted commanders, Ayas Pasha, who had commanded the attack on the Post of Auvergne, into gaol. Two days later, when his temper had cooled, he pardoned all of them, though Mustafa was dispatched to Egypt in semi-disgrace as governor there. But if the Turks had suffered a defeat, the triumph of the Knights was something of a pyrrhic victory, magnificent as it had undoubtedly been. The extent of their casualties is not known, but it was more than they could afford, even though they had probably lost only one man to every fifteen or twenty dead or wounded Turks; and what made matters worse was that they were beginning to run out of powder and shot and wood for repairing the fortifications. There was still enough food in the city but it would not last for ever, and it began to look as if Suleiman was prepared, if necessary, to spend the winter on the island; whether the food and ammunition would last until the spring was a moot question and a worrying one.

But better news arrived in early October; a relief force was at last being assembled in Italy, and the English were about to dispatch a body of trained men to the island under the command of the veteran soldier, Sir Thomas Newport; they would come by sea, and they were due to sail from Dover almost at once. In fact, Newport sailed half-way through the month only to be wrecked in the Bay of Biscay in a storm with the loss of all hands, and the Italian relief was slow to come. On the island, the siege dragged on as the weather turned wet and cold with frosts at night and snow on Philerimos and Mount Elias. Sickness thinned the Turkish ranks, but that did not deter the Turkish commanders from driving their men into attack after attack regardless of the losses they suffered each time; there were plenty more men where the dead had come from, and as long as the Christians were being steadily worn down it did not matter to Suleiman or his commanders how many of their own men died; and the Christians were indeed being worn down slowly but also relentlessly. Even two or three casualties a day was a serious loss, for as the numbers of men in the city capable of bearing arms was gradually reduced, gaps inevitably appeared at vital points on the walls; and the same thing was true of weapons as of men. There were not many guns left in working order, and as they too became casualties they could not be replaced. When the long-awaited reinforcements from Italy arrived they turned out to consist of four Italian Knights and a young recruit, who was admitted to the Order on arrival and promptly killed in action three days later. It was a bitter disappointment, and although another handful of men arrived a few days later from Crete and a dozen more from the Knights' outpost at Lindos, as the elation of the victory in late September wore off it gave way to an uneasy sense of depression.

Two events deepened the general gloom. Gabriel Tadini was wounded by a bullet which entered his right eye and smashed its way through the side of his face to emerge near his right ear. It was a miracle that he was not killed, but he was invalided out of the battle for six weeks, and his loss was sorely felt. A fortnight later another man was caught trying to pass a message to the Turks by attaching it to the bolt of a crossbow and firing it into the enemy lines. An alert sentry spotted him in the act and caught him just before he could raise the bow to his shoulder and fire it. He was a Portuguese named Blasco Diaz, and he was in the service of the Prior of Castile, Andrea D'Amaral, who had ransomed him from the Turks many years ago and made him his personal servant. The man tried to keep silence but it took only a little physical persuasion to make him speak, and what he had to say appalled those who were questioning him; for he told them that he had been acting on the orders of his master D'Amaral, who had been corresponding with the enemy throughout the siege and indeed long before it.

The news spread like wildfire. D'Amaral had been a candidate for the position of Grand Master at the time of de L'Isle Adam's election; he had spent a lifetime of service in the Order, and was as senior as anyone could be without actually being given supreme power. It seemed unthinkable that he should be a traitor, and yet people tumbled over each other to believe in his guilt. In part, this was a result of his unpopularity; he had always been arrogant, aloof and a disciplinarian, and he had made many enemies. But in part, too, the readiness of so many to believe the worst of him may well have been influenced by the atmosphere of the time; ever since the Jew, Apella Renato, had been caught red-handed, paranoia had gripped the city. No one trusted anyone else, and rumours of treachery were rife, while a mad Spanish woman was to be seen wandering about the streets with wild hair and bare feet, screaming half-intelligible threats, prophesying doom for the city and warning traitors in high places of the wrath of God to come. It was known, too, that D'Amaral had always hated de L'Isle Adam; the two men had been rivals for years.

Arrested and brought before de L'Isle Adam, D'Amaral contemptuously refused either to deny or confirm the accusation of treachery brought against him, and when put to the torture, which he bore with his accustomed courage, he simply repeated that he had nothing to say, no guilt to confess. Was he to tell a lie and to sell his honour in order to save his old limbs from the rack? he asked. But his silence did him no good. The evidence against him, though flimsy by modern standards of what is and what is not admissible in a court of law, was sufficient to convince everyone at the time that he was guilty, and he was condemned to die. Whether he was a traitor or not has been endlessly discussed, and the truth will probably never be known. He died in proud silence.

Despite a trickle of reinforcements which arrived on the island as the garrisons on Kos, in the castle of St Peter at Bodrum and in other outlying stations were brought in to supplement the few able-bodied men left in the besieged city, it became more and more obvious to everyone as the winter wore on that they could not hold out for much longer. Suleiman launched another general assault on 30 November, St Andrew's Day, and it proved to be as bloody as the last one, but by some miracle no more effective. In pouring rain the Turks attacked the bastions of Spain and Italy, only to be slaughtered by the remaining Knights and Sergeants. Exactly how many men the Turks lost will never be known for certain; Nicholas Roberts said that 'upon Saint Andrew's evin was the last battall that was between the turkes and us, at that battall was slain eleven thousand turkes'. But such a figure is incredible. Von Hammer says that they lost three thousand men, and this is probably nearer the truth. But whatever the exact number of casualties may have been, it was too much for the invaders. After the battle, to quote Nicholas Roberts once again, 'the turkes purposed to give us no more battall, but to come into the towne by trenches'.

A few days later on 3 December, a man emerged from the Turkish lines and approached St John's Gate between the Posts of England and Auvergne waving a large white flag. He proved to be a Genoese named Girolamo Monile, who had been sent by Suleiman to invite the defenders to surrender, and to promise that their lives would be spared. He was waved away. Two days later he returned, asking if he might be allowed to speak to a friend in the city in order to give him a letter from Suleiman for the Grand Master, but once again he was rebuffed, a shot being fired over his head to speed him on his way. Then on the following day a different envoy appeared, but he too was sent packing. When news of these approaches reached the Rhodians, however, it gave them hope for the first time for weeks; for unlike the Knights they were more interested in survival than in dying in obedience to a chivalrous code of honour, and they formed a deputation which waited upon their two fathers-in-God, the bishops Clement and Balestrieri, to whom they stated their case. The bishops listened to them with sympathy, and in their turn waited on de L'Isle Adam, and warned him that if he did not receive the Sultan's envoys the Rhodians might revolt.

The Grand Master summoned the Chapter, and the senior members of the Order – the Prior of the Church of St John, the Piliers of each *langue*, the Conventual Bailiffs and the Knights Grand Cross – took stock of the situation; it was grim. Although the Turks had suffered vastly higher casualties than they had themselves, their own numbers were now reduced to such a point that there were not enough men to form even a skeleton crew to man what was left of the walls; powder and shot were almost finished, and there was no more material of any kind for repairs. These were facts that no one could deny, and the conclusion was inescapable: there was no way in which the city could be saved. There were therefore only two courses of action open to them: they could fight until the last man, or they could see what terms Suleiman was prepared to offer. De L'Isle Adam had no doubt at all that they should all fight and die, and a number of those present agreed with him; but a high-ranking Spaniard, Lopes de Pas of the *langue* of Aragon, argued that such a course would merely make the enemy's victory more splendid. He argued that where all human hope was gone, it was better to come to terms, so that they might vindicate their loss at another time and place. Wise men surrendered to necessity. No matter how laudable their deaths might be, they should ask themselves whether they might do more harm to the cause for which they were fighting than their surrender. As the argument continued a deputation of islanders arrived on the scene, begging the Grand Master to remember their wives and children, and although it was obvious to everyone that the idea of surrender was utterly

Suleiman besieging Belgrade. The two men in tall white hats with white plumes in front of the dark horse and rider are Janissaries. Some of the Christian defenders seem to be drowning in the moat.

The fortress built by the Knights of St John on the ancient acropolis at Lindos on Rhodes with the modern village of little white houses at the foot of the hill. It played little part in Suleiman's siege of the city of Rhodes, and eventually its small garrison was called in by Philip Villiers de l'Isle Adam, the Grand Master, to reinforce the defenders of the city.

Two of Suleiman's granite cannonballs at the foot of a tree in the city of Rhodes. They are massive things and were used in great numbers to batter down the city walls. The superiority of Turkish artillery was a major factor in their successful capture of Constantinople in 1453 and remained a factor in Suleiman's victories on Rhodes and in Hungary.

OPPOSITE ABOVE: A gate into the city of Rhodes. The foot-bridge crosses the great ditch between the massive outer and inner walls of the city. The coat of arms over the gate is that of Pierre d'Aubusson, who was Grand Master of the Knights of St John at the time of the unsuccessful attack on the place by Mehmed II the Conqueror.

OPPOSITE BELOW: The view from the foot-bridge in the photograph above, looking down the moat between the formidable walls of Rhodes.

The siege of Rhodes by Mesih Pasha in 1480 as depicted by a Christian miniaturist, who has included more dead Turks than slaughtered Christians. Although it does not illustrate Suleiman's attack on the place, it provides a good picture of the warfare of the time with galleys attacking the harbour, the city walls and towers being manned by armoured defenders, and the Turkish camp being set up outside the city.

repugnant to him, de L'Isle Adam was sufficiently moved by the islanders' plea to agree to listen to what Suleiman had to say.

As a signal that they were prepared to talk, on 10 December a white flag was hoisted over St John's Gate, where there had been so much fighting during the past few months, and it was not long before a senior Turkish officer appeared with an interpreter. Gabriel Tadini and the Prior of St Gilles met them, and were given a letter from Suleiman to de L'Isle Adam in which the Sultan promised to allow the Knights to leave the island in peace with their belongings once they had surrendered the city; any citizens who wanted to accompany them could do so, but if the Grand Master refused to surrender, every man, woman and child in the city would be slaughtered. The Sultan demanded an immediate reply. After another session of the Chapter, Suleiman's terms were accepted, and one of the Knights, Antony of Grollée, together with a Rhodian judge named Robert Peruzzi, was sent across into the Turkish lines to ask for a three-day truce in which to make all arrangements for the surrender. Peruzzi was sent back to the city with a message from the Sultan saying that he agreed to the truce as long as no work on the defences was undertaken during the cease-fire, but Grollée was retained as a hostage. He was treated with great courtesy by Ahmed Pasha, the commander of the Turkish line opposite the Post of Aragon, who entertained him to dinner and discussed the fighting with him. Later, Grollée claimed that during the conversation Ahmed had told him that the Turks had lost 'sixty-four thousand men killed and dead of wounds and another fifty thousand from sickness' during the siege. Although there is no doubt that the Turkish losses were enormous, they cannot possibly have lost over 100,000 men, and it seems certain that either Ahmed or Grollée was exaggerating for reasons best known to himself.

What followed is a matter of dispute. Some historians have said that de L'Isle Adam was genuinely worried about Turkish good faith, not trusting Suleiman's word, and that therefore he sent another deputation to the Sultan's tent to ask for an extension of the truce and for further guarantees that the Rhodians would not be harmed after the surrender. Turkish historians have tended to say that de L'Isle Adam was playing for time in order to strengthen the city's defences, and that he had no intention of surrendering if he could fight on until reinforcements arrived. Whatever may be the truth of the matter, on 15 December the truce broke down, and Suleiman ordered the resumption of hostilities. The guns opened up along the entire front once again, and two days later the Turks launched an attack upon the Posts of Aragon and England, which were already battered almost beyond recognition; but Ahmed's men had little heart for the renewed fighting, and the defenders, few as they were, stopped them in their tracks and threw them back, having killed enough of them to discourage the rest. As Brockman has said, the Knights 'had fought Islam to a standstill'.

But the Rhodians, too, had had enough. With the two major opponents locked together in something very like a stalemate, the islanders insisted upon making overtures of their own to the Sultan, and de L'Isle Adam was in no position to prevent them. The result was yet another truce which began on Christmas Eve. With the guns silent once again, the Grand Master received Suleiman's terms for the surrender of the city, and they were an improvement on the old ones; the Knights were not only to be allowed to depart with their belongings and their honour intact, but the Sultan offered to provide shipping for them if they had not a sufficient number of vessels of their own. Once again he promised to respect the lives and property of the islanders, and even to allow those who wished to do so to leave the island at any time during the next three years; the Knights were given twelve days to depart.

They were extraordinarily generous terms, even though the Turks had been fought to a standstill, and de L'Isle Adam accepted them. There has been argument as to whether they were strictly observed or not, some people saying that the Janissaries desecrated churches and maltreated the islanders as soon as they entered the city, while others have asserted that the Turks scrupulously observed the terms of the treaty and behaved with great humanity; the probability is that, if a few of Suleiman's men behaved badly, they were in the minority, and that on the whole the terms of the surrender were observed. The Grand Master and the Sultan met on three occasions, and everyone is agreed that Suleiman treated his adversary with remarkable courtesy and respect; he was not called 'the Magnificent' for nothing. They met on St Stephen's Day, the day after Christmas, and according to the German historian, J. F. von Hammer-Purgstall, as he was about to leave Suleiman turned to his Grand Vizier and said, 'It is with regret that I am compelled to drive this brave old man out of his home.' On the following day, the Feast of St John the Evangelist, Suleiman returned the Grand Master's call, appropriately enough riding into the city by way of the Gate of St John, where he dismissed his guard, saying, 'My safe-conduct is guaranteed by the word of the Grand Master of the Hospitallers, and that is better than all the world's armies.' It is said, too, that he gave orders that the escutcheons of the Knights and of their *langues* carved on the walls of the city in various places should not be destroyed, but left as perpetual memorials of their bravery.

The Knights left the island on 1 January 1523, led by de L'Isle Adam, and sailed for Crete. One of their number was a young Frenchman from Provence named Jean Parisot de la Valette, who was destined to prove the wisdom of the advice given by Lopes de Pas to his fellows of the Chapter when he told them that in his view it was better to come to terms with the enemy so that their loss might be vindicated at another time and place; for nearly fifty years later, when Suleiman in his old age launched an even greater attack on the new home of the Knights Hospitaller on the island of Malta, La Valette had become their Grand Master, and the old Sultan was to regret bitterly that he had ever allowed him to slip through his fingers when he had had the chance to hold him. But that is another story.

VI

✠ ✠ ✠

Kings and Their Games

War's a game, which, were their subjects
Wise, Kings would not play at.

Cowper, *The Winter Morning Walk*

Suleiman left Rhodes on 6 January 1523 and returned in triumph to
Constantinople, where he was greeted with wild excitement by the
people of the city. Their enthusiasm was not surprising, for his
achievement was remarkable; in just over two years he had succeeded,
where all his predecessors had failed, in conquering two of the most
formidable Christian strongholds which for years had blocked the
way to further Turkish expansion. Even his redoubtable great-
grandfather had been defeated both by Belgrade and by Rhodes, and
the last thing anyone could have expected when the new young Sultan
had succeeded his father was that he should outdo the Conqueror
before he was thirty. Like everyone else, the princes of Europe –
whose disunity had been a major factor in his success – were
astonished by it, though unlike the Turks they were also appalled by
it; for the young man of whom they had had such high hopes now
seemed likely to be as great a menace to the Christian nations of the
West as any of his Ottoman forebears. It was a painful discovery.

The Doge of Venice was the only western ruler to congratulate
Suleiman on his victory, wishing no doubt to make sure that the
lucrative Venetian trade with Turkey and the Middle East should
continue to meet with the Sultan's approval; the other Christian
princes kept silence, though it may have been at about this time that
Francis I of France began to toy with the idea of making a secret
alliance with the Turks to help him in the war he was waging with the

Emperor Charles V. They had begun to fight each other in April 1521, just at the moment when the Hungarians were asking Charles for help to meet the imminent invasion of their country by the Turks, and indeed it was this war which so distracted both the Emperor and the King of France that neither of them – the principal Christian monarchs of Europe, as they were – was able to help either the Hungarians or later the Knights of Rhodes in their struggle against the militancy of Islam under Suleiman.

The constant state of war between Francis and Charles was destined to affect the course of events in eastern Europe so profoundly and for so many years that it is time to look briefly at the roots of their mutual hostility. That the two men grew up to be enemies surprised no one at the time, for as Marguerite of Angoulême, Francis's sister, remarked, they were born to hate each other. The fact that Charles was heir to the duchy of Burgundy, and had been crowned duke at the age of seven, would have been enough to ensure that the two should be rivals; for no King of France could have tolerated a situation in which the King of Spain and ruler of the Spanish Netherlands should also be the ruler of such a large and historically troublesome part of France as the duchy of Burgundy, and Charles was known to be immensely proud of his Burgundian inheritance and determined to claim it for himself when the time was ripe. When, in addition to all this, Charles was also elected King of the Romans and Emperor in 1520, defeating Francis, who had been the other principal candidate for the imperial crown, the lifelong hostility between the two men was made doubly sure; for with Charles supreme in Spain, the Netherlands, and now in Germany and Austria too, Francis inevitably felt himself to be encircled by his over-powerful rival, while Charles knew that Francis was in a position from which he could strike at any of his possessions, whenever he chose to do so; for the central position of France gave her monarch the power to pick and choose his target in any quarrel with the Emperor.

In view of all this, it is not surprising that when in 1521 a petty dispute broke out over the ownership of a castle in the Ardennes between one of Francis's subjects, the Duke of Bouillon, and one of Charles's vassals, tension should have mounted. In itself it was the pettiest of petty quarrels, and if relations between France and the Empire had been friendly it would have been settled without any difficulty; but they were not friendly, and fighting broke out. Shortly afterwards there was a much more serious breach of the peace at the other end of France under the shadow of the Pyrenees. The King of Navarre, whose father had been forcibly deprived of his little kingdom by Ferdinand of Aragon, Charles's grandfather, decided to take advantage of some trouble Charles was having with certain of his subjects in Spain to invade his erstwhile realm. The fact that his army consisted almost entirely of French and Gascon troops infuriated Charles, who protested in the strongest terms to the French King. On 22 April Francis answered by declaring war.

Two things now happened which were to prove of great importance. Pope Leo X, who up to this time had championed Francis, backing him against Charles in the imperial election and generally protecting his interests wherever he had been able to do so, decided to change sides, and this altered the whole balance of power in Italy in Charles's favour; for the Pope gave him the investiture of the Kingdom of Naples and recognized him as Emperor, although he had promised Francis that he would never do either of these things. Leo's *volte face* soon encouraged others to defy the French and in the duchy of Milan, which was one of Francis's most treasured possessions, the people rose in revolt against their French overlords, whom they detested.

The second event destined to influence the course of history was the death at about his time of William of Croy, the Lord of Chièvres, who had been Charles's principal adviser since his boyhood. All his life, Chièvres had worked for peace and good relations with France, concentrating on consolidating Charles's position in the Lowlands while hoping for the eventual recovery of his Burgundian inheritance. Italy had not interested him. When he died, his place was taken by a Piedmontese, Mercurino Gattinara, whose influence upon Charles was to be radically different from that of Chièvres. Italy was the centre of Gattinara's world, and he had long been convinced that if Charles could turn the French out of Italy he would be in a position thereafter to control the whole of Europe. As far as Gattinara was concerned, Chièvres could not have died at a more opportune moment, for Gattinara became the Emperor's principal adviser at the precise moment when Leo abandoned the French interest, thus presenting him with the perfect opportunity to persuade Charles to take a more active part in Italian affairs. The immediate result was that in June 1521, a month after the death of Chièvres, Charles sent an expeditionary force to Lombardy to help the Milanese fight the French, and his war with Francis spread to Italy. There, despite a few short intermissions, it dragged on wearily for many more years than anyone could possibly have guessed at the time of its outbreak; directly or indirectly it was to influence the lives and fortunes of an astonishingly varied number of people, ranging from the Italian peasants whose homes were destroyed and the inhabitants of Italian cities which were sacked and pillaged again and again as the years went by, to German and Bohemian Protestants, Turkish pirates, Popes, and the crowned heads of almost every country in Europe.

At first, all went well for Charles, and by November his imperial troops had captured Milan. A few days later, Leo X unexpectedly died, and even more unexpectedly the man who had once been Charles's tutor was elected Pope in his stead. Most people thought that Giulio de' Medici would be elected to succeed his first cousin, Leo, but they underrated the reluctance of the assembled cardinals to see the papacy become vested *de facto* in the Medici family. As a result there was a large number of indecisive votes, until someone casually put forward the name of Cardinal Adrian of Utrecht, even though everyone knew that, as a Dutchman, he stood no chance at all of being elected. In this instance, however, everyone was mistaken. Adrian was elected, and duly took the name of Adrian VI. As the American historian, Royall Tyler, has remarked in his biography of the Emperor Charles V, 'Afterwards, the cardinals could not explain their having elected a barbarian, who had never even been in Rome. At a loss for a more plausible excuse, they supposed that they must have been inspired by the Holy Ghost.' This was a suggestion greeted at the time by the chronicler, Francesco Guicciardini, with the scorn it deserved. 'As if,' he is said to have exclaimed, 'the Holy Ghost, who loves the pure in heart, would deign to visit minds possessed by worldly ambition, incredible greed and thirst for pleasure!' But Holy Ghost or no Holy Ghost, Adrian's election was a piece of luck for Charles, who had known him and trusted him all his life, and a blow for Francis, who suddenly found the papacy ranged against him.

Henry VIII, not wishing to be left out, offered to mediate between the warring parties, and Cardinal Wolsey, accompanied by the Bishops of Durham and Ely, travelled to Calais to discuss the possibility of making peace. It is doubtful whether Henry really wanted to stop the war. Wolsey made little pretence of impartiality, more or less openly taking sides against the French from the beginning of the conference in Calais, and a few days after it was over he travelled to Bruges, where he arranged a secret treaty between his master and the Emperor, in which Henry agreed to make war on France when the time was ripe, and Charles agreed to marry Henry's daughter Mary when she was of an age to do so; at the time she was five years old. It was during the course of these negotiations that news reached the assembled statesmen of the fall of Belgrade to the Turks, but although one might have expected such a calamity to give them pause it did not do so. They were shocked, of course, but they were too deeply committed to their own quarrels to turn back and unite against the infidel, and in March of the following year Henry kept his side of the bargain and declared war on France.

On 26 May 1522, while the war in Italy continued and Suleiman in Constantinople inspected his armada as it prepared to sail for Rhodes,

Charles crossed the Channel and landed at Dover, whence he took the road for London. Not unnaturally he wanted to see his future bride, who by now had attained the age of six; what he thought of her or she of him is not recorded. He stayed in London until mid-June, when he travelled to Winchester by way of Windsor, staying eventually for a few days in the episcopal palace at Bishop's Waltham, which was described at the time of his visit by a contemporary as 'a right ample and goodly Manor Place moted aboute, and a praty Brooke renning hard by it'. While he was there he made his first will; it seems to have been a place which put people in mind of their mortality, for William of Wykeham and William Wayneflete, both of them bishops of Winchester in their respective times, also made their wills there, and so did Henry II, while Cardinal Beaufort, remembering the place in his will, bequeathed to Queen Margaret of England his 'blue bed of gold and damask at my palace at Waltham in the room where the Queen used to lie when she was at the palace, and three suits of the arras hangings in the same room'. His visit at an end, Charles sailed from Southampton on 6 July, the day after his mistress Jeanne van der Gheenst gave birth to one of his illegitimate children – a daughter who was later to become the Duchess of Parma – and he landed at Santander ten days later. There he received the Venetian ambassador in audience, and listened attentively while the man urged upon him the idea of mounting a crusade against the Turks to win back Constantinople for Christendom. The Emperor's interest was not feigned; he had always dreamed of recovering the 'city defended by God', but in view of the events of the day there was a certain irony in the ambassador's enthusiasm and the Emperor's interest; for as their conversation was taking place Suleiman was landing on Rhodes amid the noisy acclamations of his troops to press in earnest the siege of the embattled Knights, while the Most Christian King of France was frantically raising money to pay for his war – not with the Turks, but with His Catholic Majesty the King of Spain – by selling jewels from the treasury of Rheims Cathedral and by melting down some splendid golden figures of the apostles which belonged to the Cathedral of Our Lady at Laon, together with a solid silver trellis which had hitherto surrounded the tomb of St Martin of Tours.

A chronic shortage of money with which to finance the war was as much a problem for Charles as it was for Francis, but during the summer of 1552 and the months which followed, while the Sultan was pounding the walls of Rhodes into rubble, the French King had an even greater cause for anxiety than lack of money. The Duke of Bourbon had been one of his boyhood friends and companions; the two had grown up together and when they had reached manhood Francis had made him Constable of France. As such, in time of war he became second-in-command to the King himself, and thus the most powerful noble in the land. He was also the richest, for at the age of fifteen he had married Suzanne, heiress of the Duke of Bourbon by Anne of France, daughter of Louis XI, and the addition of this duchy with its vast fortune to his own considerable inheritance made him the wealthiest man in France. As he grew to manhood he proved himself to be an able and courageous soldier, and when he was made governor of the Milanese at the age of twenty-five he showed himself also to be a capable administrator. But shortly afterwards the relationship between him and the King began to show signs of coolness, and as time went by it became chillier and chillier; when Francis declared war on the Emperor in April 1552, the Constable of France did not take his place with the army and Francis did not summon him to do so. Instead he stayed at home on his estates in an icy silence.

One of the reasons for the estrangement of the two men was no secret. Suzanne of Bourbon, the Constable's wife, had died in April 1521. Their three children had all died in infancy before their mother, and thus there was no heir to the huge Bourbon fortune and estates or to those lands which Suzanne had inherited from her mother, Anne of France, and under strict French law much of both was now liable to revert to the Crown. Of course the King could have waived his right to her inheritance, had he wished, and this would have been the friendly thing to do. He did not choose to do so, however, and Bourbon was faced with the prospect of being stripped of more than half of his fortune, estates and titles by his erstwhile boyhood companion and friend. He was not pleased.

All this was common knowledge. For a long time the kings of France had been clipping the wings of their over-powerful nobles and concentrating more and more political power in their own hands, so that France should never again be torn to pieces by their wars and revolts as it had constantly been in medieval days; and Bourbon was the last of the great barons to be reduced to manageable size by the Crown. On the whole, it was a process which was good for France, even though it led in the end to the absolutism of Louis XIV and the violent reaction of the revolution. But there must have been more to Francis's resolve to humble Bourbon than a determination to take the opportunity of his wife's early death to put the last of the great French nobles in his place; for after all it had been Francis who had actually increased Bourbon's power by making him Constable of France and governor of the Milanese a few years earlier, and he would hardly have done that if he had regarded him as a potential danger at the time. Something or someone must have turned Francis against him, and it has been suggested that the King's mother, Louise of Savoy, was at the bottom of the affair. 'Rumour has it,' wrote le Bourgeois of Paris at the time, 'that Madame pursues the Lord of Bourbon, because he did not want to marry her sister.' Louise's sister was Philiberte of Savoy, Duchess of Nemours, and it is possible that after the death of Bourbon's wife she may have set her cap at him; he was handsome, eligible and extremely rich. But it seems a little unlikely that Louise of Savoy should have become as implacably hostile to him, as she undoubtedly did become, simply because he had slighted her sister, and there have been those who have suggested that it was not Philiberte who tried to capture this desirable and wealthy widower, but Louise herself. She was forty-seven years old at the time, and he was thirty-three, and it is not impossible that she cast amorous eyes upon him; after all, she had been a widow since she was twenty. If she did indeed make some sort of overture to him, and if Bourbon betrayed an understandable, if deeply offensive, reluctance to entertain the idea of marrying someone fourteen years his senior, then the slighted Louise may well have had grounds for animosity. But there is no certainty that all this happened. Whether it did so or not, Bourbon's relationship with the King went from bad to worse until, driven to desperation by the unceasing persecution to which he was subjected by Francis, he made a momentous decision. He turned traitor, and offered his services to the Emperor Charles.

But Charles, too, had his problems, and in some ways they were worse than those besetting Francis. Like the French King, he was perennially short of money; having disbursed enormous sums to make sure that he was elected Emperor, he was forced to tax his long-suffering subjects in an attempt to repair his fortunes and pay for his wars, and they did not like it. The resulting unrest was widespread, and the *Communero* revolt in Spain was a warning to him that there were limits to his subjects' patience. His Habsburg patrimony was too far away from Spain for him to give it much attention, and in 1521 he lightened his own responsibility by making it over to his younger brother Ferdinand with the title of Lieutenant of the Empire; but disorders similar to the *Communero* revolt in Spain broke out there too, and Suleiman's invasion of Hungary inevitably cast its ominous shadow westwards over Austria. But perhaps the worst problems facing Charles were religious. The Church had been in manifest need of reform for longer than anyone cared to remember, and attempts had been made to persuade successive Popes to do something about the various abuses which were widespread; but although more than one Council had been called to tackle the problems facing potential reformers, nothing had been done. The situation had been so scandalous for so long, and the princes of the Church had proved so conclusively by their inaction that they had no intention of being party to any reforms if they could help it, that in the end Christians in humbler circumstances had got tired of waiting. John Hus had been burnt at the stake a century before Charles's time, but his death had served only to convince many Christian people that the Popes and their minions, the bishops and archbishops, were servants of the Devil not ministers of Christ, and the cause of reform had gained more and more adherents in the hundred years since his martyrdom; for martyrdom it was taken to be by many people.

This is not the place to describe the course of the Reformation; it must suffice to say that by the time that Charles was elected Emperor many people in Germany, the Lowlands, and central and northern Europe were convinced that the only hope of restoring the Christian faith to its original purity was to reject all claims to human authority, such as those made by Popes and bishops, and to return to the Bible as the repository of the word of God and thus the sole authority to be unreservedly trusted. It is not surprising therefore that when in 1517 Martin Luther nailed his famous ninety-five theses against papal indulgences to the door of the *Schlosskirche* at Wittenberg he caused great excitement. Within a fortnight his theses were known throughout Germany, where they were welcomed by everyone in favour of reforming the Church. Three years later, he published three more revolutionary works, which were promptly censured as heretical in the bull *Exsurge Domine*, and he was threatened with the ban unless he retracted within sixty days. He replied by burning the bull together with some other Catholic writings, and on 3 January 1521 he was excommunicated. In April of the same year, just at the time that the Hungarian envoys were imploring the Emperor Charles to help them in their coming war with the Turks, as already mentioned Luther was summoned to appear before him at the Diet at Worms, and ordered to recant. Instead he made a vigorous speech, defending himself and refusing to withdraw a word of his former pronouncements. Although Charles knew as well as anyone that the Church was in desperate need of reform, and although he had some sympathy for Luther's ideas, he deeply distrusted Luther's violent – indeed, almost fanatical – challenge to the established authority of the Church. After all, it was St Paul who had said that 'the powers that be are ordained of God', and who was this German monk to set himself up against St Paul? So Charles put Luther under an imperial ban, albeit reluctantly, for he suspected that by doing so he would alienate many of his subjects both in Germany and in the Netherlands; and events were to prove that he was right. Indeed, for the rest of his life he was destined to be plagued by people calling themselves Lutherans, who were virtually impossible to control or govern for the simple reason that they were not deterred from doing what they considered to be right by the threat of physical violence or even death. Two years after

Luther was put under the ban two of his disciples, John van Essen and Henry Voes, proved this to be the case by refusing to repudiate their beliefs and by being burnt to death as a result on 1 July 1523 in the market place in Brussels. They were the first of many Lutherans to suffer.

But if there was no easy solution to the religious problems confronting Charles, at least the war with Francis continued to go more and more in his favour, and a month after the *auto-da-fé* in Brussels a league was formed by Charles, his brother Ferdinand, Pope Adrian VI, Henry VIII of England, the Doge of Venice, Milan, Florence, Siena, Lucca and the Duke of Bourbon against Francis. It was a formidable combination, and things looked black for the French; but the key figure in the new alliance was the Pope, and he died unexpectedly a few weeks later on 14 September 1523, to the undisguised relief of the papal court, which could not wait to see an Italian again on the throne of St Peter. This time the cardinals made no mistake; they elected Giulio de' Medici as Pope Clement VII with exemplary speed, hardly a vote being cast against him, so determined were the electors not to allow the Holy Ghost to saddle them once again with a barbarian as Pope. But if the Italians were delighted with their new pontiff, Charles was less well pleased for the new Pope's first political action was to repudiate his predecessor's commitments and to show clear signs of reverting to the traditional papal policy of trying to hold the balance of power evenly between the great powers, while playing one off against the other and staunchly resisting all efforts to reform the Church; and in fact it was not long before the alliance fell apart having accomplished nothing worth recording. But although this was a disappointment to Charles it was more than offset a little later, when he received the astonishing news from Italy that a battle had taken place at Pavia on his twenty-fifth birthday, 24 February 1525, in which the French had been routed and Francis I had been captured.

No such disaster had befallen a reigning European prince since King John the Good of France had been captured by the Black Prince at the battle of Poitiers in 1356, and Europe was stunned. The accounts of the battle of Pavia are confused and at times contradictory, but the main outline of events is clear enough. Against the advice of most of his advisers, in the autumn of 1524 Francis decided to make an attempt to recover the duchy of Milan, even though it meant embarking on a winter campaign. At first all went well, and Milan was retaken without difficulty; but then things began to go wrong. Not content with this initial success, Francis decided to lay siege to Pavia in the belief that it would succumb as easily as Milan; but Pavia was defended with great skill and even greater courage, and all Francis's attempts to storm the place were beaten off with considerable loss of life to the attackers. The morale of the French soldiers suffered and as the winter weather deteriorated, making life more and more uncomfortable for them, disease took its toll and the whole enterprise began to look more and more misconceived.

Francis then made a bad mistake. Wishing to create a diversion, he sent 10,000 of his men supported by some of his artillery under the command of the Duke of Albany to attack Naples, in the hope that the enemy would chase them, while leaving him alone to complete the reduction of Pavia. But Lannoy and Pescara, the commanders of the imperial army, refused to be drawn and stayed where they were, while Francis found himself worse off to the tune of 10,000 men and a significant number of guns. On the eve of St Matthias's Day, Lannoy and Pescara held a conference, and decided to attack. Moving up quietly under cover of darkness, the imperial troops took up their positions undetected, and when day broke the French found themselves between the walls of Pavia and their newly arrived enemy.

All accounts agree that at first the fighting went well for the French, whose artillery gained an early advantage and inflicted heavy casualties on the Spaniards. In fact it may have been this early success which led, paradoxically, to their eventual defeat, for Francis, who was in command of the French centre, seems to have been misled by premature cries of 'Victory! France! Victory!' into ordering his light cavalry to attack too soon. As they advanced, the French artillery had to stop firing for fear of hitting their own men, and with the French guns silenced the Spaniards turned on their attackers and forced them back to their original positions in considerable confusion. Hoping to retrieve the situation, the King now charged the enemy at the head of the heavy cavalry, ordering some Swiss mercenaries and French infantrymen to support him, and the weight of his attack bore down his opponents, while he himself killed their commander, the Marquis of Sant Angelo, with his lance. But the infantry failed to keep pace with him, and when the Duke of Bourbon's men came hurrying to the rescue of Sant Angelo's hardpressed troops, the Swiss mercenaries turned tail and fled. Unsupported by his infantry, Francis found himself in the thick of the battle, fighting for his life. His plumed helmet and splendid armour, partly covered with a surcoat of cloth of silver emblazoned with the arms of France, made sure that everyone, both friend and foe, should know exactly who he was, and as a crowd of Spanish soldiers clustered round him, thrusting and stabbing, he was in imminent danger of losing his life despite the courage with which his knights fought to protect him. La Trémoille, aged seventy-five and known by everyone as *le chevalier sans reproche*, was killed fighting by his side, and so were the young Bastard of Savoy, whose first battle it was, the Count of Saint-Pol, and the two brothers Galéas and Jules de Saint-Séverin, respectively the King's principal equerry and his chief *maître d'hôtel*, while Francis himself was saved only by the excellence of his armour. Lannoy, seeing the King's danger, spurred his horse through the fighting, and reached him just after his horse had been killed under him; he was trying to defend himself on foot surrounded by Spaniards who were vying with each other in their eagerness to kill him and strip him of his armour and jewels, and only Lannoy's arrival saved him from death. Exhausted and out of breath, he lifted the visor of his helmet, gasping for air, to show a face streaming with blood from a flesh wound, and stripping off his gauntlet he handed it to Lannoy in token of his surrender. It was almost ten o'clock in the morning, and as the news that the French King was a captive spread through the ranks of both armies, there were cries of 'Victory! Spain! Spain! Spain!' from the imperial soldiers, while the men of Normandy and Lorraine and Provence, routed and in terror for their lives, fled in disorder, leaving the plain of Pavia littered with corpses and slippery with pools of blood. Between 6,000 and 8,000 Frenchmen died that morning; some were killed in battle, some drowned as they tried to swim the River Ticino, and some had their throats cut by the Spaniards who pursued them.

While his countrymen were stumbling across the fields of Lombardy or dying in its ditches, Francis was closely guarded by Lannoy, who still feared for his life. After a day or two he was taken to a castle at Pizzighetone where he remained until the following summer, when he was taken to Spain. His imprisonment gave him plenty of time to think and to pray, and Francis did much of both. Meanwhile, the people of France rallied round his mother the Regent, Louise of Savoy, and prepared to ride out the storm which everyone expected to break over their heads at any moment. When the story got about that immediately after being made captive Francis, still covered in blood and the sweat of battle, had been allowed by his captors to turn aside for a moment into the Charterhouse of Pavia, where the monks were singing Psalm 119, they were deeply impressed; for the words which Francis heard were, '*Bonum mihi quia humiliasti me . . .*' – 'It is good for me that I have been in trouble, that I may learn thy statutes . . .' – and they confirmed his subjects in their belief that they could see the hand of God in the events of that terrible day.

VII

✠ ✠ ✠

The Flight of Kings

Kings with their armies did flee, and were discomfited: and they
of the household divided the spoil.

Psalm 68

Fortunately for everyone in western Europe, when Suleiman returned
to Constantinople from Rhodes in triumph after his victory there he
decided not to take advantage of the distracted state of the Christian
world to press home his attack upon it. Once again, a shadow was cast
over his homecoming by the death of one of his infant sons, Abdullah;
but the little boy's death, though sad, could hardly have caused his
father much surprise, so commonly did babies die in the first few
months of life, and Suleiman does not seem to have allowed it to
depress him for very long. It was the will of God, and only a fool wept
for long when God's will was done. So Suleiman put it behind him,
and got on with the affairs of his daily life. When he was not occupied
with the business of government he spent much of his time hunting,
which he greatly enjoyed. His favourite sport was falconry, and when
he went out hunting with his falcons, he was accompanied by his chief
falconer, a very remarkable man named Ibrahim.

Ibrahim had been born at Parga on the west coast of Greece opposite
the southern tip of the island of Corfu in the Ionian Sea. He was the
son of Christian parents, but while still a boy he had been captured by
Turkish pirates, who had taken him back to Turkey and sold him as a
slave to a widow of Manisa in Asia Minor. She had treated him
well, giving him a good education and bringing him up almost like
one of her own children; but when Selim had made Suleiman
governor of that part of the world, Ibrahim had somehow passed into

Suleiman's service, though whether the widow sold him or gave him to his new master is not known. He was exactly the same age as Suleiman, who seems to have been captivated by his charm. He was handsome, quick-witted and highly intelligent, and he seems to have had an aptitude for languages, for in addition to Turkish and Greek, both of which he spoke fluently, he also spoke Persian and Italian passably well. He was fond of music and could play the viol, while his favourite pastime was reading, especially reading history, which he loved. At first, Suleiman made him one of his principal pages, but his rise was rapid and when his master came to the throne after Selim's death, Ibrahim was promoted to be chief falconer, and this was the position he still occupied when the Sultan came home from Rhodes in January 1523.

He was not to remain in it for very long, however, for when Piri Pasha, the Grand Vizier, died, to everyone's astonishment Ibrahim was put in his place, despite the fact that he was junior to many other members of Suleiman's staff. As Vizier, he saw even more of his master than he had done as his chief falconer, and this was natural enough; but the degree of intimacy in which the two men lived after Ibrahim's new appointment exceeded anything which had been seen in Turkish court circles before this time, and was truly astonishing. They became virtually inseparable, Suleiman often eating at the same table as his servant – something no Sultan had done since the days of Mehmed the Conqueror – and even sleeping in the same tent. Today this kind of behaviour would be taken by many people to be strong presumptive evidence of a homosexual relationship between Suleiman and Ibrahim, but for various reasons this is unlikely to have been the case. For one thing, both men married; Suleiman had a number of women at his disposal in the harem, and Ibrahim married Suleiman's sister. This does not preclude the possibility that they also had a homosexual affair, but there are other reasons for dismissing the idea as at best improbable; for even though the Ottoman Sultans were autocrats whose every whim was law, they were not regarded as being superior to the laws of God, nor did they regard themselves as such, and homosexual relationships were strictly forbidden and condemned as sinful in the *Sheriat* or sacred law of Islam. Admittedly, drinking wine is also condemned, and this did not stop many Sultans from getting regularly drunk; the great Mehmed was a heavy drinker, and Suleiman's successor was seldom sober.

Admittedly, too, there is evidence that sodomy was not rare among the Turks. J. F. von Hammer-Purgstall, describing the Turkish poet Ishak Tschelebi, said of him that 'he never wore a turban, neither in the house, nor outside; his language was consistently filthy, and all his life he indulged an infamous passion which is not rare among the

Turks; in his last years he gave it up in favour of drunkenness, though he never gave up his aversion to women. Always barefoot and bareheaded, he would run after young boys in the street, and in his poetry after acid witticisms.' Another Turkish poet, Deli Burader, who was a contemporary of Suleiman, built some public baths on the European shore of the Bosphorus near Constantinople, and they 'appealed so strongly to the voluptuous passions of the Turks by the various esoteric pleasures provided there by Deli Burader, and by the beauty of the young boys who provided them, that the city flocked to the place in crowds, until Ibrahim had it closed in the interests of public morality'. Not discouraged, the enterprising and indomitable Deli Burader departed for Arabia, where he built some public baths and a mosque, perhaps praying in the latter to be forgiven for what he did in the former. It was not a few eccentric poets only, however, who were addicted to the pleasures of buggery, for when cities fell to Turkish arms in war the victors were as pleased to carry off a few pretty boys and youths as they were to capture the most appetizing and attractive girls and young women, and there is little doubt about the nature of the fate reserved for them. But the fact that many Turks were addicted to sodomy cannot be regarded as evidence that Suleiman was in love with Ibrahim, let alone that he translated his desires into action. Indeed, this is highly improbable, for if any such arrangement between the two men had existed tongues would certainly have wagged, and rumours would have spread through the palace and the city; and yet no such rumours have come down to us. The most that can be said is that there may have been an unconscious homosexual element in Suleiman's affection for Ibrahim; though whether this was indeed the case or not, we shall never know, nor does it matter very much. Meanwhile, the bizarre suggestion by the American historian, Hester Jenkins, that Ibrahim may have been a eunuch has even less to be said for it than the idea that Suleiman was homosexual. The one thing that is historically sure is that, from the moment of his appointment as Grand Vizier until the day of his eventual downfall, whatever his relationship with the Sultan may have been, Ibrahim, the son of a Greek fisherman of Parga, became the most powerful man in Turkey after his master. In fact, it may have been Ibrahim who suggested to Suleiman two years after his conquest of Rhodes that he should invade Hungary once again, and renew the war in the West.

During those two years, however, Suleiman was not without troubles of his own, even though they were nothing compared with those surrounding Charles and Francis and the other western monarchs. Egypt, which had been conquered as lately as his father's time after centuries of Mameluk rule, did not like its new Turkish masters. Ahmed Pasha, one of the commanders during the siege of Rhodes, had been so disgusted by Ibrahim's appointment as Grand Vizier that he had asked for the post of governor of Egypt in succession to Mustafa, who had been sent there in semi-disgrace. He was a proud and ambitious man, and in January 1524 he rose in revolt, renouncing his allegiance to the Sultan and proclaiming himself to be the sole and independent ruler of Egypt. Suleiman did not allow the news of his rebellion to interrupt his well-earned rest from the cares of office, and he continued hunting and enjoying himself in the country as though nothing had happened; but early in 1525 he sent Ibrahim to Egypt at the head of a large punitive force with instructions to restore order there. Ibrahim landed near Alexandria on 24 March, and by the second week in June he had accomplished the task entrusted to him, and Ahmed was dead.

With the Grand Vizier out of the way in Egypt, however, and with the Sultan still enjoying himself in the country near Adrianople, there was no one in Constantinople to take note of the fact that the Janissaries were becoming more and more disgruntled, and when Suleiman returned to the capital in the spring of 1525 they were seething with discontent. Trained from childhood for war and denied most of the pleasures of peace such as wives and families and homes, if they were deprived of the excitements of war for long they became restive; for nearly three years since the fall of Rhodes they had been in Constantinople, condemned to endure the boredom and inactivity of life in the capital while the Sultan went out hunting in the country and the Grand Vizier was busy in Egypt, and they did not like it. So when Suleiman returned to the city they decided to show him just how displeased they were with the way in which he had neglected them, and they broke out into a riot. They attacked the Customs, plundered houses in the Jewish quarter, and broke into the homes of any senior officials who happened to have incurred their displeasure; last but not least, a group of them forced their way into the presence of Suleiman, who it was said killed three of them with his own hand before being forced to withdraw when the others threatened him with their bows; though exactly how he managed to do this safely is not known. No details are available of how the revolt was eventually suppressed, but suppressed it was, and a number of senior officers were executed for their part in it while others were relieved of their commands. During the whole affair Suleiman showed no sign of weakness or fear, and his resolution seems to have impressed the Janissaries for their loyalty to him never wavered again, and this Suleiman knew; from this time forward he was so sure of their complete reliability that during the years which followed their revolt he increased their numbers until their strength had been raised to 20,000 by the year 1530.

However, if Suleiman had not been intimidated by them he had learned the lesson that nearly all his successors were to be forced to learn by bitter experience, namely that it was extremely unwise to deprive the Janissaries of the pleasures and excitements of war for longer than was necessary; they needed an annual campaign, in which to indulge themselves if they were not to become insubordinate and disorderly; and their rebellion was almost certainly one of the factors which decided him to renew the war against Hungary. Ibrahim had already urged him to do so and, perhaps even more significantly, so had the King of France, who had written secretly to Suleiman warning him of the dangerously megalomaniac ambitions of the Emperor Charles. There is a sense in which this was an entirely understandable move on Francis's part; hemmed in on every side by Charles and humiliated at Pavia, he turned for help to the head of the one great power who was at loggerheads with his over-powerful rival: power politics in action. But in another sense it was a most extraordinary thing to do, which was symptomatic of the death of one age and the birth of another; for it would have been virtually unthinkable at almost any time during the three or four previous centuries for a great Christian King to make secret overtures to a Turkish sultan to encourage him to bring in the armies of Islam to redress the balance of Christendom: to attack another Christian country, as Francis now encouraged Suleiman to attack Hungary and thus indirectly greatly add to Charles's difficulties. The fact is that the concept of Christendom was dying and that of Europe, a geographical grouping of rival nation states, was taking its place for better or for worse, while nationalist policies and politicians were taking the place of competing creeds and militant missionaries. The age of the Crusaders was passing away, and that of Machiavelli and his Prince was replacing it.

Preparations for the new campaign began in the spring of 1525, and little attempt to hide them was made by Suleiman or his commanders; the Golden Horn resounded to the hammers of his shipwrights, while the city's quays were piled high with great mounds of military equipment destined for transport up the Danube – cannonballs, powder kegs, military clothing, rope, tents and other stores. The furnaces in the various foundries in Constantinople's industrial quarter down by the Bosphorus were so busy that their light illuminated the sky at night; while outside the walls a forest of tents sprang up to accommodate the troops which were being collected systematically from all over the Ottoman empire together with thousands of camels and other pack animals. The various representatives in the capital of Europe's Christian monarchs watched these open preparations for war with anxious eyes, hoping that they might be intended for an expedition against Persia, with whose new Shah, Tahmasp, Suleiman had recently chosen to pick a quarrel when he had come to the throne after the death of his father Ismail; their hopes were increased when the Persian ruler wrote to Charles V suggesting that they might make an alliance against the Turks, but their optimism was short-lived. On 23 April 1526 Suleiman left Constantinople at the head of an army of over 100,000 men and 300 cannon, and took the road which led westwards towards the Hungarian frontier. The world now knew where his next blow was about to fall.

There was no need for Suleiman to declare war, for he had never made a formal peace with the Hungarians after his last campaign there, and indeed during the years which had elapsed since the capture of Belgrade sporadic fighting between the two countries had continued. A year after the fall of the city a large Turkish force under Ferhad Pasha had overrun the country between the Rivers Save and Drave, having first invaded Croatia, where they had captured a number of small cities. Two years later 15,000 *akinji* were routed in southern Hungary by a bellicose archbishop, Paul Tomori, who sent the head of Ferhad Pasha to King Louis of Hungary as a present together with forty battle standards, a large number of horses, and some magnificent arms encrusted with gold and silver. The Turks retaliated by pouring into Dalmatia, laying the countryside waste and burning the villages as they went, and eventually capturing a castle at Jacse belonging to a noble named Karlovitch with its garrison of 300 men and a number of other nobles. Since this was not to be tolerated, a dashing Hungarian count of Italian extraction, Christopher Frangipani, who was later to be beheaded for treachery, earned himself the title of 'Protector' by defeating the Turks in Croatia, driving them out of some of the cities they had taken there and liberating their inhabitants.

This intermittent warfare of raids and counter-raids gave rise to its own crop of semi-legendary tales of heroic exploits and feats of arms, among which the David-and-Goliath story of a diminutive Hungarian commander, who was challenged to single combat by an enormous giant of a Turk named Djem, was typical. The two men met on horseback, while their men clustered round to watch them fighting each other, and at first the Turk seemed to be sure of the victory; but then the Hungarian made a supreme effort and with a mighty blow of his sword severed his opponent's right leg at the thigh. As it fell to the ground, still booted and spurred and spouting blood, the Hungarian soldiers roared their approval, while the Turkish ranks groaned to see their giant of a commander fall dying from his horse. As a story symbolic of gallant little Hungary engaging the greatly superior forces of the Turkish giant in single combat, while the other Christian nations of Europe neglected her in her hour of greatest need, it was understandably popular.

When messengers arrived in Buda with the news of Suleiman's approach, it was greeted by the Hungarians with their usual mixture of blind courage and chaotic improvidence. Rousing speeches, full of defiance and confidence in victory and unrelieved by the faintest glimmer of intelligence, were made in the Diet even though everyone knew that there was not enough money in the Treasury to pay the messengers who had brought the tidings of the Turkish advance, still less to raise or pay for an army with which to meet it. A decision was made to requisition as much gold and silver plate and precious vessels from the Church as could be secured before the clergy hid them, and this at least was a sensible plan; but when it was put into action the nobles, whose task it was to collect the plate and surrender it to be turned into coin, appropriated most of it for themselves without a thought for the country's financial problem. There was an even greater dearth of soldiers than there was of money. At the time when Suleiman was crossing the southern frontier there was not a single soldier anywhere near King Louis, for most of the cities had bought their exemption from military service with cash, and now refused to supply any men, while the great nobles were dilatory in the extreme, preferring to cling on to their own retainers as personal bodyguards rather than surrender them to the nation.

Worst of all, perhaps, the nation was still deeply divided into two, one faction supporting the King and consisting of the great nobles, and the other following John Zapolya, the nearly autonomous governor (or *Voivode* to give him his Hungarian title) of Transylvania, who was the champion of the lesser nobility. Neither of them was particularly impressive as a man or suitable as a candidate for the appallingly difficult task of rallying the country to face the greatest threat to its life which it had ever encountered. Louis was a nice young man, but feckless and more interested in enjoying himself than in the stern realities of politics; as Suleiman came ever closer to the frontiers of his country he seldom rose from his bed until midday, and then he spent the rest of the daylight hours out hunting before returning to the palace, where he would usually dance with Mary of Austria, his wife, and the other ladies of the court until the small hours of the morning. Such frivolity did not inspire his subjects with much confidence in him; but they did not trust Zapolya either, for what sort of a man would lend himself to party-political bickering and self-seeking political postures at such a time? So the country continued to be divided despite its danger, and preparations to meet the Turkish invasion made no progress at all. Eventually King Louis, realizing belatedly the seriousness of the threat to his country, marched out against the enemy alone in an attempt to shame his people into coming to his aid, and by the beginning of August about 4,000 men had rallied to his banner, while others were preparing to follow their example; but it was a late and hopelessly inadequate response to the danger which was facing them, and despite their apparent self-confidence most Hungarians recognized their weakness and continued to hope for help from the West.

The West, however, was otherwise engaged. Pope Clement sent 50,000 ducats, but even he was reluctant to do more since he knew that any assistance he gave to the Hungarians would indirectly help Charles V and his brother Ferdinand, and he was deeply suspicious of the growing power of the House of Habsburg. Meanwhile King Sigismund of Poland, who had recently experienced the full horror of a raid by the Turks into Podolia as far as Lwow, had no intention of exposing his people to such an experience again if he could help it, and he had made a treaty with Suleiman which bound the two countries to keep the peace for three years. Better things were expected from Austria, which was bound to Hungary by a dual marriage alliance, Ferdinand having married King Louis's sister Anna, and Louis himself having married the sister of both Ferdinand and the Emperor Charles; but the German world was only just recovering from the terrible Peasants' War, which had devastated Swabia and Franconia, and the country was still convulsed by the religious problem. Attempts were made to awaken the various petty princes who ruled Germany to the Turkish danger and to their duty to help their hard pressed fellow Christians in Hungary, but since Luther had said that the Turks were the instruments of God's anger against his faithless people to chastise them into obedience, there were many who thought that to resist the Turks would be to resist the will of God and therefore would be akin to blasphemy; since it would also be to aid and abet a cause espoused by the Pope, whom many people considered to be far more devilish than any Turk, this made it doubly blasphemous. The Diet eventually met at Speyer where, after agreeing to disagree in religious matters and adopting the famous formula, *cuius regio, ejus religio*, it also rather reluctantly agreed in general terms to take defensive measures against a possible Turkish attack, and to send a deputation to discuss matters with the Hungarians; but by this time the Hungarians were on the eve of the most decisive battle in the history of their country. Once again, the other Christian nations had left them to fend for themselves, and the symbolic story of gallant little Hungary taking on the Turkish giant in single combat was about to be turned into the hard reality of a historical event.

Suleiman was in no hurry. He had recalled Ibrahim from Egypt in time to put him in command of this new expedition, and he and his

Vizier maintained an iron discipline while the army was on the march. If a soldier strayed from the road or allowed his horse to eat the young crops in the fields by its side, he was immediately beheaded or hanged; looting or stealing cattle belonging to the local peasants was also forbidden on pain of death. When it is remembered that the country through which the army was marching, even though it was part of the Ottoman empire, was inhabited almost entirely by Greek-speaking Christian peasants, the strictness of these somewhat ferocious rules throws much light on the impartiality of Turkish justice where their Christian subjects were concerned. At a slightly later date but still in Suleiman's time, de Busbecq was full of praise both for the impartiality with which the Turks treated the various ethnic and religious minorities in their empire and for the remarkably disciplined behaviour of their soldiers.

The first thing that I noticed [wrote de Busbecq, when staying near a large military camp], was that the soldiers of each unit were strictly confined to their own quarters. Anyone who knows the conditions which obtain in our own camps will find difficulty in believing it, but the fact remains that everywhere there was complete silence and tranquillity, and an entire absence of quarrelling and acts of violence of any kind, and not even any shouting or merrymaking due to high spirits or drunkenness. Moreover, there was the utmost cleanliness, no dungheaps or rubbish, nothing to offend the eyes or nose, everything of this kind being either buried by the Turks or else removed from sight. The men themselves dig a pit in the ground with their mattocks and bury all excrement, and so keep the whole camp scrupulously clean. Moreover, you never see any drinking or revelry or any kind of gambling, which is such a serious vice amongst our soldiers, and so the Turks know nothing of the losses caused by cards and dice . . . Thus all is quiet, and silence reigns in their camp, especially at the season of their Lent, if I may so call it. Such is the powerful effect of their military discipline and the severe traditions handed down from their forefathers. There is no crime and no offence which the Turks leave unpunished. Their penalties are deprivation of office and rank, confiscation of property, flogging, and death. Flogging is the most frequent punishment, and from this not even the Janissaries are exempt, although they are not liable to the extreme penalty . . . The endurance of the Turks in bearing punishment is quite marvellous. They often receive more than a hundred strokes on their calves, the soles of their feet, and their buttocks.

Toughened perhaps by this sort of treatment, Turkish soldiers were also trained to put up with the minimum of comforts while on campaign in the field. To quote de Busbecq again:

They are careful to avoid touching the supplies which they carry with them as long as they are marching against their foes, but reserve them, as far as possible, for their return journey, when the moment comes for retirement, and they are forced to retrace their steps through regions which the enemy has laid waste, or which the immense multitude of men and baggage animals has, as it were, scraped bare like a swarm of locusts. It is only then that the Sultan's store of provisions is opened, and just enough food to sustain life is weighed out each day to the Janissaries and the other troops in attendance upon him. The other soldiers are badly off, if they have not provided food for their own use; most of them, having often experienced such difficulties during their campaigns – and this is particularly true of the cavalry – take a horse on a leading string loaded with many of the necessities of life. These include a small piece of canvas to use as a tent, which may protect them from the sun or a shower of rain, also some clothing and bedding and a private store of provisions consisting of a leather sack or two of the finest flour, a small jar of butter, and some spices and salt; on these they support life when they are reduced to the extremes of hunger. They take a few spoonfuls of flour and place them in water, adding a little butter, and then flavour the mixture with salt and spices. This, when it is put on the fire, boils and swells up so as to fill a large bowl. They eat of it once or twice a day, according to the quantity, without bread, unless they have with them some toasted bread or biscuit. They thus contrive to live on short rations for a month or even longer if necessary.

The Turkish soldiers needed all their powers of endurance during the long march to Hungary, for the weather was appalling with almost continual rain and bitterly cold winds. Outside Philippopolis on 22 May the army was battered by a violent hailstorm, and Suleiman noted in his diary that 'during the afternoon the countryside is covered with hailstones the size of hazel nuts'. A few days later on 29 May he wrote, 'the army arrived at Sofia in driving rain. 30 May, halt; all the streams break their banks, and wash many tents away . . . 9 June, the army arrives at Nissa; the waters of the Semendra having flooded their banks, we take the road to Aladja in torrents of rain and hail . . . 11 June, the first day of Ramadan, halt; rain . . . 23 June, halt at Kozarun in continual rain with floods everywhere. 24 June, the army crosses the little river Ire, but the waters of the Morava are so swollen that it cannot be crossed.' Ibrahim, who had gone on ahead of the main body, had endured the same frightful weather. 'It rains night and day,' he wrote on 23 June, 'the water falling in torrents washes away the tents, and two soldiers are drowned . . . The army suffers greatly because of the rain.' And so their journey went on in misery and acute discomfort, which might well have almost destroyed the morale of a less formidably disciplined fighting force than Suleiman's army; but the Turks, though soaked to the skin and half-frozen, were as formidable as they had ever been when eventually they reached the Hungarian frontier, and the prospect of action delighted them.

They did not have to wait long. Ibrahim arrived below the walls of Peterwardein (the modern Yugoslav city of Petrovaradin) on 15 July, and on the following day it was attacked. Scaling ladders were thrown up against the walls and as the Hungarian garrison of less than a thousand men retreated to the comparative safety of the citadel, the city itself was taken almost without a fight; but the citadel was defended much more vigorously and the Turks lost a good many men in the course of two abortive attempts to take it. Furious at the delay, Turkish engineers spent the next two weeks laying two huge mines under its walls, and when they were blown a breach was made through which the Janissaries poured in triumph, crushing all opposition. Of the men of the garrison, 500 were immediately beheaded and 300 were reserved for sale as slaves, and to celebrate his success Ibrahim arranged a ceremonial parade during which his men marched past Suleiman with the 500 Hungarian heads lolling repulsively like bits of butcher's meat on their pikes as the first fruits of victory and as a warning not to resist the forces of the Sultan. Suleiman was so delighted by Ibrahim's success that he held a special divan during which he distributed large sums of money in largesse to the various commanders who had taken part in the attack, and sent his congratulations to their men.

Understandably, if not heroically, the next small town on the army's route surrendered without delay, and a dozen of its leading citizens were rewarded by being ceremoniously invested with kaftans of honour, after which they were graciously allowed to kiss the Sultan's hand. In pouring rain the Turks pressed on to Esseg, which also surrendered in the hope of a similar escape from the wrath to come, but it was only partly successful; the lives of its citizens were spared but the town itself was sacked and some of its houses were burnt. Meanwhile, Ibrahim supervised the construction of a pontoon bridge across the swollen waters of the River Drave, which was the last great natural barrier between the invaders and the Hungarian army, of which the Turks had still seen no trace. Suleiman had been amazed when he had reached the Drave only to find it undefended; but the truth was that his enemies were still arguing among themselves as to the best way to check his advance, while leaving Archbishop Tomori to fight a rearguard action against him with an utterly inadequate force, if he was given the opportunity to do so. Needless to say, no such chance was afforded him, and as the Turkish host poured across the Drave Tomori led his men back across the great Hungarian plain, made marshy by the rain and flooded rivers, to join King Louis near the little town of Mohács on the west bank of the Danube, where events were forcing a decision on him and his divided country-men.

King Louis had reached Mohács with only about 4,000 men but as the days had passed, more and more reinforcements had straggled in to join him, and on the eve of the battle which took place a few days later he probably had about 25,000 men with him, more or less equally divided between infantry and cavalry, and perhaps as many as eighty cannon; some authorities put the number under his command a little higher at 28,000, but everyone is agreed that if he had not chosen to fight at Mohács he would have been heavily reinforced. John Zapolya was only a couple of days' march away with 15–20,000 men; some Bohemians were approaching from the west as fast as they could, and Count Frangipani was bringing a contingent of Croatians to join the King. But although the wiser members of Louis's entourage begged him to retreat to Buda, thus leading the Turks ever further and further away from their bases and at the same time giving the various Hungarian reinforcements time to join him, the mere idea of retreat proved unacceptable to the proud and defiant Magyar nobles, whose ignorance of fear was more admirable than their equal ignorance of even the most elementary of military principles and their remarkable stupidity. Moreover, they disliked John Zapolya, and were determined to fight and win an immortal victory before he could arrive and share in their triumph; it never occurred to them for a moment that they might be defeated. The word 'defeat' was not to be found in the vocabulary of the Magyar nobility; and anyway, since God would be fighting for them against the infidel Turks, the issue of the battle could not be in any doubt; atheists, heretics and cowards might advocate retreat, but the cream of Hungarian society would fight, and God would not desert them.

Although Suleiman had left Constantinople at the head of about 100,000 men, by no means all of them were front-line troops and a few men had been lost in battle and through sickness on the journey; but even if only half of those with whom he had marched out of the capital four months earlier were available to face the Hungarians at Mohács, the Turks must still have outnumbered their opponents by almost two to one, while in cannon they had an even greater advantage. It is extraordinary that King Louis and Archbishop Tomori, instead of choosing their ground and waiting for the Turks to attack them, should have chosen to attack them first. They could have resorted to a well-tried tactic – forming up behind a barrier of the armoured carts, which they always had with them, rather as the American settlers later defended themselves behind a screen of covered wagons when attacked by Indians; but once again such prudence was not to the taste of the Hungarian nobility, and even Archbishop Tomori, who should have known better, scorned the idea. With a self-confidence bordering on the insane, the Hungarian heavy cavalry thundered into action under a forest of plumes and banners at just three o'clock in the afternoon of 29 August 1526.

The sheer weight of this charge by the massed chivalry of the Magyar nation was enormous, and the Turkish centre gave way before it. It is almost impossible to re-create in the imagination the feelings of an ordinary Turkish infantryman as he stood his ground while this great phalanx of thousands of armoured knights, saddle to saddle, on huge horses, sweating and snorting and each weighing over a ton, came galloping down on him over the grey and sodden plain of Mohács with the inevitability and terrible destructiveness of an avalanche or a landslide. He would not have been human if he had not been sweating and afraid, but being a Turk and by nature immensely brave, he would not have given ground, even under this approaching avalanche of steel and bone and sweat, if he had not been ordered to do so; instead he would have stood his ground and died. In the event, however, Ibrahim gave the order to give way before the Hungarian charge, and as their horses crashed through the Turkish front towards the point at which the Sultan himself was stationed, King Louis's infantry, scenting victory, charged after them, cheering and screaming with excitement.

For a time, it looked as if the lunatic courage of the Hungarians had carried the day, and the Turks seemed to be reeling under their onslaught; there was even a moment when Suleiman himself seemed to be in some danger, as a handful of Magyar nobles broke through to within yards of his bodyguard. But Ibrahim knew what he was doing, and as soon as almost all the Hungarians had been drawn into the midst of their enemies, he ordered his infantry to stand back while his gunners began systematically to destroy them. From both sides the Turkish artillery poured a barrage of cannonballs into the struggling mass of men and horses, mowing them down in great swathes. By four o'clock, the fate of Hungary was sealed and the flower of the nation was dead. Before the battle the Bishop of Grosswardein, a man named Perenyi who was noted for his wit, had predicted that 'the Hungarian nation will have twenty thousand martyrs, and it would be as well to have them canonized by the Pope'; the Bishop's witticism proved to be an under-estimate. The Turks took no prisoners, and the slaughter was appalling; very few Hungarians escaped. 'On the orders of the Sultan,' wrote Kemal Pasha Zadeh, the Turkish historian, 'the Janissaries, aiming their blows at the cruel panthers who had opposed us, caused hundreds, or rather thousands, in the space of a moment to descend into Hell.' King Louis was killed while trying to escape from the battlefield on his horse, which fell back on him as it struggled up the steep bank of a stream, burying him under its weight in the waters below. Archbishop Tomori, too, was killed, together with two other archbishops, many bishops, and the great majority of the Magyar nobility. Suleiman, in his diary, is at his most terse: 'August 31. The Emperor, seated on a golden throne, receives the homage of the viziers and beys; massacre of two thousand prisoners; the rain falls in torrents. September 2. Rest at Mohács; twenty thousand Hungarian infantry and four thousand of their cavalry are buried.' When someone called Mohács 'the tomb of the Hungarian nation' he was not exaggerating; after the battle Hungary was destined to form part of the Turkish empire for 150 years.

But the battle was not the end of Suleiman's campaign; with no one to stand in his way he marched up the Danube to Buda, which he reached on 10 September without encountering any opposition, and the few people who had stayed there hurried to send him the keys of the city as a token of their submission. In return, Suleiman promised that the place would not be given over to his soldiers to be sacked, and he himself took up residence in the castle, which had always been the home of the Kings of Hungary; but for once the Sultan's iron control of his army proved inadequate to the occasion. The Turkish troops, after months of exertion and privation, decided that they were not going to be cheated of the pleasures of a sack despite the Sultan's orders, and they ran riot through the city. Fires were started; palaces, churches, and private houses were looted; a few women were raped, and the repressed fears and frustrations of months of danger and discomfort were let loose in an orgy of violence and destruction. Suleiman, always a man of few words, wrote in his diary: 'A fire breaks out in Buda, despite the efforts of the Sultan; the Grand Vizier seeks in vain to put it out.' In fact, the city was burned to the ground, the royal palace alone escaping, and while the Janissaries and other infantry were pillaging the burning city, the *akinji* were spreading out over the country like a plague, burning the villages and farmhouses and raping and murdering their inhabitants.

A week later on 20 September, the troops in the capital crossed the Danube on a newly constructed pontoon bridge and entered Pesth, this time apparently on orders from the Sultan, and they promptly burnt and sacked this city too; but to everyone's surprise it proved to be their last act of violence. For on the next day Suleiman gave the order to start for home, apparently having decided that the ruins of the twin cities were not worth garrisoning; they were a long way from Constantinople, the winter was approaching, and the weather was appalling. Moreover, he probably reckoned that he could annex the whole of Hungary at any time he chose to do so now that he had utterly destroyed its fighting forces; so, carrying with him the accumulated treasures of the royal castle in Buda together with most of the famous library which had been assembled by Matthias

Corvinus, and two huge cannon which the Hungarians had captured from Mehmed II after his abortive siege of Belgrade seventy years earlier, he set out for Turkey. Supplies were desperately short and this time the army was not only allowed but ordered to pillage the country, until it reached the Turkish frontier, and on the way it met a good deal of resistance from the peasants whose stores of winter food and whose flocks and herds stood between them and starvation. Casualties on both sides were heavy, and it is said that the Turks actually lost more men during their march home than had perished at Mohács, but however this may have been they reached Constantinople on 13 November, which they entered to a hero's welcome as the people of the city cheered themselves hoarse. Suleiman, who had been on the throne for a mere six years, had proved himself to be a greater conqueror than any of his predecessors. If he could conquer the island of Rhodes, capture Belgrade, annihilate the Hungarian army and push the frontiers of Islam almost as far west as the borders of Austria before he was thirty-two years of age, what were the limits to what he might accomplish in the years to come? The Turks were not the only people to ask themselves that question; there was hardly a western statesman who did not tremble at the possible answer. The battle of Mohács and the burning of Buda-Pesth had at last alarmed every Christian capital in the West. It was not too soon.

VIII

✠ ✠ ✠

Turks, Popes and Neighbours

Here is a talk of the Turk and the Pope, but my next door neighbour does me more harm than both.

M. P. Tilley, *Dictionary of Proverbs*

The Emperor Charles set Francis free on 17 April 1526, nine days before Suleiman marched out of Constantinople on his way to Mohács and Buda-Pesth. The French King had been his prisoner for just over a year, and the experience had not made him any fonder of his rival and captor than he had been before the battle of Pavia, nor had agreement on terms for his release been easy to reach. Francis, under duress, had expressed himself as willing to pay the Emperor three million crowns, to leave Italy, and to renounce all claims to Flanders and Artois; but he was not prepared to cede the duchy of Burgundy to him and this was the one thing which Charles wanted above all. Gattinara did his utmost to persuade the Emperor to accept Francis's offer, for he knew how badly Charles needed money and as we have seen, he was more interested in ridding Italy of the French than in the fate of Burgundy; but Charles was stubborn and no agreement was reached. In retrospect, it is possible to say that Charles may have been acting with greater realism and indeed greater wisdom than his advisers; for once he had freed Francis, any promises made to withdraw all French troops from Italy would not have been worth the paper they were written on, as subsequent events were to prove all too clearly, and it may be that Charles realized this. As for the three million crowns, where were they to come from? Francis could not lay his hands on such a huge sum of money, and Charles knew it. Once safely back in France, the French King could laugh at any demands

Charles might make for payment. In the end, however, an agreement was reached in Madrid; Francis promised to hand over Burgundy to Charles and to marry his sister Eleanor, the Queen Dowager of Portugal, who would bring a dowry of a million crowns with her, and Charles appeared to be satisfied. Francis was released, having twice given his word of honour that he would abide by the terms of his liberation, and Charles set off for Seville, there to marry Isabel of Portugal.

Predictably, Francis had not been back in his own country for more than a few days before he publicly repudiated his promises to Charles on the grounds that they had been forced upon him, and less than a week later he formed an alliance with the Pope, Venice and Count Sforza, all of whom were afraid of the growing power of the Emperor. Matters then deteriorated into farce; Charles informed the French ambassador that he considered that his King had not behaved like a gentleman, and challenged him to a duel, whereupon Francis, agreeing to this transformation of *realpolitik* into the stuff of *opéra bouffe*, sent a herald to Spain to accept his rival's challenge. Needless to say, however, nothing more came of the affair, and the two men never met in single combat. Instead, Charles was forced to realize that his problems in Italy had not been solved by the battle of Pavia, and he was as bankrupt as ever. A few weeks later, he heard of the death of his brother-in-law, King Louis of Hungary, and of the disaster that had befallen the Hungarians at Mohács. The news was bad, but there was worse to come.

After the defeat of the French at Pavia, the imperial troops in Italy had had nothing to do, and they had become bored. An army consisting of German mercenaries commanded by George Frundsberg and a large number of Spaniards under the Duke of Bourbon were camped near Bologna, and as the weeks followed each other and lengthened into months the men became more and more restive. They were badly clothed, badly nourished, unpaid, feared and detested by the local people and condemned to idleness. They had been promised the soldiers' rewards of conquest, booty, wine and women, and they did not like rotting away in an obscure corner of Italy with nothing to do. So early in 1527 they rebelled. Frundsberg was so shocked by the mutiny that he died of a stroke, while Bourbon, who just managed to escape being cut to pieces by the mutineers, eventually succeeded in asking them what they wanted. Action, they told him, and he had little alternative but to provide it for them, or at any rate to go along with them as they provided it for themselves.

Crossing the Apennines, their first objective was Florence; but the Florentines had been warned of their coming and were prepared for them. Bourbon, not wishing to risk a battle and having been informed that Rome was without troops and defenceless, persuaded his men to follow him in a lightning dash upon the city, and on 2 May they reached Viterbo. On hearing of their approach, Clement VII was terrified; he appealed to Renzo da Ceri, an experienced soldier who had already met Bourbon in battle on a previous occasion, to man the walls of the city, and by the time that the imperial troops arrived Renzo had somehow found 4,000 volunteers to defend the place against them. On the morning of 6 May, just before dawn, Bourbon led his men to the foot of the great wall of the Borgo, where he leapt from his horse and seized a scaling ladder; but before he could put it into position, he was shot in the right groin by a man on the wall with an arquebus, and fell dying to the ground. Having braved the initial fury of his insurbordinate troops, and then having led them successfully to within spitting distance of a prize as rich as Rome, Bourbon had become something of a popular hero with his men, and his death enraged them. As he was given the last rites of the Church they stormed the walls of the city, while the head of that Church was scuttling for safety into the embattled fastness of Castel Sant Angelo together with some of his cardinals and a number of ambassadors. Once inside the walls, the imperial troops fanned out into the streets, and went on a rampage of violence which, if later accounts are to be believed, has few parallels even in the annals of an age as violent as the first half of the sixteenth century. Nothing was sacred, and no one was spared; some German mercenaries, fiercely Lutheran in their conviction that all Catholics – and especially Italian Catholics – were idolaters, broke into St Peter's, where they stabled their horses, defecated on the altars and imported some prostitutes, with whom they acted out a number of obscene and somewhat childish burlesques. Outside in the streets bands of drunken soldiers roamed, noisily indulging themselves in an orgy of rape and murder. Thus far, there is nothing extraordinary or improbable in the contemporary accounts of the sack of Rome; it is more difficult to know how much credence should be given, however, to some other atrocity stories which spread like wildfire throughout Europe after the event and deeply shocked the whole of Christendom. Whether they were true or not, however, they had their importance, for they were widely believed at the time, and Charles was blamed for the alleged behaviour of his troops. Women, it was said, who tried to resist being raped were disembowelled and left in the gutters of Rome to die; nuns were publicly stripped in the city's squares, violated, and then impaled on stakes or pikes; householders who refused to say where they had hidden their jewels and other treasures were forced to watch as their children's throats were cut before their eyes, while others were hung up to the ceilings of their own houses by their testicles until they told their torturers where they had concealed their money, whereupon they were cut down by being castrated. When at last the soldiers were so sated with violence that they became tired of it, Rome smelled like a charnel house, and disease spread through the stricken city, killing many of those who had somehow managed to survive the attentions of the imperial troops. The Pope, meanwhile, held out against them in Castel Sant Angelo for a month until 5 June, when he surrendered.

None of this made Charles any more popular than before, and shortly after the sack of Rome Henry VIII broke off relations with him. One might have thought that the disaster at Mohács would have been enough to alert the various western powers to the seriousness of the Turkish menace, and so make them pause in their quarrelling; the need to unite against the common danger was so obvious that they must have been aware of it. Indeed, Charles and his brother Ferdinand, who were more immediately menaced than the other European monarchs by the western surge of the Turks, probably saw the true nature of the threat to Christendom clearly enough, and would have been both relieved and delighted to have escaped from the tangled web of old quarrels, petty jealousies and inherited rivalries in which they found themselves enmeshed, if they could have done so; but it was easier to pray for such a political miracle than to achieve it. As to Francis, who had encouraged Suleiman to attack Hungary in the hope that such a move would frighten and embarrass his Habsburg rivals, he may have been secretly a little appalled at the magnitude of the disaster inflicted with his tacit consent upon the Hungarians by the Sultan, but if so he showed no sign of dismay; and twinges of conscience which he may have felt seem to have been strictly subordinated, at any rate in public, to his delight at the discomfiture of Charles and his brother, for the greater the threat to Austria, the more they would both be distracted from their quarrels with France.

As for Henry VIII, although he publicly deplored the Turkish victory, England was too far away from Constantinople for him to feel personally threatened by it; he was more concerned with his domestic problems, and in some of these Charles was deeply involved. At the time Henry was trying to get rid of Catherine of Aragon, and not surprisingly this did not please her nephew, Charles. Predictably, Henry regarded the Emperor's opposition as a tiresome and unnecessary additional complication to an already complicated and tiresome problem, and the relationship between the two men noticeably cooled. If this had been all, however, matters would probably not have deteriorated. But Charles had recently announced his intention to marry Isabel of Portugal, and Henry was furious. As everyone knew, the Emperor had been betrothed to the Lady Mary Tudor ever since she was five, and to throw her over in favour of a

Portuguese princess, simply because she would bring with her a much larger dowry than Henry could afford to give his daughter, was insufferable: so insufferable that Henry changed sides, made an alliance with France, and declared war on Charles in January 1528. By this time, however, Charles, who must have become so accustomed to receiving bad news that he expected nothing else, was given cause for rejoicing for a change; for not only had he begun to fall in love with his unspectacular and rather frail little Empress from Portugal, but she provided him with a son, the future Philip II: an event which Charles celebrated in true Spanish style with a *corrida*, killing a bull with his own hand. Two months later, his brother Ferdinand's wife, Anna of Hungary, also gave birth to a son and heir, the future Maximilian II, thus ensuring that however unpopular the Habsburgs might have become, they would not lack for champions in the immediate future.

Apart from celebrating the birth of his son, in the aftermath of Mohács Ferdinand was also busy establishing his claim to the thrones of Hungary and Bohemia. Now that his brother-in-law King Louis was dead, he had a much stronger claim to the two kingdoms than anyone else through his wife Anna; for since Louis had died childless, his sister was his nearest of kin and his heir. But there were some people who were bitterly opposed to his claims, for to be patriotic in Hungary was synonymous for many people with being anti-German; but his opponents were divided among themselves and still suffering from shock at their country's disastrous defeat by the Turks, and their opposition had little effect. The two kingdoms badly needed the support of the two Habsburg brothers, and Ferdinand was chosen to be King of Bohemia less than two months after Mohács, while a little later the Diet at Pesth followed suit and recognized him as King of Hungary.

With Ferdinand's claims to the two thrones accepted, his opponents routed, and his triumph assured, the question of the Hungarian succession seemed to be settled; but it was not so. There were still some people who did not like either Ferdinand or Austria, and who did not believe that their country could any longer afford to resist the Turks or even be allied to the Austrians, who were bound to resist them; Hungary, they argued, would then simply become a battlefield over which the two super-powers, Turkey and the Habsburg Empire, would fight each other, while preserving their own lands undamaged. So they looked for another man to become their King, a man who would make peace with the Turks and rescue their country from the greedy hands of the Habsburgs before it could be turned into a mere satellite of Austria. They had no difficulty in finding such a man, for John Zapolya was eager to play the role of anti-German patriot assigned to him, and he was duly elected King in opposition to Ferdinand. The result was civil war.

At first, everything went in Zapolya's favour. He was in command of the only disciplined body of Hungarian troops left after the débâcle at Mohács, and with them at his back he entered Buda in triumph. Venice sent him messages of congratulation; Henry VIII recognized him; France announced that she was delighted by his election; the Pope murmured encouraging things about him, and Frangipani assured him of the loyal obedience of Slavonia. With nine-tenths of the country behind him, it looked as if he had completely outmanoeuvred Ferdinand; but he was no match for the Austrian as a politician and he allowed himself to be persuaded to make a truce with his rival, from which he stood to gain nothing, while Ferdinand was given the time he needed to plan a counter-attack. After six months the truce expired, and Ferdinand invaded Hungary at the head of 11,000 regular soldiers, only to encounter almost no opposition from Zapolya, who had made no preparations to meet him. City after city fell to the Austrians, and Zapolya's support melted away; droves of Hungarians changed sides and joined Ferdinand; and after being beaten in a battle near Tokay, Zapolya fled into his native Transylvania. Even there people turned against him, and after yet another battle in which he was again beaten, he took refuge in Poland, leaving Ferdinand the undisputed master of both Bohemia and Hungary.

But Zapolya was unwilling to accept defeat. Instead, he turned to his country's greatest enemies, the Turks, and asked for help. Suleiman was happy to step in and make life difficult for Ferdinand, but at first he played a haughty and elusive role. Zapolya approached him through a Polish intermediary, a nobleman named Hieronymus Laski, who had already served for some years as Polish ambassador in Paris and elsewhere, and was an accomplished diplomat. At first, however, he was not well received in the Turkish capital; he was shunted unceremoniously from one petty official to the next without ever getting near to the all-powerful Ibrahim, who was the one man he wanted to see, for by this time it was only through Ibrahim that anyone could hope to reach the Sultan. Frustrated by the difficulties of finding his way through this bureaucratic jungle, Laski turned for help to a remarkable man named Ludovico Gritti, the bastard son of a former Venetian ambassador to Constantinople by a Greek woman. Ludovico had been born in 1480, and he had grown up in the Turkish capital; when his father was recalled to Venice to become Doge, he had taken Ludovico with him. The boy was sixteen at the time, and in Venice his father gave him the best education available to the sons of wealthy Italians of the High Renaissance, and since he was a brilliant pupil there should have been no limits to the possibilities open to him; but in fact Venetian law forbade bastards from holding high office in the city, and so at the age of twenty-seven he had returned to his birthplace, where he had soon made a huge fortune and a name for himself in commerce. He spoke Turkish, Italian and Greek perfectly, French and German fluently, and a number of other languages well enough to make himself understood; he was charming, devious and untrammelled by scruples of any kind. He lived in a splendid palace on the shores of the Bosphorus, where he entertained visiting Europeans and helped to arrange meetings between them and the Grand Vizier, who was his friend. With his wealth, his brilliance and the skill with which he exploited his position as an intermediary between the Christian West and the Islamic East, Ludovico Gritti was one of the most fascinating minor characters produced by an age which was rich in such people; indeed, in some ways he was a typical Renaissance man.

Laski had no difficulty at all in procuring Gritti's help, for as soon as he met him he offered him an annual honorarium of several thousand ducats and the income from a rich Hungarian bishopric, and Gritti was always prepared to do almost anything for money. As a result, all doors were miraculously opened to the Pole and, just before Christmas, on 22 December 1527, he was ushered into Ibrahim's presence. Von Hammer has described their meeting: the Grand Vizier did not mince his words. 'Why has your master not asked the Sultan's permission before being crowned King of Hungary?' he asked. But Laski was a diplomatic man, and he managed Ibrahim tactfully enough to be granted another interview six days later. Once again, the Grand Vizier was blunt to the point of rudeness. 'We killed King Louis,' he told his visitor; 'we captured his palace, and ate and slept in it. His kingdom is ours. It is stupidity to imagine that a crown makes a man a King; it is not a lump of gold or a set of jewels which makes anyone a King, but a sword.' Ibrahim was no fool, however, and although he treated Laski with scant courtesy he realized that it would suit the Sultan's purpose to strengthen Zapolya's hand against Ferdinand, and thus to ensure that Hungary remained divided. Laski was therefore allowed to speak to Suleiman, who treated him with more grace than he had received from Ibrahim, and when Laski left Constantinople he carried with him the Sultan's promise to support Zapolya in his struggle against the Austrian usurper.

News of his rival's diplomatic success did not take long to reach Ferdinand, who had little alternative but to emulate him by sending two representatives of his own, John Hoberdanaz and Sigismund Weichsleberger, to Constantinople to sue for peace or at least for a truce. Heinrich Kretschmayr, Gritti's biographer, has described how, on arrival, they behaved with an astonishing lack of tact, browbeating Ibrahim and demanding that the Turks immediately withdraw from the whole of Hungary and hand over their bases to the Archduke Ferdinand. If they thought that they could bully the Grand Vizier into agreement, they greatly mistook their man. He was surprised, he told them with icy sarcasm, that their master had not asked for Constantinople. When they were eventually admitted into the presence of the Sultan, they fared no better. 'Tell your master,' Suleiman said to them with no attempt to hide his hostility or the underlying menace of his words, 'that although he has not yet discovered what it is like to be our friend or neighbour, he will soon do so. You can tell him that I myself shall soon come to see him, bringing all my forces with me, and that I shall give him what he demands. Tell him to prepare well for our visit.' In fact the two envoys could not deliver this message for they were forbidden to leave Constantinople; instead, they were thrown into prison in the *Yedikule Hisar*, or Fortress of the Seven Towers, where they languished for months while Ferdinand was left without any knowledge of their fate or that of their mission.

Fortunately, however, Suleiman was too busy suppressing revolts in Cilicia and Karamania (the present Cappadocia) to do much to help Zapolya or to harm Ferdinand for the time being; but by the end of the year 1528 he had succeeded in coping with both insurrections, and there was little doubt in anyone's mind that the spring of 1529 would see him leading yet another great expedition up the Danube, this time ostensibly to support his protégé, John Zapolya, but actually to attack the House of Habsburg. Suleiman made no secret of the fact that he considered himself to be the Lord of the Age, and that the pretensions of the Emperor Charles and his brother Ferdinand to be his rivals for the title were not only intolerable but ridiculous. It was time to teach them a lesson.

IX

✠ ✠ ✠

Enemies about the City

Deliver me from mine enemies, O God . . . In the evening they
will return, grin like a dog, and will go about the city.

Psalm 59

In the first ten years of his reign, Suleiman's military victories were so
spectacular that it is easy to forget that he spent most of his time at
home, where domestic affairs and his private life occupied him for
months on end; and yet it was here in the Sultan's private world that
the people moved who had most influence on him. In fact it was a dual
world; for on the one hand he was surrounded by his household staff
and his ministers of State, while on the other he enjoyed the company
of the ladies of the harem. The two worlds were so rigidly separated
that the inhabitants of the one never met those of the other, though
they often influenced each other.

During his first few years in power, the most important of the
people in this private world of Suleiman's was his mother, Hafiza, the
Sultan Valideh as she was called. She was the exception to the general
rule that the women of the Sultan's harem started life as slaves who
had either been captured in war or bought in the market place, for, as
has been said already, originally Hafiza was the daughter of the Khan
of the Crimean Tatars. Much of Suleiman's childhood had been spent
with her, while his ferocious father enjoyed himself making war on all
and sundry, and by all accounts he was devoted to her. Although she
ruled the harem with a rod of iron, she seems to have got on well with
the other woman in her son's life at this time, a Montenegrin girl of
great beauty by whom he had had a son in his early days before
ascending the throne. She had been captured in a Turkish raid and

named Gulbehar or 'Flower of the Spring' because of the loveliness of
her complexion and general grace, and Suleiman seems to have been
comparatively faithful to her, despite the opportunities open to him,
especially when he became Sultan. By later standards these were
modest, for where some of his more enthusiastically sensual
successors kept eight or nine hundred women in their harems,
Suleiman's harem was much smaller than that; there may have been
two hundred females living in the harem in his day, but many of these
were children, who might or might not take his fancy when they grew
to maturity, but who were much more likely to be married off to
members of his household when they reached the age of twenty-five;
for any girl who had not attracted his attention by that time was either
sold or given to someone else in need of a mother for his children.

A Genoese ambassador to the court of Suleiman's father, Selim, has
left a graphic account of the way in which the Sultan chose his
bed-fellows in his time:

When the Sultan decides to go to the Serai of the ladies, sometimes in
disguise, and sometimes openly on horseback, the chief of the eunuchs
arranges the girls, all beautifully dressed, in line in the courtyard; and when
the Sultan has arrived and the door has been shut, he and the eunuch move
along the line of girls greeting each one politely as they pass. Then, if there is
one who specially pleases him, he puts a handkerchief on her shoulder, before
walking on with the eunuch to stroll in the garden amongst the ostriches and
peacocks and many other birds kept there. Later, he returns to his rooms to
dine and to sleep. Once in bed, he asks someone to tell the girl, to whom he
gave his handkerchief, to bring it to him; a eunuch duly calls her, and she
comes with the handkerchief, while the eunuch leaves the room. The next
day, the Sultan commands that she be given a golden dress, an extra nine
aspers a day, and two more personal maids. Sometimes he remains in the
Serai for three or four days, sleeping with whom he will, before returning to
his own palace.

Interesting and accurate as no doubt this is as an account of Selim's
sexual habits, there is reason to believe that Suleiman was a less
frequent visitor to the harem than his father; when he did go there,
often enough it was to visit his mother, and when he wanted to sleep
with someone, it was nearly always Gulbehar who shared his bed. But
there were exceptions to this rule, and at about the same time as
Ibrahim began to rise to power a new recruit to the harem began to
attract his attention. She was a Russian girl, by birth a Christian and
the daughter of an Orthodox priest, who had been captured during
the course of a Turkish raid into Galicia – the border country between
Poland and the Ukraine – and on arrival in Constantinople, where she
was bought for the Sultan's harem, she was named Khurrem. It is the

Turkish word for 'Laughing One' or 'Smiling One', and apparently her smile was so radiant and irresistible that everyone was enchanted by it. Certainly she captivated Suleiman, and as the years went by he became ever more and more enamoured of her; small and fair-haired, she was not particularly beautiful according to all contemporary accounts, but she had enormous charm, great intelligence and a will of steel. As rumours of her growing ascendancy over the Sultan spread outside the walls of the harem, the small European community in Constantinople dubbed her 'La Russelane' because of her Russian birth, which became corrupted to Roxelana, the name by which she is known to history. In 1524, two years before the battle of Mohács, she bore Suleiman a son, who was named Selim after Suleiman's father, and as the years passed she gave him two more sons, Bayezid and Jehangir, who was a hunchback. This is not the place to enlarge upon the influence which Roxelana was destined to have upon the fortunes of Turkey – that must come later; it must suffice here merely to record her arrival in the harem in Constantinople and her growing influence over Suleiman.

In the spring of 1529, the great military expedition which the western world had been both expecting and dreading was ready to leave Constantinople, and on 10 May Suleiman set off at the head of the largest army which had ever been mustered there. It was a good deal more powerful than the army with which he had invaded Hungary before the battle of Mohács, and although it is always difficult to know how much reliability to put on contemporary statistics, most authorities are agreed that this time the army probably numbered about a quarter of a million men and 300 cannon. There is no need to describe their journey in detail; indeed, it would be tedious to do so, for it did not differ greatly from that which had culminated at Mohács three years earlier; discipline was extremely strict again, and once again the weather was atrocious. (It is sometimes suggested in our own time that the climate of Europe is deteriorating; there never used to be such cold, wet springs or such rain-sodden summers in the old days, or so it is argued; but if the spring and summer of 1529 are anything to go by, this is not true.)

The march of the Turkish army in 1526 had been made acutely uncomfortable by persistent rain, but the discomforts of the Mohács campaign were nothing to the suffering and indeed the dangers endured by the Turks three years later. At Philippopolis the waters of the Maritsa were so swollen with rain that the bridge over the river in the centre of the town was washed away, and on the night of 9 June the flood waters rose to such a height that the plain upon which the army was encamped at what was believed to be a safe distance from the river, was inundated; many soldiers were drowned while others only saved themselves by climbing trees, where some of them nearly starved to death before they were rescued. The cold was almost as bad as the rain; men shivered in wet clothes all day, only to be huddled together for warmth at night in bedding from which it was impossible to wring the water, so sodden had everything become. Nothing escaped the rain; the food was sloppy with it, weapons rusted, harness grew green with mildew, and water seeped into powder kegs and ruined them.

As for the roads, which by modern standards were extremely bad at the best of times, the combination of incessant rain and the passage of an army of 250,000 men with their wagons, artillery, horses, mules and camels turned them into quagmires. It was not unusual in the early sixteenth century for roads in countries as civilized and comparatively advanced as France, for instance, to become so bad in winter that those who were foolhardy enough to travel upon them risked being drowned in enormous waterlogged pot-holes or great morasses of liquid mud. It can be imagined, therefore, what a summer like that of 1529, combined with the passage of Suleiman's army, did to the roads of eastern Europe: men slithered and squelched in the mud; wagons and cannon got bogged down and had to be abandoned; horses, mules and camels fell and broke their legs, or stood, stubborn and shivering, while their grooms swore at them and tried to drag them another few yards along the eight-hundred-mile journey upon which they were embarked.

When at last the Turks reached Mohács on 19 July, Zapolya accompanied by Laski and about 6,000 cavalrymen came to do homage to Suleiman, who received him with great pomp, presenting him with three racehorses with saddle cloths of gold and four ceremonial robes of cloth of gold; but he made it abundantly clear in the process that, although he was prepared to help Zapolya make good his claim to be the King of Hungary, he was welcoming him as a vassal. He rose to meet him and stretched out his hand in greeting, but Zapolya was expected to kiss it, not to shake it. Thus the field of Mohács, upon which the pride of the Hungarian nation had already been humbled in battle, became the scene of a second humiliation, as Zapolya sacrificed any true patriotism he may once have felt to his personal ambition to be King.

Reinforced by this Hungarian contingent but already badly delayed by the weather, Suleiman moved on towards Buda. This time his men were forbidden to plunder the countryside, for they were not at war with Hungary but only with the usurper Ferdinand and his Austrians, and of them so far there had been no sign at all. Various towns such as Szeged, which might have been expected to resist the Turkish advance, surrendered without a murmur. A small garrison of German mercenaries offered a rather feeble resistance at Buda, but surrendered on being promised that their lives would be spared: a promise which was immediately and cynically broken by the Janissaries, who were angry at Suleiman's ban on looting the city and who worked off their bad temper by massacring the Germans in defiance of the Sultan. Seven days later, Zapolya was installed on the throne of the Arpads by a minor Turkish official, and the army took to the road again, marching slowly westwards under a grey and water-laden sky, while the *akinji* went ahead in haste to enter Austrian territory, where they would once again be free to enjoy a little arson and rapine.

Ferdinand had had plenty of time to prepare for the coming of the Turks. He had made one more attempt to make peace with the Sultan before his country was invaded, but his ambassadors had been treated with even greater contempt than they had received on their previous visit. Ibrahim had asked them sarcastically how their master could possibly call himself King of Hungary after the Sultan had twice conquered that country without once meeting Ferdinand in battle; it was obvious that he was no King, but merely a little fellow in Vienna, hardly worth noticing. The Vizier had gone on to say that the Sultan was seeking only 'the King of Spain', whom he pointedly refused to call Emperor; and Suleiman himself, when eventually the ambassadors met him, also made it clear that he was bent on war with Charles. Having been thus warned that war was now inevitable, both Ferdinand and Charles had set about to prepare for it, but his had not proved easy.

The Empire was still distracted by the religious problem, and although recently Luther had changed his tune, in a pamphlet entitled 'On the War against the Turks' where he had urged all Christians to stand together against them, many of his followers still made no bones of the fact that they considered the Pope to be a far greater menace to true religion than Suleiman, and Roman Catholics to be more benighted than the Turks. It had been difficult, too, to persuade the German princes to do much to help; they were bitterly jealous of the Habsburg brothers, and not at all averse to seeing them in difficulties, even though they had reluctantly to admit that if the Turks were allowed to conquer Austria, it would inevitably be their turn next time. In the end, therefore, when it was almost too late, they agreed to a *Reichshilfe* for the defence of the Empire, and belatedly the slow business of raising troops had been begun.

If the weather had not slowed up Suleiman and his waterlogged army, who took much longer to reach their objective than they had expected, these German troops would never have arrived in Vienna in time to defend it; but as it turned out the Austrian garrison of about 12,000 men was strengthened by the arrival of 8,000 Germans a few days before the Turks arrived at the walls of the city. Even so, the defenders were hugely outnumbered by their enemies; moreover, they had only seventy-two cannon with which to defend the place, and the walls of the city were old-fashioned and quite inadequate to resist a bombardment by the heavy modern guns of the day. Fortunately, most of the defenders were veteran soldiers, who enjoyed war and were good at it, and they had built earthworks wherever they were needed to reinforce the old walls. With all their enthusiasm and military expertise, however, they would not have stood much chance of repelling Suleiman if he had not been forced by the weather to abandon nearly all his heavy guns during the course of his journey; some had sunk irretrievably into the mud of the roads; some had been lost when a bridge over the River Drave had collapsed under their weight; and some had been left behind in Buda, as it had become more and more obvious that unless the army abandoned them it would not arrive at its destination before the winter closed in.

The first sign which the people of Vienna had of the approach of the enemy was the sight of a few thin black columns of smoke rising lazily into the sky in the far distance as villages were set on fire by the marauding *akinji*; and as the Turks approached nearer to the city, so they grew in number and proximity until they rose like a forest all round the city from horizon to horizon. At the same time refugees from the countryside began to arrive in the capital to the terrifying accompaniment of the slow ringing of 'Turk-bells', as the church bells were tolled from every nearby tower and steeple until the air was filled with their sonorous alarm. On 23 September the Turkish horsemen reached the walls of Vienna with their pikes lifted high, each with an Austrian head on the end of it, and as the silent men on the battlements watched them arrive the Turks whooped and screamed in defiance. Four days later on the eve of St Wenceslas's Day, 27 September, Suleiman joined them with the main body of the army. He pitched his tent at a safe distance from the city near the village of Simmering, and the Janissaries camped round his headquarters while the rest of his men spread out round the city. The siege of Vienna had begun.

With a few exceptions, historians have seen the battle which followed as the most crucial challenge to western Christendom since the battle of Tours eight centuries previously, when a Moslem army of Moors was defeated by Charles Martel. Ferdinand himself was not in the city; he was trying to raise more troops in Germany, having given command of the garrison to Count Nicholas von Salm, a veteran of Pavia and many other battles and a highly competent soldier. When Suleiman heard from some prisoners taken by his cavalry that neither the Archduke nor his brother, the Emperor Charles, was in the city, he told them angrily that he intended to chase

Ferdinand and chastise him wherever he might be; then he sent them into the city to tell the defenders and citizens that if they submitted their lives would be spared, but that if they did not surrender at once, they and their city would be utterly destroyed.

His army was so enormous and the garrison of the place so small by comparison, being outnumbered by at least ten to one, that it is surprising that the idea of accepting the Sultan's offer occurred to no one; they were few in number, and their means of defending themselves were meagre with only seventy-two cannon in the city, but their morale was high and their hatred of the Turks intense: indeed, even more intense than it had ever been, for everyone had heard the stories of atrocities committed by the approaching Turks on the women and children of the outlying villages, recounted by the refugees who had sought safety in Vienna. Moreover, they had made their preparations well; the suburbs had been burnt to the ground so that the invaders should not be able to use the houses there as cover, the garrison was on full alert, and every able-bodied citizen of the place had been mobilized and was ready to help in the coming struggle. When they received Suleiman's ultimatum, their answer was delivered by a task force of 2,500 men, who made a sortie from the Carinthian Gate and killed 200 Turks under the Sultan's very eyes, as his tent was being pitched at Simmering.

Without heavy artillery the Turkish bombardment, which began at once, did little damage to the fortifications of Vienna, old-fashioned as they were, and von Salm felt safe enough at the top of the tall spire of St Stephen's Church, from which vantage point he could watch every movement of the enemy outside the city walls; if a stray ball hit the spire, it was too small and spent to do much harm, and the Count spent most of his time there. The Turks realized that they would never breach the walls by using their artillery alone, and they began mining operations early in the siege, driving shafts beneath the Carinthian Gate and the monastery of St Clare; but some prisoners taken during another sortie on 6 October gave away the secret of these mines, and counter-mines were begun immediately by some German sappers and blown successfully a few days later. Frustrated by the failure of their attempt to blow up the Carinthian Gate, the Turkish gunners subjected it to a furious bombardment, and early in October scaling ladders were prepared and great bundles of faggots were bound together in bundles with which to fill the moat at the foot of the city wall in preparation for an assault. In order to forestall this attack, the Austrians made a dawn sortie from the city, hoping to surprise the Turks, but the Janissaries were waiting for them, and 500 of them were killed while others were taken prisoner; almost certainly their plan of attack had been betrayed to the enemy by an informer.

Although this was a disaster, which the defenders could ill afford, it might have been worse; for as the survivors fled back to the safety of the city walls they were so hotly pursued by the Turkish infantry that for a moment it looked as if Suleiman's men would carry one of the city gates before it could be shut against them. Fortunately for the Viennese, they just failed to do so, and when they tried to scale the walls beside the gate which had been slammed in their faces, they were beaten back by the Austrians, who killed and wounded many of them in the process. Honours were not exactly even, for the Turks could afford their casualties much better than the Austrians, but if the Christian forces had not won a spectacular victory at least they had not suffered an irreversible defeat; and time was on their side. Indeed, their most powerful ally was fast approaching, and the longer the defenders could hold out, the more surely could they rely on this imminent support. That ally, of course, was winter.

After the near-disaster of this sortie by the Austrians, the two sides settled down again to a war of mining and counter-mining, the defenders not wishing to risk another adventure outside the walls and the Turks not daring to launch another immediate assault upon them until they had been breached by a mine. At about three o'clock on the afternoon of 9 October, however, two mines were detonated, one on either side of the Carinthian Gate, and for the next three days the city was under constant attack. At first, the Turks sent in waves of half-trained troops, most of them conscripted peasants, to wear down the defenders before launching the Janissaries and other trained soldiers on them. The fact that most of these wretched people were either killed on the spot or wounded did not worry their commanders; there were many other peasants where they had come from, and they were regarded as expendable, especially since even in death their bodies performed the useful function of filling the ditches and moats over which the Janissaries would later have to move up to the attack. As for the peasants, if they refused to oblige their commanders by advancing like sheep to the slaughter, they were promptly shot for disobedience. Thus under a furious artillery bombardment of the wall on either side of the two great breaches in it, while trumpets were blown and drums beaten, wave upon wave of terrified conscripts rushed screaming at their objective, only to be mown down in hundreds by the Austrians and Germans armed with arquebuses.

Nicholas von Salm fought with immense bravery shoulder to shoulder with his men, appearing again and again at the point of maximum danger to rally the defence. On the second day two more mines were blown near the Carinthian Gate, and the beys of Yannina and Valona led their men forward into the attack only to be repulsed with the loss of 200 men; but by this time the soldiers of the garrison had had no sleep for almost three days and nights, and although they had not suffered as many casualties as their enemies, inevitably some of them had been killed and others wounded, while the rest were hungry, thirsty and exhausted.

On the morning of 12 October, two more Turkish mines were blown, opening huge new breaches in the city wall near the Carinthian Gate, and things looked so bad that for the first time the Viennese came near to despair. They managed to smuggle a messenger out of the city with an urgent plea for help, but they knew that he could not possibly summon help in time to repulse the formidable ranks of shouting, triumphant Janissaries, who would either carry the city by dusk or die in the attempt. From the top of St Stephen's spire, the Turkish pashas and beys could be seen exhorting their men, and in some cases striking them with the flat side of their swords, as they drove them into battle, and crying loudly to heaven and each other of the greatness of God and the glory of Islam, into battle they continued to go all day. Yet by some miracle of steadfastness and sheer endurance, the exhausted soldiers in the city continued, too, to drive them back over the heaps of corpses lying below the ruins of the city wall. As darkness fell that night, after the confusion of the past three days' fighting with its rubble of blood and stones and its mountain of dead bodies, most of the soldiers on both sides must have been too tired even to think of what the next day might hold for them; and yet, in fact, the fate of the battle had been decided. For that night Suleiman wrote in his diary, 'October 12, two new mines open great breaches. Council is held in the Vizier's tent of all the beys of Rumelia; the cold and lack of food, making themselves felt more and more, the decision is made to retreat after one more effort.' Winter had arrived.

The Sultan's 'one more effort' was a fiasco. The Turkish soldiers had reached and indeed passed the limit of human endurance, and when they were ordered, cajoled, bribed and browbeaten to attack once more the next morning, they did so, but so half-heartedly that the issue was never in doubt and the defenders of the city never in much danger. Later in the day, they even launched an offensive sortie against their enemies, and returned to the city with a number of prisoners. Ibrahim wanted to retreat at once, but Suleiman had not entirely given up hope of a last-minute miracle, and on 14 October two more mines opened up a new breach in the wall and the Sultan ordered the army to attack yet again; but the assault was no more successful than before, though von Salm was badly wounded by a splinter of stone which shattered his thigh. Otherwise Christian casualties were light. That evening the Sultan gave the order to retreat, and at midnight the watchmen on the walls of Vienna saw flames rising from the enemy camp as the Janissaries burnt their tents and everything else which they could not carry with them. The *sipahis* (or regular cavalry) and the *akinji* had taken a number of prisoners in the countryside round the city during the course of the siege, and they disposed of these too; the older ones, both men and women, were burnt with the rest of the camp rubbish, while over a thousand more were systematically massacred by a squad of soldiers detailed for the task. Only those in the flower of their youth and beauty were allowed to live, to be sold later as slaves. Meanwhile, the watchers on the wall were forced helplessly to witness the scene, as their countrymen were butchered and the night air was rent by the hysterical screams of frightened children and the cries of the dying.

In the morning, as the news spread through the city that the Turks were striking their camp and preparing to leave, everyone rushed into the streets in huge excitement and relief. Every cannon in the place fired salvoes of rejoicing to salute the victory they had won, the church bells were set pealing and pealing over the battered roofs of the city, and even the clocks, which had been stopped during the siege, were started again and made to chime the hour of triumph. When Ibrahim heard the noise, he asked one of the more aristocratic prisoners, who had been spared in order to be ransomed, what it was all about, and when he was told that it was a sign of rejoicing, he sent the man into the city to try to arrange the release of the Turkish prisoners, perhaps hoping to catch the Viennese in a good mood; but they were in no frame of mind to treat with Ibrahim, and nothing came of it.

In fact, it was not until 16 October that Suleiman finally struck camp and set off on the long march to Constantinople, which the jubilant Austrians and Germans, aided and abetted by the winter weather of central Europe, were determined to make as dangerous and uncomfortable for them as they possibly could. The Sultan's rather pathetic attempt to prove to his troops that their defeat had really been a resounding victory by handing out huge rewards to all and sundry, with specious messages of congratulation upon the glorious triumph they had all just won, deceived no one, and did little to improve the temper of the Janissaries, who were in an ugly mood. Harassed by imperial cavalrymen, who picked off all stragglers and inflicted casualties on the retreating host whenever they could, famished with hunger because of a really desperate shortage of food, frozen to the bone by appalling weather, and humiliated by the first major defeat which they had suffered for years, the Turks vented their anger and frustration upon the unfortunate people of the country through which they passed; the memory of their atrocities was to sink so deeply into the consciousness of Europe and win them such an

indelible reputation for barbarism that three centuries later Mr
Gladstone could still refer to 'the unspeakable Turk', while for
hundreds of years on successive Good Fridays every parson in the
Church of England was in duty bound to pray for 'all Jews, Turks,
Infidels, and Hereticks' as the prime murderers of Christ and haters of
God. Two days after leaving Vienna, it snowed, and as the army
crossed the Danube on the next day both men and baggage were lost
in the icy waters of the swollen river. Suleiman's diary is a catalogue of
minor disasters; every day it either rained or snowed; each river to be
crossed took its toll of men and equipment, while horses and camels
died or were drowned in increasing numbers as the journey
continued; to crown it all, as the army at last drew near to its
destination, there was a violent earthquake and the Greek and Turkish
villages through which it passed were in ruins and filled with weeping
people. The next day, 9 November, Suleiman ordered a local
governor, a man named Mahmoud, to be hanged for some reason or
another, and two days later he and what was left of his army marched
wearily into Constantinople, where he set about celebrating his
'victory'.

Thus ended his most ambitious attack by land upon the Christian
West. Numbers are always difficult to estimate, but it had probably
cost the lives of about 40,000 Turkish soldiers and 20,000 Christians,
most of them countrymen and peasants caught up in the war and
killed by marauding bands of *sipahi* and *akinji* or by the army in
retreat. The cost in human suffering cannot be estimated.

Suleiman receiving a foreign ambassador, possibly de Busbecq who closely resembled the man in the picture bowing to the Sultan. On his arrival at the Palace, de Busbecq 'was introduced into the Sultan's presence by his chamberlains, who held our arms. . . After going through the pretence of kissing his hand, we were led to the wall facing him backwards, so as not to turn our backs towards him.' De Busbecq remarked on the Sultan's expression which was 'anything but smiling, and has a sternness which, though sad, is full of majesty.'

Suleiman hawking. Ibrahim was his Chief Falconer before he made him Grand Vizier.

Giannizzere andando alla guerra

A Janissary with a sword and an arquebus. The arquebus was an awkward weapon, fired by a match and usually supported on a notched stick when discharged. As the 16th century progressed, it was gradually replaced by the more advanced musket. The plumes on Janissaries' hats were not as imposing as those depicted here.

OPPOSITE BELOW: Two early 16th-century engravings of Turkish women by an Italian, who travelled widely in Turkey and published an account of his travels. The lady on the left is a person of distinction, while the one on the right with long hair and a little bouquet of flowers is described as 'Cortigiana'; whether this means a concubine, of whom there were many in Turkey, or a prostitute is not clear.

Suleiman besieging Vienna in 1529. The line-up of artillery in the picture is impressive, but in fact Suleiman failed to take the city at least partly because he lost so many of his heaviest cannon en route; the state of the roads was made appalling by atrocious weather, and the distances involved were enormous.

X

✠ ✠ ✠

Princes' Favours

O how wretched
Is that poor man that hangs on princes' favours!
Shakespeare, *King Henry VIII*

As was all too often the way of things, after uniting to meet the Turkish invasion of Austria, the various Christian powers fell out among themselves and began squabbling again as soon as the danger was past. If the German princes had continued to co-operate with Ferdinand after the victory at Vienna, he would probably have been able to drive the Turks out of Hungary altogether; but they were jealous of the Habsburgs and as soon as the threat to their own lands was removed, they ordered their troops to return home. They were not prepared to take sides in Ferdinand's quarrel with John Zapolya for the Hungarian crown; in fact some of them probably hoped that Zapolya would win, for the last thing they wanted to see was yet another extension of Ferdinand's power. So the chance to recapture Belgrade and defeat Zapolya, Suleiman's puppet, was thrown away; instead, Ferdinand sent envoys to Constantinople to make peace with the Sultan.

On his return, Suleiman had arranged a vast programme of festivities to celebrate the circumcision of his sons by Roxelana and his 'victory' at Vienna. That these jollifications were expressly designed to disguise the extent of his defeat is obvious, and all historians have remarked upon the fact; but it would be interesting to know whether Suleiman himself saw it this way. It is possible that, even as early as this in his career, the *folie de grandeur* from which he was to suffer more and more as he grew older had already gripped him, and that he had managed to convince himself, if no one else, that he had not really been defeated. His object in invading Austria, he told all and sundry, had been to chastise Ferdinand and to bring him and his brother Charles to battle, and since neither of them had dared to face him, he had returned home unsatisfied, but by no means defeated. As for Vienna, since Ferdinand had not been in the city at the time, he had not really been interested in capturing it; of course, he could easily have done so, had he chosen to continue the siege, but it had not been worth his while. These were the things Suleiman said, and he may have believed them.

But if Suleiman was deceiving himself with his victory celebrations he was deceiving no one else, though the people of Constantinople enjoyed the various free festivities with which he supplied them. There were games, tournaments, sham fights and horse races in the Hippodrome, where a huge tent had been installed for the Sultan who sat there on a golden throne supported by columns of lapis lazuli to enhance his splendour; while in other parts of the city each evening plays were staged, concerts given, dances held, circuses thrown open to the public free of charge, and displays of fireworks organized in the parks and public gardens. But the arrival of Ferdinand's envoys did more than anything else to save the Sultan's face. Their mission was a major blunder on Ferdinand's part, for if the Austrians had been the victors, what were they doing coming cap in hand to Suleiman suing for peace? Neither he nor Ibrahim was the man to miss such a splendid opportunity to turn the diplomatic tables upon his enemies, and although the ambassadors were welcomed honourably enough, Suleiman kept them waiting for nearly a fortnight before he graciously consented to see them. When they did meet him, it soon became apparent that agreement was going to be impossible; Ferdinand's main demand was for Suleiman to recognize him as King of Hungary, and this the Sultan flatly refused to do, insisting, too, that he would not remove the Turkish garrison from Buda. Deadlock was soon reached and in November they left for home having achieved none of their objectives.

But diplomatic triumphs were not enough for Suleiman and he pressed ahead with yet more military preparations for another invasion of Austria. He was determined to bring Ferdinand to battle somehow, and even more determined to humiliate Ferdinand's brother Charles, who had only recently succeeded in persuading the Pope, chastened by his experience during the sack of Rome, to crown him as Holy Roman Emperor: a formal act which, surprisingly, had never been performed. At long last, however, Clement VII had placed the imperial crown on his head at Bologna on 24 February 1530, and the news of his coronation had enraged Suleiman; there could be only one

Emperor in the world, and he was that Emperor. How dare anyone challenge his unique pre-eminence? It was plain that 'the King of Spain' needed putting in his place, and Suleiman intended to prove his point by force of arms.

He was, however, in no hurry, and it was not until the spring of 1532 that he made his move. Everything seemed to play into his hands; his military preparations were complete, his army stronger than ever before, and Charles was known to be no longer in Spain, but in the Empire, having for the moment made his peace with France. At last, therefore, Suleiman believed that he would be able to lure his rival into battle and then he would annihilate him; of that he had no doubt. So once again he marched out of Constantinople and headed for Hungary and Austria.

There is no need to describe the resulting campaign in detail. It is interesting chiefly because it shows how much Suleiman had learned from his previous campaigns, though owing to the military astuteness of the Habsburg brothers he failed to achieve his main aim. The news of his coming was not long in reaching Vienna, where a much stronger army than that which had defeated him three years earlier was soon assembled. Whether Suleiman knew of this concentration of Christian forces and of its strength or not – and he probably did, for he was always very well informed – he never challenged it. His previous siege of Vienna had taught him two things: first, the city was so far from his bases in Turkey that his communications were stretched to the limit, and these communications were very vulnerable indeed to such things as the vagaries of the weather; and secondly, without heavy artillery, which was almost impossible to transport so far over the existing roads, he would never be able to reduce the city. He may also have remembered the huge cost of the siege of Rhodes, and it is certain that he remembered only too well the cost of the retreat from Vienna in winter. In view of all these things, he led his army into Austria, where he besieged the little town of Güns a few miles from the frontier, hoping no doubt to draw Charles and the imperial army out of Vienna to its rescue. It was a good idea, but in fact Charles was in Ratisbon, and had no intention of being drawn by Suleiman on to ground of the Sultan's choosing; as a result the two great armies never met, while the people of Güns paid the penalty by taking on the entire Turkish army single-handed, and resisting everything it could throw at them for a whole month, thereby winning an immortal name for themselves. In the end they were forced to surrender, but their courage and resolution had so impressed Suleiman that he agreed to a virtually nominal capitulation of the city, refusing to allow his soldiers to sack it or to harm its people.

In a last attempt to draw Charles and Ferdinand out of their defensive position in Vienna, Suleiman turned south and led his army in a great raid into the Austrian province of Styria. From a military point of view, apart from providing bait to lure his enemies into the open the raid into Styria had no real objective other than to give his men a chance to pillage the country and to inflict the maximum damage upon its economy and its wretched inhabitants with the minimum risk to themselves. The entries in his diary are, as usual, revealing; at one time the army seems to have got almost out of hand as it spread out in search of plunder. On 15 September Suleiman made a note of the fact that he had had to halt 'in order to gather together again the army, which was widely dispersed; fog so thick that it was impossible to tell one man from another'. A week later, when he reached the River Drave, 'the three army corps arrive simultaneously at the bridge in turmoil and confusion. The Grand Vizier and the other commanders take charge, remaining on the bridge on horseback directing the traffic all day.' But despite these moments, when the iron discipline of the Turkish army seems to have broken down, it returned safely to Constantinople by the end of October, where once again Suleiman organized a number of 'victory' celebrations to disguise the truth about his abortive expedition.

Both sides were now ready for peace. Suleiman could not afford to challenge the Emperor again, at least for the time being, for trouble was brewing in Persia; and Charles was eager to waste no more time cooling his heels in Austria for he had urgent business to attend to in Italy and in Spain. He had moved from Ratisbon to Vienna at the time that the Turks were crossing the River Drave on their way home, and he had stayed there until the beginning of October just in case Suleiman might decide to turn round and make a sudden dash for the city in the hope of surprising its defenders; but as soon as he was reasonably sure that the Sultan did not intend to return, he left for home. So when Ferdinand tentatively inquired whether the Sultan would welcome an embassy to discuss an end to hostilities between the two powers, he was assured that his envoys could be certain of a safe-conduct and a sympathetic hearing. Encouraged by this, Ferdinand chose a certain Hieronymus of Zara to be his chief ambassador in Constantinople. He was an impressive man who had greatly distinguished himself during the recent siege of Güns, and he reached the Turkish capital on 10 January 1533, where he was received with all due ceremony. He was granted interviews both by Ibrahim and by the Sultan within a few days of his arrival, and it was obvious that the whole diplomatic climate had changed since the last Austrian embassy had visited the place; this time the Turks plainly wanted the negotiations for peace to succeed, though they made it clear that they intended to insist upon Ferdinand's recognition of the Sultan's supremacy, even if it should be a token affair. Consulted by his ambassadors, Ferdinand agreed, and by early summer a treaty of peace was signed, and in July the Austrians set out for home.

But if the negotiations were uneventful and of no particular interest, Ibrahim's bearing and behaviour throughout his conversations with the Austrian ambassadors were remarkable. He was at the height of his power at the time, and he made no bones about boasting of its extent. A record of his remarks is to be found in the massive collection of Austrian and Turkish state papers edited by Anton von Gévay in the nineteenth century.

'Although I am the Sultan's slave,' Ibrahim said on one occasion, 'whatsoever I want done is done. On the spur of the moment I can make a stable lad into a pasha. I can give kingdoms and provinces to anyone I like, and my master will say nothing to stop me. Even if he has ordered something, if I do not want it to happen, it is not done; and if I command that something should be done, and he happens to have commanded the contrary, my wishes and not his are obeyed. I can make war and grant peace, and I can make men rich. The Sultan is no better dressed than I am, and what is more he pays all my expenses, so that my fortune never decreases. He trusts his power to me, his kingdoms, his wealth, everything both great and small, and I can do what I like with them.'

The Austrians were astonished at the openness with which the Vizier spoke, but in fact what Ibrahim said was true enough; his power was absolute. The one thing he seems to have forgotten by this time was that it was also precarious; for, as Ludovico Gritti said drily to one of the Austrians during a later conversation recorded in von Gévay's papers, 'If one day the Sultan should choose to send one of his scullions to slay Ibrahim Pasha, there would be no way of preventing the killing.' That proved to be a prophetic remark, for if no one had yet challenged the unique position which Ibrahim had held for ten years, the time had now come when he had a rival for the Sultan's favour: a rival who had no intention of sharing Suleiman's affection with anyone and every intention of supplanting Ibrahim as the power behind the throne.

Roxelana's rise from obscurity to eminence took place behind the silken curtains and closed doors of the harem, and was therefore largely hidden from the eyes of the world. When her children were born the news was made public, and those with noses sensitive to the scents borne abroad on the diplomatic breezes of Constantinople sniffed the wind, and drew their own conclusions; but it was not until after Suleiman had made peace with Ferdinand that anything dramatic enough happened to confirm their suspicions that a new power was at work behind the scenes in the Sultan's private world. In 1533, however, the Sultan Valideh, Suleiman's mother, died. The old lady had been undisputed ruler of the harem for years, and her passing left a power vacuum which inevitably precipitated a contest between Gulbehar and Roxelana for the succession, and less than a year later it became clear to the world who had won it; in 1534 Gulbehar, who by rights should have taken the old lady's place, was exiled to Manisa. Of course, the word 'exiled' was not used, and indeed she was not sent to live there in perpetuity but only for part of the year; but in fact her banishment from the capital was the work of Roxelana, who was left without a rival for Suleiman's affections in the harem and, except for Ibrahim, in the private and enormously powerful world of the inner circle of his intimate companions.

As soon as Gulbehar was safely out of the way, Roxelana set about making quite sure that no one else in the harem should do to her what she had done to the Montenegrin Rose of Spring. She persuaded Suleiman that, since nowadays he slept with no one but herself, it was unfair to keep the prettiest girls of his harem locked up there for ever, and that it would be much better if he were to arrange marriages for them to suitable members of his household. In this way she got rid of most of the best qualified competitors for the Sultan's bed, and having thus assured her own ascendancy in the harem, she turned her attention next to Ibrahim; at least, it seems overwhelmingly probable that she did so, though there is no hard historical evidence that she plotted his downfall. Nevertheless, at the time no one was in any doubt that the course of events during the next few years was largely due to Roxelana's determination to oust the Grand Vizier from his position of supreme power as Suleiman's right-hand man, so that she herself could assume his mantle. In the event, Ibrahim had become so over-confident of his influence over the Sultan that he played into her hands. It is hard to blame him for being so sure of himself, for after the campaign of 1532 and the subsequent peace with Ferdinand in 1533, Suleiman seems to have been content to leave the whole business of government to Ibrahim, while he himself spent his time enjoying himself in the country, hunting and living the life of a carefree country gentleman. When war broke out with Persia in 1535, he simply told Ibrahim to take command of the Ottoman army while he himself remained at home. He would join him later.

This arrangement did not please the Turks, who liked their Sultans to be warriors and to take command of their armies in the field. Moreover there were those, both at home and with the army in Persia, who resented Ibrahim's usurpation of the Sultan's position and authority, even though he was acting on the Sultan's orders. Many people were bitterly jealous of him, and the combination of resentment and jealousy which surrounded him should have warned him to be on his guard; but his enemies were careful to conceal their hatred behind smiling faces, and by this time Ibrahim was so confident of the Sultan's favour that the idea of caution seems never to have occurred to him. He was the Grand Vizier, the Sultan's *alter ego*, almost indeed the Sultan himself; so Ibrahim began signing various orders and documents not simply as Commander-in-Chief (the Turkish word is *Serasker*), but also as Sultan. There are those who say that the title 'Sultan' was sometimes given to men of high rank, and that Ibrahim may not have been arrogating to himself royal status by using it; but even if this is true, at the time there were men around Ibrahim who were only too eager to seize on any excuse to accuse him of treason, and he could not have provided them with a better opportunity to do so than by signing himself in such a way. But he was powerful and no one dared say anything to him, with the possible exception of a man named Iskander Chelebi.

Chelebi was the Chief Treasurer or *defterdar*, who had long hated Ibrahim, and the two men had a violent quarrel at this time, which may have been the result of remonstration by Chelebi about Ibrahim's use of the title 'Sultan'. What is certain is that the two men fell out during the first weeks of the Persian campaign in 1535, and that shortly afterwards Chelebi was accused by Ibrahim of embezzling army funds. Whether he was guilty or not it is impossible to say after so long, but on Ibrahim's orders he was arrested, tried and convicted. A few days later, he was publicly executed, but not before he had written a letter to Suleiman accusing Ibrahim of conspiring against the Sultan's life, and citing as evidence the fact that the Vizier had taken to signing himself as Sultan.

The letter was delivered to Suleiman when he joined the army in time to enter Baghdad in triumph at its head. It could not have been the first time that he had received a scurrilous letter accusing his minister of malpractices, for Ibrahim had made many enemies over the years, and at first sight it is a little difficult to understand why Suleiman should have believed it; he had trusted Ibrahim so completely for so long that one might have expected him to dismiss Chelebi's letter as a piece of libellous malice and throw it away in disgust, had it not been for two things. First, words either spoken or written by a man about to die were always treated with special respect by Moslems, and Suleiman may have found it hard to believe that Chelebi would have deliberately lied just before dying on the scaffold. But even this need not have been conclusive, for it must also have occurred to a man as intelligent as the Sultan that, even if Chelebi had believed his accusation to be true, he might easily have been misled by his hatred and jealousy of Ibrahim. But if such a thought passed through Suleiman's mind, plainly it did not convince him, and it seems sure that someone else must have already begun to undermine his faith in Ibrahim. Roxelana was a single-minded and ruthless woman, and she did not like competition. She had got rid of Gulbehar; now it was Ibrahim's turn.

Ten or a dozen years previously, when Suleiman had begun to confer more and more powers upon Ibrahim, showering him with honours and increasing his authority almost daily until even Ibrahim himself had become a little alarmed at the dizziness of his rise to eminence, it is said that he had turned half-jokingly to his benefactor and begged him not to advance him so high that his fall would inevitably be fatal, when and if it were to take place. The story goes that Suleiman had laughed, praising him for his modesty and swearing that Ibrahim should never be put to death as long as he remained Sultan, no matter what accusations might one day be brought against him. But this incident had occurred a long time ago, and it is doubtful whether either Suleiman or Ibrahim remembered it. So in the spring of 1536, after the campaign in Persia had been brought to a successful conclusion and both men were once more at home in Constantinople, when Ibrahim was summoned to dine with the Sultan and spend the night in the palace, as he had done on hundreds of occasions in the past, he duly presented himself for dinner, suspecting nothing. Very early the next morning, however, his body was found at the gate of the palace and the marks on his neck left no doubt that he had been strangled, while other marks were proof of the fact that he had fought fiercely for his life. On Suleiman's orders his corpse was loaded on to the back of a horse with black trappings, and carried across the Golden Horn to Galata, where it was buried in an unmarked grave. Ibrahim had become too powerful, and not for the first time or for the last, Roxelana had got her way.

From this moment onwards, she went from strength to strength. She had already astonished the diplomatic world by persuading Suleiman to break with all precedent and make her his legal wife; despite the fact that for six generations no Ottoman Sultan had married any of the women with whom he had slept and by whom he had had his children, after Gulbehar's banishment to Manisa Suleiman had married Roxelana. He had done it quietly in the palace, but since he had also ordained that his marriage should be the occasion of public rejoicing, the news of Roxelana's triumph had spread throughout a startled world like wildfire. A Genoese banker living in Constantinople at the time recorded the fact that 'this week took place in the city an event without precedent in the annals of previous Sultans. The Grand Signor took to himself as Empress a slave woman from Russia named Roxelana, and great feasting followed.' After Ibrahim's death, she took further steps to consolidate her position, and although to describe them here is to anticipate events, her subsequent influence was destined to be so great that perhaps the story of the way her power increased almost daily behind the scenes should be told now, if only in outline.

The first thing she did once Ibrahim was safely out of the way was to make sure that his successor should never wield enough power to become her rival. This was not difficult, for she simply persuaded her husband to appoint as Grand Vizier a man who was, if not exactly a nonentity, a highly undistinguished and slightly unsavoury political hack with none of Ibrahim's brilliance or ability. In fact, Ayaz Pasha was a lecher more interested in enjoying the many venereal pleasures of his bulging harem than in attending to affairs of state, and he did not last long; worn out perhaps by his excessive fondness of amorous indulgence, he succumbed to the plague after only three years in office. But at least he died in the knowledge that, whereas it had only been with the help of God that the seed of Abraham had been multiplied as the stars of heaven, he had not done badly on his own; for even though many of his offspring had predeceased him, dying in infancy like so many others, when he himself departed this life Ayaz Pasha left 120 living children, of whom forty were still in their cradles.

He was succeeded by the second Vizier, an Albanian named Loutfi Pasha, who was very different from his predecessor in his tastes; for far from being a womanizer he made no secret of his contempt for women. Furthermore, he not only despised and disliked them, but he hated those who disagreed with him and showed their disagreement by openly admiring the opposite sex. Despite his aversion, he had married one of Suleiman's sisters in order to advance his political career, and although little is known of their life together there is a record of one occasion when they had a flaming row. Apparently, Loutfi's attention had been caught by the affair of a lascivious Turk, who had been found *in flagrante delicto* in the midst of an orgy with a number of naked ladies, and the Vizier had been so disgusted that he had immediately ordered one of his minions to mutilate the sinner's genitals with a razor. When his wife heard of this barbarity she was so appalled that she accused him of being a monster, a savage and a tyrant, whereupon Loutfi flew into a towering rage and attacked her physically; her cries for help brought a number of eunuchs and ladies-in-waiting to her rescue, and Loutfi was dragged out of the room still screaming at her. When Suleiman heard of it he was incensed that his sister should be treated in such a way, and a little later when Loutfi also came under suspicion of treasonable correspondence with the Austrians, he was dismissed and sent into enforced exile in Demotika, where eventually he died. His wife remained in Constantinople as her brother's guest, thankful, one would imagine, to see the last of her misogynistic spouse.

The next man to be appointed Grand Vizier was even less impressive than either of his two peculiarly unimposing predecessors; it is difficult to imagine what made Suleiman appoint him. Suleiman Pasha (for he shared the Sultan's name) was a eunuch aged eighty, who somehow managed to last four years in office before being ignominiously sacked; perhaps Roxelana persuaded her husband to appoint him as a stop-gap while her own long-term plans were coming to maturity, and then the old man was tiresome enough to live longer than she had anticipated. However this may have been, in 1544 he was dismissed and in his place her son-in-law, Rustem Pasha, a Bulgarian who had married her daughter by Suleiman, Mihrimah, was appointed Grand Vizier. Her power, already great, now became not only unchallenged but almost unchallengeable, and the government virtually passed into her capable hands.

Although no one could possibly know it at the time, this was a political fact which was destined to settle the fate of the Turkish Empire and to ensure its abrupt decline after Suleiman's death; for although Roxelana was intelligent, able and determined, she was not exempt from one very common human failing: as a mother she was blind to the faults of her children. Gulbehar's son, Mustafa, was heir apparent to the throne, and she was determined to change that. Unluckily for Turkey, when Roxelana was determined to do something, she pursued her purpose with a relentlessness which knew no limits.

XI

✠ ✠ ✠

Pirates and Kings

It is, it is a glorious thing
To be a pirate King . . .

W. S. Gilbert, *The Pirates of Penzance*

From the time of Suleiman's accession until the end of the
inconclusive campaign of 1532, during which the little town of Güns
withstood the whole might of the Turkish army unaided and alone,
the war had been fought primarily on land; there had been a few naval
skirmishes and minor battles at sea, but they had been of little real
importance. However, after his failure to take Vienna or to bring the
Emperor Charles to battle, Suleiman began to turn his attention to the
Mediterranean; the capture of Rhodes had opened the way for his
ships to challenge the enemy by sea, and if he could not reach Charles
by land then the alternative was to carry the war to his back doorstep
by attacking the coastal cities of Italy and Spain itself. The only thing
wrong with this excellent plan was that, as sailors, hitherto the Turks
had proved themselves to be greatly inferior to their Christian foes.
However, Suleiman was not the man to allow that to deter him and so
he set about repairing the deficiencies of his navy and greatly
strengthening it; and to do this he called upon Khaireddin Barbarossa,
a North African corsair, who was already about sixty-seven or
sixty-eight years of age and one of the most colourful products of a
colourful age.

He was one of four brothers. They had been born on the island of
Mytilene, the ancient Lesbos, the sons of a Greek potter, and like most
of the islanders they had learnt the ways of the sea early in life. Their
father was a Christian renegade, who had served as a Janissary for

many years before retiring from the army and returning to his native island, where he had taken up pottery and married the widow of a Greek Orthodox priest, by whom his sons had been born. Ishak, the eldest, became a merchant, but the other three – Uruj, Khaireddin (pronounced Haireddin) and Elias – became pirates. At the time piracy was a traditional occupation in the islands, and no one regarded it as a dishonourable or even a disreputable profession. As Christopher Lloyd, who has recently written a history of the English corsairs of the Barbary coast and their exploits, has remarked, 'In the Mediterranean the word "corsair" denoted a member of one of the oldest professions. From time immemorial the seizure and plunder of ships sailing in that sea had been customary. Merchantmen were well armed because it was accepted that they might be attacked by galleys darting out of the bays and inlets of the North African coast or the isles of Greece, even by those of the Knights of St John from Malta, or St Stephen from Pisa, who, though dedicated to protecting Christendom from the infidel, frequently indulged in what can only be called piracy.'

Ishak was soon killed in a fight with the Knights of St John, but the other two pirate brothers prospered. The time could scarcely have been more favourable for aspiring pirates, for the extinction of the Fatimid Caliphate had left the whole of northern Africa at the mercy of a number of petty Moslem dynasties, which had been declining for years. The Beni Merin of Morocco, the Beni Zian of Algeria and the Beni Hafs of Tunis had degenerated to such an extent that in effect their rule was purely nominal, while their realms were in fact ruled by petty chieftains who called themselves 'governors' and paid lip service to their respective governments, but who behaved like independent princelings and made their living as pirates. The geography of the northern coast of Africa was perfect for the job, for it was rich in shallow, half-hidden inlets and easily defended small harbours, while its winds were notoriously unpredictable except to those familiar with the area, who could usually outsail anyone who pursued them. In the first quarter of the sixteenth century, while Suleiman was growing to manhood, Uruj and Khaireddin succeeded in establishing themselves as the acknowledged leaders of these petty pirate chiefs, making a great name for themselves, and being dubbed 'Barbarossa' because of their bushy red beards.

War at sea in the early sixteenth century, whether waged by pirates or by sailors employed by their respective national rulers, was still dominated by the galley, as it had been since Roman days. Galleys varied a little in size, but all were long and narrow and capable of a turn of speed which was beyond the power of the larger square-rigged merchant vessels of the day. Some were about 150 feet overall with a beam of about eighteen or twenty feet. They carried one or two triangular lateen sails, but in battle or when trying to overhaul a prize they were propelled by oarsmen, who sat in banks on either side of the ship, three rowers to a bench, heaving at oars thirty-five feet long and almost as massive as modern telephone poles. A normal crew numbered about 200 men excluding any soldiers who might be aboard, and usually the rowers were prisoners of war. These galley slaves were shackled by one leg to make sure that they did not rise in revolt against their taskmasters and take over the ship. They were driven to work by the ship's boatswain armed with a whip, who walked up and down the gangway between the banks of sweating, half-naked oarsmen, as they strained at their huge oars by rising from their benches with their free foot against the bench in front of them, and then throwing their whole weight backwards until they collapsed on their own bench again, only to begin the whole process all over again. It was a notoriously hard life even in an age in which hardship was the lot of most men, and it could not have been made any more endurable by the nauseating condition of the ships in which they heaved and sweated their hearts out year after year; for a galley could be smelt a mile away.

Those who regard the exploits of sixteenth-century pirates as suitable subjects for romantic novels or films tend to forget that the goddess Hygeia, Aesculapius' daughter, had not been worshipped for a thousand years. It would never have occurred to the officers of a war galley, whether they happened to be Moslem or Christian, that their galley slaves should be allowed to wash from time to time; stinking of sweat, the men at the oars were expected to urinate and defecate as best they could in the well of the ship while still shackled to their benches, and the scuppers of a galley were permanently awash with human excrement. In a battle, wounded men fell into this filth to die, and the blood and guts of others added to the vileness.

A galley's main armament consisted of a gun or two mounted in the bows. They were fired at an enemy ship from a range of about 200 yards in the hope of damaging and immobilizing it, whereupon it would be rammed with an iron-tipped ram designed for the purpose and the soldiers on the galley would board it, screaming and yelling at the tops of their voices to intimidate their opponents. It was not until nearly a century later that both warships and merchantmen began to mount a much larger number of guns broadside, and thus greatly to increase their fire-power, and even then it was done only at the expense of their mobility; and mobility was a galley's greatest virtue. A Benedictine monk who lived in Algiers towards the end of the sixteenth century described the galleys of his own day and deplored the fact that the Moslem vessels were superior to those of the Christians, because they were so extremely 'light and nimble and in such excellent order; whereas the Christian galleys are so heavy and in such bad order and confusion that it is utterly vain to think of them giving chase . . . The Algerines are very expert withal and (for our sins) so daring and fortunate that in a few days after leaving Algiers they return laden with infinite wealth and captives.'

The brothers Barbarossa rose to fame at a time when the Moslems of Africa were seething with hatred for Christians in general and Spaniards in particular, for after the fall of Granada in 1492 thousands of Moors from Spain had escaped and taken refuge in Africa. They had lost everything and they were thirsty for revenge; knowing the Spanish coast intimately, and its vulnerability to attack from the sea, they had harried it unmercifully, making the lives of everyone who lived within ten miles of the sea a nightmare. In fact, their raids had become so frequent and destructive that the Spaniards had retaliated by invading North Africa, where they had captured a number of towns and established naval bases. Oran, Bougie, Algiers, Tripoli and some smaller places had all fallen into their hands by the time the Barbarossa brothers appeared on the scene, and this was a state of affairs which they decided to rectify. Uniting the Moors behind them, they embarked on a war of reconquest, and at first they were remarkably successful; but in 1518 Uruj was killed and Khaireddin became the sole leader, taking unchallenged command of the anti-Christian coalition of little pirate states. It was not long before he gave unmistakable signs of a potential stature much greater than that of a mere pirate chief; for he recognized that, if he was to compete on anything like equal terms with the Spaniards, he would need the support of someone on a more or less equal footing with their King. He therefore turned for help to Selim the Terrible, and in return he promised to be his most loyal subject. Selim was delighted. He sent Khaireddin back to Africa as *beylerbey* or provincial governor with a small force of about 6,000 Turkish soldiers.

During the next few years, Khaireddin Barbarossa went from strength to strength. During the first years of Suleiman's reign, the young Sultan was too busy conquering Rhodes and campaigning in Hungary and Austria to spare much time or thought for Barbarossa, and the Emperor Charles was too busy fighting Francis I to send much help to the scattered and hard pressed Spanish garrisons in northern Africa. As a result, Barbarossa succeeded in regaining most of the places held by the Spaniards. In the end he made such a nuisance of himself in the western Mediterranean that Charles was forced to take him seriously and to plan a counter-attack against him. The opportunity to put his plan into action came in 1530, when he had at last made peace with France – if only temporarily – and Suleiman had just retreated ignominiously from the walls of Vienna. He had just gained another asset, too, for the most celebrated Christian seaman of the day, the Genoese Admiral Andrea Doria, had changed sides, deserting the service of Francis I and offering himself to the Emperor. Confident in Doria's ability to teach Barbarossa a lesson, Charles ordered him to take the offensive against his various naval bases in northern Africa, and the Genoese duly obeyed. In July he attacked the Algerian port of Cherchell, and although he did not capture the place he damaged it seriously, and a year later he captured a small port near Oran. But it was not until September 1532, at the precise moment when Suleiman was besieging Güns, that Doria made his master stroke. Sailing through the Strait of Messina with a fleet of forty-four galleys, he attacked and captured the fortified port of Coron on the south-western tip of Greece.

It was a serious loss for the Turks, for in the days of sailing ships most seafarers preferred to hug the coasts whenever they could do so, rather than risk the dangers of a long voyage out of sight of land. But following the coastline had its disadvantages too, for if the winds were contrary weathering a point or a rocky headland was both difficult and dangerous, and it might take weeks. If there happened to be a natural harbour near such a place, commanding the approaches to it, once it was fortified and garrisoned it could not only offer invaluable hospitality and shelter to friends in trouble, but it could virtually deny passage to enemy shipping; and of course it could keep an eye on all passing traffic and keep itself well informed of the movements of friend and foe alike. Coron was just such a place, and its loss was a double embarrassment to Suleiman, for coming as it did only ten days after his retreat from Güns, which had defied him so successfully on land, it was a most unwelcome advertisement to the world of his weakness at sea. Such weakness could not be tolerated, and so he summoned Khaireddin Barbarossa to Constantinople.

The old man obeyed, but he did so in his own fashion. He was well aware of his own importance and he took his time on the journey to Constantinople, eventually sailing through the Sea of Marmara and into the Golden Horn at the head of a fleet of forty ships with flags flying, as befitted the escort of a potentate of his stature. A few days later he presented himself in the palace accompanied by eighteen of his captains, and was received by Suleiman with every mark of honour. The Sultan then charged him with the task of enlarging the Ottoman navy and turning it from the clumsy and inefficient force which it had always been into the finest fighting force afloat in the Mediterranean. It was a formidable undertaking, which was made no easier by the envy and petty jealousy with which he was greeted by many of the Turkish naval officers over whose heads he had so suddenly been placed. They regarded him as, an upstart, and so did some of the

Ottoman bureaucracy, who were not used to being pushed around by someone as forceful and as contemptuous of their dilatory ways as this formidable newcomer with whom they now had to contend. But after a year, during which Barbarossa travelled to Persia to meet Ibrahim and enlist his support, most of these petty difficulties had been overcome, and Suleiman formally appointed him *kapudan-i deryâ* or 'admiral of the sea': Grand Admiral of the Ottoman Fleet, in fact.

It was not long before Charles was made aware that he could no longer safely regard the western Mediterranean as his own naval preserve. In June 1534, Barbarossa sailed from the Bosphorus in command of eighty-four ships. Leaving the majority of them in the Aegean to protect Turkish shipping there, he himself sailed westwards with a small but powerful flotilla manned by his best-trained men, and slipped unseen through the Strait of Messina by night. Like a pack of wolves breaking into a sheepfold, the Turkish ships descended upon the coastal towns of Italy with savage efficiency. Reggio was the first to suffer; those of its inhabitants who resisted the invaders were immediately killed, the better-looking girls and women were raped, and the town was stripped of its treasures before being left desolate and dark with pools of blood. Further up the coast eighteen galleys were caught unawares and destroyed, while town after town was pillaged and burnt after the people had fled in terror on hearing of Barbarossa's approach. At Fondi he landed a party with orders to capture the castle, where one of the most celebrated beauties of the day was believed to be living at the time. Stealing up to the place under cover of darkness, the Turks were almost upon it before the lady was awakened and warned of her danger; leaping from her bed in nothing but a nightgown or, as one version of the story would have us believe, not even in that, she was just in time to leap upon an unsaddled horse and to gallop away through the night accompanied by an esquire, who escorted her to safety. It did the poor man little good, however, for the lady in question was Julia Gonzaga, the widow of one of the Colonnas and the sister of Joanna of Aragon, and the fact that her gallant escort had seen the lovely Julia naked or virtually so was enough to enrage the Gonzaga family, who had the luckless young man murdered for his pains. The story was immensely popular at the time, and it has been repeated with understandable gusto by many historians since then; whether it is strictly true or not is another matter.

But Barbarossa's real target was in northern Africa, and having terrified the people of Italy he doubled back on his tracks and attacked the port of Tunis, a place of immense strategic importance, before anyone had realized that he was no longer at large in the Tyrrenhian

Sea. The Hafsid rulers of Tunis were both effete and unpopular, and they had recently made the cardinal mistake of accepting Christian help to keep themselves in power, and the ordinary Tunisians did not like them. Their dislike had turned to something very like hatred when an unsavoury young man named Muley Hassan, a member of the royal family, had seized the throne and promptly murdered forty-four of his forty-five brothers in order to make sure that he would meet no family opposition to his rule in the future; it had been annoying that one brother should have escaped this domestic holocaust, but even so Muley Hassan had felt reasonably safe with all but one of the family dead, and he had relapsed happily into a life of debauchery in his harem of 400 ravishing young boys. Thereafter, when his subjects had rioted, he had repressed them with great brutality, and as a result there had been several attempts on his life, which had only encouraged him to indulge in even more brutal measures of repression. So when Barbarossa appeared with his Janissaries, the people welcomed him as a deliverer and Hassan fled. Barbarossa entered the city in triumph, and annexed it to the Ottoman Empire.

Tunis commands the narrow sea between Africa and Sicily, and its loss to the Turks was not only an obvious threat to that island but also posed an immediate threat to shipping passing along the Mediterranean. The safety of Christian ships had already been in jeopardy when the older Barbarossa brother, Uruj, had captured Algiers, but it was a thousand times worse now that Khaireddin had taken Tunis, and Charles decided to take action. He was still at peace with France, and the Lutherans in Germany were not causing him as much trouble as they often had in the past, so the time seemed right for a move to oust Barbarossa from his new conquest. Moreover, Pope Clement VII had died on 25 September 1534, and three weeks later Alessandro Farnese had been almost unanimously elected to succeed him as Paul III; he was hardly seated on St Peter's throne before he began to urge Charles to mount a new Crusade against the infidel Turks, whose naval activities on his own back doorstep in the Adriatic had highly alarmed him, as well they might have done. So Charles could count on papal support for any move he might make against Barbarossa. No help could be expected from England, however, for one of the last things Clement had done before his death had been to order Henry VIII to take Catherine back as his lawful wife, and Henry was furious; but Portugal, the Empire and the Netherlands all promised to join in the great adventure against the enemies of Christ, and Charles's own subjects in the Cortes were sufficiently well disposed to the project to be willing to defray the cost of it.

But Charles was a cautious man and at heart a peaceful one, and before embarking on a new war against the Moslems he tried to get his way by intrigue. He sent a Genoese named Luis de Presenda, who spoke Arabic like a native, to Tunis in disguise with orders to get in touch with Muley Hassan in the hope that he might be able to stir up a revolt against Barbarossa. If this plan failed, he had orders to make contact with Barbarossa himself and to find out whether he could be persuaded to change sides, in which case Charles would make him ruler of the whole of northern Africa. If this plan also failed, then it should not be too difficult to arrange for Barbarossa to be murdered one evening when, as was his regular habit, he devoted himself to the important business of getting hopelessly and enjoyably drunk. Whether any of these plans might have succeeded will never be known, however, for the unfortunate Genoese was arrested and put to death before he had had the time to put them to the test.

The failure of Presenda's mission left Charles with no alternative but to attempt to recover Tunis by force of arms, and in the early months of 1535 his preparations were nearing completion. By the spring he was ready, and 30,000 troops were assembled in Sardinia waiting to embark at Cagliari, where a fleet of 400 ships had been gathered. At the beginning of June, Charles arrived accompanied by Andrea Doria, and on the 14th the great armada set sail. The voyage took three days, and on the 17th the imperial army began to disembark near the site of the ancient city of Carthage. The landing was unopposed, for Barbarossa did not dare to challenge so large a fleet at sea or even attempt to prevent the troops coming ashore; instead, he ordered fifteen of his best ships to sail secretly to Bône, where they would be safe from the enemy, and the rest of his fleet was stripped of its guns, which were needed for the defence of Tunis itself, and moored in the inner basin of a shallow salt-water lake, which provided the only approach to the place by sea. It was defended by a formidable fortress known as La Goletta (or The Throat), so named because it stood on a narrow neck of land between the outer part of the lake and the inner basin which formed the city's harbour, and Charles decided to make it his first target; for it was obvious that whoever held La Goletta did indeed hold Tunis by the throat.

Barbarossa was well aware of the importance of this fortress, and he had put a number of Moorish soldiers and 5,000 of his best Turkish troops into it under the command of a celebrated corsair known as Sinan the Jew with orders to defend it to the last man. As a result they fought with courage and grim determination and the siege, which lasted for twenty-four days, was extremely costly to both sides. But despite their losses Charles's men fought as bravely and with as much determination as their enemies, and on 14 July their efforts were crowned with success. A tremendous cannonade by land batteries was opened on the already badly battered fortress, while one of the most powerful ships afloat, a great carrack with eight decks, the *Saint Ann*, belonging to the Knights of St John, was brought up to bombard it from the lake, and under the weight of this attack from two sides, La Goletta at last fell to the Knights, who led an assault upon one of the breaches in its walls. Some of the defenders under their leader, Sinan, managed to escape and fight their way back towards the city, and Barbarossa came out to meet them in some trenches which had been prepared for just such an emergency. The position had been chosen in order to prevent the invaders from reaching the next watering point along the road to Tunis, and in the end this proved to be decisive, though not at all in the way anticipated by the men who had dug the trenches; for the weather was appallingly hot and Charles's men were beginning to suffer badly from thirst. With lips cracking in the heat and tongues beginning to swell, they were not going to allow anyone to stop them reaching the wells which lay ahead, and they rushed in to attack those blocking their path with a ferocity born of physical desperation.

Charles, despite the fact that he was suffering from gout, was conspicuous during the sharp little engagement which followed, fighting in the forefront of the battle, as indeed he had throughout the siege of La Goletta, even though this was his first personal experience of war. As a result, he had completely captured the affection of his troops, who would have followed him anywhere; for it was not often that emperors shared the same hardships as their men, and they loved him for it. It did not take them long to overrun the trenches which stood in their path, and Barbarossa was forced to withdraw as fast as he could to the safety of the walls of Tunis. Charles and his imperial troops reached the city on the evening of 20 July.

Recorded history is an abstract of events: a written or spoken record of a tiny section of past happenings which all too often are reduced to bare facts. At the time, however, no fact or event is bare, and history consists of a myriad of interlocking events in which a multitude of men and women are involved with their emotions of hope and fear, anger and desire, tiredness and hunger and longing for peace. It is difficult to re-create in the imagination an idea of how the men of the imperial army felt the next morning as the African sun came up over the eastern horizon into a brazen sky, bathing the walls of Tunis with the first light of the day. As they braced themselves for one more effort, they must have known that an attack on a city as well fortified as Tunis would cost many of them their lives. But on this particular morning the inevitable tension and fear ended unexpectedly in a great wave of relief, as the news spread throughout the waiting army that within the city several thousand Christian prisoners had broken their chains and risen in revolt against their Moslem guards. Encouraged by tidings of Charles's victories outside the city and led by a Knight of St John, they had stormed the arsenal, armed themselves and launched a violent attack upon Barbarossa's men. Attacked from within and without, the city could not be defended, and Charles and his men entered it in triumph without meeting any serious opposition, to be welcomed ecstatically by their fellow Christians whose revolt had made that triumph possible.

During the next three days, the victors went on the usual rampage of violence. The town was sacked by gangs of drunken Spaniards and Germans, who murdered and raped, burned and looted, until they were too tired to continue; to describe the events of these three days in detail would be repetitive, for much the same sort of thing happened whenever a city fell, and at the time everyone accepted the fact that a conquered city must expect to be treated thus; both sides regarded the excesses committed by the conquerors as quite normal. There is some evidence that Charles was revolted by the behaviour of his men, but even he did not try to prevent them from running amok; they had suffered much, they had fought hard, and no one could have denied them what they regarded as their just reward now that they had captured the place. They believed that they had won an important victory, and they were right; for the Spaniards were destined to hold Tunis for the next forty years, during which time it was invaluable to them. They lost it eventually through the negligence of Don John of Austria, Charles's illegitimate son by Barbara Blomberg, and a certain Cardinal Granvelle, who was Viceroy of Naples at the time. At the time, Don John was so absorbed by the game of tennis and the Cardinal so preoccupied by amorous dalliance with his various mistresses that the defence of Tunis went by default; or so it was said. As a result, some wit in Madrid coined a ribald little jingle, which made people laugh:

> Don Juan con la raqueta,
> Y Granvela con la braguete,
> Perdieron La Goletta.

The American historian, Royall Tyler, from whose biography of Charles V the story comes, has translated it as: 'Don John with his racket, and Granvelle with his flies undone, lost La Goletta.'

But though the capture of Tunis was an important victory, it would have been much more important if Barbarossa had not escaped. While the imperial soldiers were busy getting drunk and roaming the streets like wild animals, he took advantage of the general chaos to slip out of the city and make good his escape to Bône, where he knew that his fifteen best galleys were safely waiting for him. The rest of his fleet had been captured by Charles in the inner basin of the lake of Tunis, and its loss was serious, but as long as he himself escaped it could be made good in time. From Bône he sailed for Algiers, and although by this time Andrea Doria was aware of his flight and trying to intercept him, he failed, and the old corsair arrived in Algiers in a furious mood thirsting for revenge. There he found another seventeen ships fit for service, and with them he promptly sailed north towards the Balearics, determined to get his own back for his defeat at Tunis before Charles returned to Spain. He dressed his own men in Spanish naval costume, flew the Spanish flag at his masthead, and sailed into the harbour at Port Mahon in Minorca to the salutes and cheers of the inhabitants, who mistook him and his fleet for their own victorious sailors returning from Africa. They were soon disillusioned. By the end of the day Barbarossa had captured two Portuguese caravels, which happened to be in harbour at the time, and taken 5,700 prisoners from the town itself, where about another 800 were left lying dead in the streets as he sailed away. On his way home he sacked various towns along the coast of Valencia, where he sold his prisoners for a ransom of 6,000 ducats, and, thus both enriched and revenged for Charles's victory at Tunis, he sailed for home. He had not been there long, however, before he was summoned by Suleiman to come to Constantinople, and in the spring of 1536 he was charged with the task of building a fleet of 200 ships for an expedition against southern Italy. Plainly, the Sultan was not going to allow the loss of Tunis to deprive him of the initiative in the naval war in the Mediterranean.

Meanwhile, the great European powers were playing their usual tortuous, tangled and deceitful diplomatic games. The Most Christian King of France was leading the way by negotiating at the same time with Charles, the Venetians and the Turks, with whom he eventually made a secret alliance. He had never had any intention of honouring the terms of the Peace of Cambrai, which he had signed with the Emperor seven years previously in 1529, and he was determined to get Milan back, either by agreement or by war. Charles was prepared to listen and indeed to make concessions, but they were not enough for Francis, who invaded the Duke of Savoy's province of Bresse in February 1536, and then crossed the Alps and took Turin.

Although the threat to Milan was obvious, Charles still hoped to solve his disagreements with the French by diplomacy. He travelled to Rome to enlist the help of Pope Paul III, Alessandro Farnese, but there on Easter Monday, 17 April 1536, his patience at last ran out. In the presence of the whole papal court and the two French ambassadors he addressed the Pope in a carefully prepared speech delivered in Spanish, in which he recalled his many and repeated attempts to come to an agreement with the French King, despite the latter's equally frequent and repeated breaches of faith. Again and again, he said, he had tried to make an alliance with France against the common enemy, the infidel Turk, and again and again his efforts had been frustrated. He had had enough. He gave Francis a triple choice: the Duke of Milan had just died, and Charles proposed that the French King's third son should marry the widowed Duchess, Christina, who was his own niece, thus uniting their houses and solving the Milanese problem; if Francis rejected that course of action and wished to go to war over Milan, he could do so, but let him be well aware that such a decision might well entail the destruction of Christendom and the triumph of the Turk, who would become master of western Europe as he had already become master of its eastern lands; and if the French King rejected both these proposals, there was a third way of settling his differences with the Emperor: Charles was willing to meet him in single combat on condition that afterwards the combined forces of the Empire and France should march together against the Turks under the command of the victor.

The Pope was – or pretended to be – appalled, protesting against such a challenge being issued in his presence, and although it seems unlikely that this display of moral indignation was sincere, his protest stimulated Charles to explain that what he was trying to do was to spare the lives of a multitude of soldiers, both Spanish and French, by resorting to the old ritual of ordeal by battle between Francis and himself instead. Everyone present was deeply impressed by the Emperor's obvious sincerity, but no one was naïve enough to imagine for a moment that Francis would agree to such a bizarre proposal. War was therefore inevitable, and it very soon followed. Determined to take the initiative, Charles ordered the Duke of Alva to invade southern France at the head of 50,000 men, but the subsequent campaign there turned out to be a disaster. As the imperial troops advanced through Nice into Provence the French retreated before them, laying waste the country as they went, and the invaders soon began to run so short of food that they were reduced to near starvation; dysentery broke out in their ranks, and when Marseilles proved to be impregnable they had no alternative but to beat an ignominious retreat.

While the two major Christian powers were thus engaged, preparations for naval warfare were being pressed ahead in Constantinople, and the fact that Italy was to be the target of the great armada was an open secret. But then a very odd thing happened. Barbarossa made secret overtures to the Emperor, suggesting that he might change sides if Tunis were restored to him as ruler. Whether he ever really intended to desert Suleiman will never be known. Those who believe that his suggestion was sincere explain it by saying that he was jealous of the new Vizier, Loutfi Pasha, and angry at the execution of Ibrahim, who had been his friend and loyal supporter; but others have believed that the whole thing was a ruse to lull the Emperor into a sense of false security. Charles himself was suspicious and took so long to reply that nothing came of the affair, and by May of the next year, 1537, Suleiman was ready to march west again at the head of the Turkish army, while Barbarossa sailed for the Adriatic. If the old pirate had ever intended to play the turncoat, the moment for action had passed.

In late July the Turkish fleet hove to off Otranto near the fortress of Castro, and Barbarossa waded ashore at the head of 8,000 cavalrymen and an even larger body of infantry, who were followed by a formidable train of siege guns as soon as the beachhead was secure. The people of Otranto were understandably terrified. The city had already had experience of what it was like to be overrun by a Turkish army, for almost sixty years earlier, on 11 August 1480, Mehmed the Conqueror had ordered his army to attack the place, which he had intended to use as a bridgehead for a full-scale invasion of Italy. The Turks had taken it by surprise, and massacred most of the inhabitants, and the people of Otranto had never forgotten the horror of their visitation.

This time, the Turkish cavalrymen were led by a traitor named Pignatelli, who persuaded the small garrison of the castle at Castro to surrender without a fight, promising them safe conduct through the Turkish lines, and speaking to them in their own language of the good will of the Turks, who had no intention of harming them. Unable to believe that a fellow Italian could be base enough to lie to them, the wretched men marched out and were promptly and unhesitatingly butchered; and the same fate was meted out to the garrisons of a number of other castles in the area. Otranto, too, was captured and sacked, and the coast for miles on either side of the city was 'laid waste like a pestilence', as one observer at the time described it. In the event, however, to the enormous relief of the people of Italy, Barbarossa withdrew after a month, re-embarking his men and taking 10,000 Italians with him for sale in the slave markets of Constantinople.

He withdrew because, in the meanwhile, Suleiman had declared war on Venice. For centuries, the Venetians had bent over backwards to ingratiate themselves with the Turks for the sake of the extremely lucrative trade which they and they alone were privileged to ply with the Sultan's dominions in Turkey itself and in the various subject countries of the Middle East; but recently they had been irritated by the concessions made by Suleiman to the French, and they had been foolish enough to show their annoyance. Later, they had been even more foolish, and had attacked some Turkish vessels as they sailed peacefully on their lawful occasions past the island of Corfu, which was a Venetian possession at the time, murdering their crews and stealing the ships' cargoes. From one of these vessels, however, a young man had escaped by throwing himself overboard and clinging to a plank until rescued by some compatriots, who had taken him to Loutfi Pasha with his tale of woe. Suleiman's patience with the Venetians was nearly exhausted in any case, and when he heard of this recent outrage he recalled Barbarossa from Otranto, and ordered him to join in an attack on the island from which these intolerable acts of piracy had been launched.

But despite a combined attack by Barbarossa and Suleiman, who took command from his headquarters on the Albanian coast, neither the island nor the city of Corfu itself succumbed. The capital was strongly defended, and for once the Turkish artillery seems not to have been as effective as that of their enemies; although they mounted a huge cannon on a rock near the city, it was capable of firing only about six of its great fifty-pound missiles a day, and it was so inaccurate that most of them flew over the city to fall into the sea, while their lighter artillery made little impression on the city walls.

The Venetians, on the other hand, plied their guns to such good effect that two Turkish galleys were sunk, and casualties among the besiegers were heavy. Indeed, if contemporary Turkish historians are to be believed, it was when no fewer than four Turkish soldiers were killed by a single cannonball from a Venetian gun that Suleiman decided to lift the siege. 'The capture of a thousand fortresses,' he is reputed to have said, 'would not make up for the death of one warrior of Islam' – a remark which, if it was ever made, might have inspired greater confidence in the speaker's sincerity had it been uttered before ordering the siege rather than at the moment of defeat. However, such noble sentiments sound good when put into the mouths of men of war after the event, and this is probably what happened in this case; for although Suleiman had many virtues, he was not a good loser, and on this occasion he was furiously angry at being repulsed. The Venetians, he decided, must be made to pay for daring to oppose him.

As a result, Barbarossa was ordered to attack the remaining Venetian possessions in the Aegean, where quite a large number of Greek islands still flew the flag of St Mark over their cities and fortresses. Syros, Paros, Tinos and Naxos in the Cyclades, Patmos in the Dodecanese, Skyros and Skiathos further north, Aegina in the Saronic Gulf, and some smaller islets had all been Venetian possessions since the sacking of Constantinople by the men of the Fourth Crusade in 1204, when the victors had sat down in the stricken city to carve up the Byzantine Empire between themselves. Now they were visitied, one by one, by the Turkish fleet; some gave up without a struggle, either for lack of means to defend themselves against such a formidable enemy, or from the sheer terror which the name of Khaireddin Barbarossa inspired; but their surrender did them little good, for they were mercilessly sacked and their inhabitants taken away to be sold into slavery. Other islands proved more resolute, resisting the Turks as best they could, but in the end most of these too were forced to submit; the odds against them were too great, and despite their courage their inhabitants were dragged off to be sold side by side with their less heroic compatriots in the markets of Turkey. It is said that when Barbarossa eventually sailed home, he carried with him a huge loot of cloth, money, a thousand girls and fifteen hundred boys valued at just under a million pieces of gold. Suleiman was delighted.

Early in the following year, there was a curious sequel to Barbarossa's punitive expedition against the Venetians in the Aegean. In February 1538 the Venetians, still smarting from their treatment there, joined the Emperor and the Pope in a 'Holy League' against the Turks. A combined fleet was gathered with the idea of sailing eastwards in search of revenge upon the Turks, whose turn it was to be taught a lesson in manners, and during the summer of the same year it assembled at Corfu. It consisted of fifty-five Venetian galleys, twenty-seven supplied by the Pope, forty-nine vessels commanded by Andrea Doria, and finally some Spanish warships which were rather reluctantly sent by Charles to join the others. The Emperor's reluctance was understandable, for he had little interest in who controlled the eastern Mediterranean, and he did not want to risk the lives of his men or the safety of his ships on an expedition from which he could expect little profit or advantage. As a result, before the fleet could sail, Charles decided to try once more to seduce Barbarossa into changing sides. Secret arrangements were made, and on 20 September under cover of darkness Andrea Doria and the Emperor's Viceroy of Sicily, Ferrante Gonzaga, met a man representing Barbarossa at a prearranged spot on the Albanian coast, and tried to persuade him to defect. For a time, it looked as though the negotiations were going to succeed, but they failed to do so in the end for two reasons: Charles would not promise to hand over Tunis to Barbarossa, for he had already promised the city to Muley Hassan, and Barbarossa would not agree to burning those Turkish vessels which he was unable to bring with him, when he changed sides. Since agreement eluded them, Andrea Doria and Gonzaga sailed back to Corfu.

What followed makes sorry reading. The Turkish fleet was lying in the Gulf of Ambrakia, almost a small inland sea with a narrow entrance guarded by a fortress at Preveza on its northern point. Here in 31 BC the battle of Actium had been fought for control of the Roman world between the forces of Antony and Cleopatra on the one hand and Octavian on the other, and here the combined Christian fleet decided to attack their enemies; but, as so often happens when an allied force goes into battle, there was little unity of command and the attack had not been well planned in advance. The Venetians were at odds with Andrea Doria and when Barbarossa, whose ships were fewer than those of his enemies, refused to oblige them by sailing out to meet them, the respective Christian commanders could not agree on the next move. At first it was decided to put a large force ashore to capture the fortress of Preveza, and then to sink a ship in the narrows and thus to block the entrance to the Gulf; but when the time for action came Andrea Doria refused to take part in it, and the whole thing had to be abandoned.

Since it would have been lunacy for the Christian fleet to sail into the Gulf to engage the Turks, and since Barbarossa was apparently determined to stay where he was, stalemate seemed to have been reached, and the allied fleet prepared to go home without having achieved anything; but then to everyone's surprise, just when Doria had already begun to sail away, Barbarossa came out of the Gulf and attacked the Venetians. Doria, who was furious, was only reluctantly persuaded to turn back and come to the aid of his allies, and having done so, he did very little to help them. The allied ships were thrown into confusion; the fleet was separated into two parts, neither of which knew what was happening to the other and, although few ships were lost, when a storm blew up and forced both sides to break off and run for shelter, there was little doubt in anyone's mind that the Turks had been the victors. Certainly, Suleiman celebrated the battle as a victory, and subsequent events were to justify him. For it is hardly an exaggeration to say that from the day of the battle of Preveza, 27 September 1538, until the day thirty-three years later when another combined Christian fleet met the Turks at Lepanto, the Mediterranean became an Ottoman preserve: a fact of which the inhabitants of the coastal cities in the Christian West were soon to be made painfully aware.

XII

✠ ✠ ✠

Sweet Enemy

That sweet enemy, France.

Sir Philip Sidney, *Sonnet XLI*

The Emperor's abortive campaign against the French in Provence had left both him and the King of France hopelessly bankrupt. Charles had sunk deeper into debt than ever, and he had lost a splendid army and much of the prestige he had won at Tunis, while Provence had been turned into a desert for years to come, and the rest of France had been squeezed dry to pay for the war there. Neither country was in any condition to mount another campaign against the other, and peace of a sort was essential to both; but where personal and national *amour propre* is concerned even political necessity has to wait upon hurt pride, and it was over a year before Francis would even agree to talk about peace with the Emperor. All that could be accomplished was a ten years' truce, which was negotiated and signed at Nice on 18 June 1538 by representatives of the two sides, while Francis and Charles did their best to avoid each other; in fact, however, they met at Aigues-Mortes in the Camargue, as Charles made his way homewards, and there Francis, with a Gasconade flourish and ill-disguised insincerity, protested undying friendship for the man whom he had hated all his life. A little later, in May 1539, Charles's fragile little Portuguese Empress Isabel, whom he had married principally for her money but with whom he had then fallen deeply and lastingly in love, died. Charles was desolate, and things were made no better for him by the citizens of Ghent who chose this moment to rise in revolt against him. For once, Francis seems to have been genuinely sorry for

Charles in his bereavement and he invited him to travel through France on his way to the Low Countries to cope with the rebels; Charles agreed to do so. He took his time, spending two months on the journey and staying at Fontainebleau as the guest of the French King for Christmas, where he was superbly entertained. Francis suggested that, now that he was a widower, the Emperor might marry his youngest daughter, Margaret of France, who was sixteen at the time; but Charles politely refused. He never married again.

Although his visit to France succeeded in making relations between him and Francis a little easier than they had been, it did not lead to the signing of a peace treaty, though the ten-year truce between France and the Empire still held good, and Charles, having chastised the rebels of Ghent, could devote his whole attention to the continuing naval war with the Turks. Venice had been knocked out of the war, and had signed a humiliating and punitive peace treaty with Suleiman, but despite her loss as an ally and the defeat of his own naval forces at Preveza, his enemies did not have everything their own way. In June 1540 one of Barbarossa's principal and most formidable lieutenants, a corsair named Dragut, who was almost as celebrated and quite as much feared as Barbarossa himself, was captured after a long chase by a superior force of Christian ships, which eventually ran him to ground on a remote part of the coast of Corsica. Like any other prisoner of war, he was shipped to Genoa and there chained to a rower's bench as a galley slave, until he was ransomed four years later.

In revenge for the loss of his lieutenant, Barbarossa attacked Gibraltar on 9 September 1540, and although he failed to capture the fortress he sacked and burned the town and took a number of prisoners. Three weeks later there was a naval battle near the small island of Alboran 150 miles east of Gibraltar, and this time the Christians were the victors, sinking one Turkish ship and capturing ten others; but the fact that Barbarossa was able to sail more or less when and where he liked throughout the whole western Mediterranean was a proof that the initiative in the war at sea had passed into his hands, even if he suffered a few reverses from time to time. Charles determined to get that initiative back.

If he was to succeed, however, it was important that he should act while the somewhat brittle truce with France remained unbroken, and on 3 July 1541 an event occurred which almost certainly presaged another outbreak of war despite the 'undying friendship' so recently expressed by Francis for the Emperor. The French ambassador to the Sultan's court in Constantinople, a man of great intelligence and diplomatic skill named Antonio Rinçon, was murdered near Pavia on his way to Constantinople. Whether the deed was done by imperial agents from Milan or not is a question which has been debated again and again without ever being answered for sure. Rinçon was a Spaniard by birth, who had entered the service of the French King, with whom his country was at war, and thus he was a traitor in the Emperor's eyes. This does not mean that Charles ordered his death, or even that he was informed of the plot to murder him, but it seems highly probable that the crime was the work of the Marquis of Vasto, who was Charles's governor of Milan at the time. Needless to say, after the event the Marquis hotly denied any complicity in it, and it is always possible that he was speaking the truth; but it is unlikely. Political assassinations were regarded as legitimate ways of furthering national policy in Renaissance Italy, and if Vasto was behind Rinçon's murder, it is unlikely that he would have felt particularly guilty for arranging it. As Royall Tyler has remarked, he would have defended himself on the grounds that 'it was a villainous thing for the King of France, then at peace with the Emperor, to egg on the Turk to attack Christendom, and to use to this end a Spaniard who had turned traitor to his own King'. Since that had been the precise purpose of Rinçon's journey to Constantinople there is much force in the argument that his murder was a minor villainy by comparison; but this was a contention unlikely to appeal to Francis, and when he heard of his ambassador's death it gave him the excuse which he had been seeking to break off relations with Charles once again.

Charles was pressing ahead with preparations for his attack on Algiers, and in the autumn of 1521 Spanish, German and Italian troops began to concentrate in Majorca and the other Balearic islands. The season was late, and Charles's military advisers were almost unanimously against risking a campaign so late in the year, but he wanted to score a success against Barbarossa before Francis was ready to come to the aid of his Turkish allies, and he overruled them. Half-way through October, sixty-five galleys and 400 troop ships manned by 12,000 sailors were ready to carry 24,000 soldiers to Africa; with them sailed 'stout' Cortez of Mexican fame, who had returned from the New World a year previously, and by 23 October this formidable force was successfully disembarked to the east of the town of Algiers; by the following morning they had mounted their artillery on the hills commanding the town, where the guns would be able to fire down into it. The citizens were terrified but the governor of the place, a certain Hassan Aga, treated Charles's demand that he should surrender with contempt. At the time, it seemed a forlorn if courageous gesture of defiance, noble but futile, for Charles and his army were in a position of such apparently unassailable superiority that nothing could possibly prevent their triumph; and so, it seems, Charles himself believed. But the weather can make nonsense of the most cast-iron military certainties, and so it did on this occasion, for at midnight a gale blew up and rain began to fall in torrents. The soldiers were unable to keep their powder dry, their muskets could not be fired, their artillery became useless, and the night was so wild and dark that no one knew where he was or who was next to him in the darkness.

The Turks in the town realized what was happening and made a sortie in force, using their swords and bows with deadly effect and spreading confusion in the imperial ranks. It was a night of chaos, and when the day broke and the invaders saw over a hundred of their ships lying helpless on the shore, wrecked by the storm, their discouragement was complete; soaked to the skin, cold and demoralized, there was no fight left in them. Andrea Doria had managed to save some of the expedition's ships in a nearby bay, and Charles had no alternative but to admit defeat and re-embark those of his men who had survived the night. When they reached home, and it was possible to count the cost, it was found that 12,000 men were missing.

It was the first major defeat suffered by the Emperor, and although he could in no way be blamed for the sudden change in the weather, which had been its sole cause, inevitably his prestige was badly damaged, while the reputation of the Turks for invincibility was strengthened once again. Francis I, of course, was delighted by the discomfiture of Charles, and no longer even tried to pretend that he was not in full and open alliance with Suleiman, whose ambassador, a remarkable man named Younis Bey, cut an exotic and colourful figure for a time at the French court. Younis had been born in Corfu, presumably of Christian Greek parents, and if the contemporary French historian, Brantôme, is to believed, he spoke both demotic and classical Greek fluently as well as Turkish, Arabic, Moorish, Persian, Armenian, Hebrew, Hungarian, Russian, Slavonic, Italian, Spanish, German, French and Latin: a remarkable achievement even for a Renaissance man. But the presence of a Turkish ambassador at court was by no means the limit of French involvement in what was called at the time 'this impious alliance with the infidel'. On the contrary, when the Turkish fleet sailed west once more in the spring of 1543 a Frenchman named Paulin was on board Barbarossa's flagship as it sailed out of the Golden Horn and began the long voyage towards the coasts of Italy and Spain with orders to attack the cities there. Reggio di Calabria was the first to suffer, where Barbarossa captured the eighteen-year-old daughter of the Spanish commander and forced her to renounce her Christian faith and embrace Islam as a preliminary to dispossessing her of her virginity. Messina was the next to fall, and as the news spread all Italy trembled. A few days later, when it became known that the Turks had forced the citizens of Nettuno and Ostia to supply them with food and water as their fleet lay in the mouth of the

Tiber, Rome panicked; the streets had to be patrolled by armed men at night to prevent a mass exodus from the city; everyone tried to escape into the country and the wildest rumours spread unchecked. But in fact the Turks were not equipped for an invasion or even for a great inland raid upon Rome, and the fleet sailed away northwards to Marseilles, where Barbarossa was received with the greatest possible respect and honour, and where Paulin was told of the King's command that the French fleet should now join that of the Turks in a siege of Nice, which was not part of France at the time but belonged to the Duke of Savoy, who was both the vassal and the ally of the Emperor.

Accounts of the events which followed vary, though some things are certain. The Turks and the French began to quarrel almost from the moment of the former's arrival in France, where the vast majority of ordinary people made no attempt to hide their horror at this sudden invasion of infidels. The Turks, for their part, were horrified by the inefficiency of the French port authorities, where the naval stores and provisions they had been promised were not forthcoming, and where everyone seemed to be totally incompetent. When the siege of Nice began, things became even worse; Barbarossa was so aggravated by the slovenly ineptitude of the French sailors that he is said to have cried, 'What soldiers are these that fill their vessels with wine casks and forget to bring their powder?' Nice would not have fallen if it had not been for the Turkish artillery, which opened a breach in the dilapidated city walls with almost no difficulty at all, whereupon the governor of the place agreed to surrender the city in order to avoid the horrors of a sack.

In the event, however, despite the convention of war which decreed that a city which surrendered should be spared, Nice was both unmercifully sacked and then burned. Although later French propaganda laid the blame for this outrage upon the shoulders of the Turks, all the evidence goes to show that it was the French themselves who ran amok in the captured city and then burned it to the ground; after the surrender, the Turkish fleet, its part in the battle completed, withdrew to its anchorage at Villefranche, leaving the French to garrison the town, and it was only then that the killing and the looting began. Sir Godfrey Fisher, in his book *Barbary Legend*, quotes the Frenchman, Marshal Vieilleville, as saying that 'the town of Nice was sacked in defiance of the terms of capitulation, and it was then burned; but for this one must not blame Barbarossa and his troops, for they were already far off when this happened . . . This slander was put upon the unfortunate Barbarossa in order to uphold the honour and the reputation of France, indeed of Christendom itself.'

After the battle for Nice, the honour of France was not enhanced in anyone's eyes and certainly not in those of many Frenchmen themselves, when the inhabitants of Toulon were forcibly evicted from their homes in order to make room for Barbarossa's men, who virtually took over the town. Those French men and women who were left were forced to endure the sight of turbanned infidels swaggering about the streets of the city, while the voices of the muezzins calling them to prayer mingled with the sound of Catholic church bells ringing for mass. A large house was converted into a mosque, and the harbour was filled with Turkish galleys manned by Christian slaves. The crowning insult came when an epidemic broke out in 1544 among these wretched creatures and they began to die like flies, whereupon the Turks sent raiding parties out to the villages in the country round Toulon with orders to find replacements for the dead and to bring them back in chains to make good the shortage of galley slaves. This was too much. The outcry was so violent that Francis was forced to bribe Barbarossa to leave.

If the French King had counted on stealing a march on Charles by enlisting the powerful assistance of the Turks in his fight against him, he had badly miscalculated; for when the news spread throughout Europe that he was playing host to an army of infidels and encouraging them to ravage the coasts of Christendom, people everywhere were outraged. Henry VIII, with whom Charles had been at odds for years, was so disgusted by the behaviour of his French ally that he forgot his differences with the Emperor, and in February 1543 signed a secret treaty with him, the purpose of which was to force Francis to give up his unnatural alliance with the Turks; he even promised to invade France at the proper time and march on Paris. The German princes, too, who in normal times were bitterly jealous of the Emperor and his brother Ferdinand, were as disgusted as the English King by the sight of Frenchmen and Turks sacking Christian cities together; they would not hear of making common cause with Francis against Charles, whom they welcomed with unaccustomed warmth when he arrived at Aix-la-Chapelle in January 1544. They even voted unanimously in the Diet at Speyer to give him as much help as they possibly could against France and the Turks. But perhaps the most remarkable evidence of how counter-productive from Francis's point of view his treaty with the Turks had proved to be was provided by Luther and Calvin, both of whom came out strongly in support of Charles, for all the world as if the Protestants of Germany and Switzerland had never been the Catholic Emperor's most bitter enemies.

With the ranks of western Christendom closed behind him more effectively than they had been for years, Charles determined to force Francis to drop his Turkish alliance. He assembled a large army at

Metz, and at the end of June 1544 he invaded northern France at the same time as Henry VIII landed near Boulogne in obedience to his treaty obligation. The progress of the imperial army was rapid, and if the English had kept their promise to march on Paris the war would probably have been brought to a successful conclusion even more quickly than in fact was the case; but Henry's men contented themselves with besieging Boulogne instead of marching on the capital, despite the fact that the panic-stricken Parisians were desperately trying to patch up the defences of the city, which had been allowed to fall into hopeless disrepair as years of peace and security had seemed to render them redundant. Even so, however, the potential threat posed by the English army in the Boulonnais immobilized a large enough part of the French army to make Charles's advance down the Marne irresistible, and as city after city fell to him Francis decided to make peace as quickly as he could. Thus on 19 September, less than three months after Charles had crossed the French frontier near Pont-à-Moussons, the French King signed a peace treaty at Crépy-en-Laonnais, and the war was over. Charles was free at last to turn his attention to Suleiman once again.

XIII

✠ ✠ ✠

An Evil Net

Man . . . knoweth not his time: as the fishes that are taken in an
evil net, and as the birds that are caught in the snare, even so are
the sons of men snared in an evil time, when it falleth suddenly
upon them.

Ecclesiastes 9:12

Even though the fighting had shifted to the Mediterranean, the
situation of the people of Hungary and the Danube valley was an
unenviable one. Their country was divided into three parts, Ferdinand
and the Austrians claiming some of it, Zapolya holding sway in the
north-east, and Suleiman himself retaining the richest district in the
south and centre by right of conquest. Meanwhile, the Sultan did
everything in his power to keep the quarrel between Ferdinand and
Zapolya alive, for a divided country was better from his point of view
than a people united under either claimant to their loyalty. As for the
people themselves, no one much cared what happened to them; they
were the puppets of the worst kind of power politics, helpless
spectators and victims of the homicidal game of diplomatic
blind-man's-buff in which the three occupying powers were
perpetually jostling for advantage over one another. Few of the minor
players in it lived for long, for most of them were murdered by their
opponents before they had learned the rules of the lethal game in
which they were involved. Even Ludovico Gritti, supple and subtle as
he was, did not last long. He was sent to Hungary by Suleiman to
support Zapolya against Ferdinand, but he so offended the Hungarians that they surrounded him in a castle, caught him as he tried to
escape, and promptly cut his head off. It is said that they found a small
bag of jewels strapped round his waist, later valued at 400,000 ducats.
    After Gritti's death, the political situation became even more

complicated when Ferdinand and Zapolya agreed secretly to share the kingship, each retaining his own part of the unhappy country and each calling himself King until the death of Zapolya, when the whole of Hungary would pass to Ferdinand. Since Zapolya was childless at the time, this suited Ferdinand, and since Ferdinand also agreed to join forces with Zapolya in an attempt to recapture Belgrade from the Turks, it suited Zapolya; but when wind of it reached Constantinople it did not suit Suleiman, who flew into a rage. Zapolya took fright, and in order to ingratiate himself once again with the irate Sultan he decided to marry the King of Poland's daughter, Isabella, knowing full well that her father was Suleiman's most trusted ally, and hoping thus to avert retribution for his flirtation with Ferdinand. The new political alliance was almost certainly made on the advice of a man at whom it is worth looking for a moment, for he was a typical product of the tortuous times in which he lived.

The son of a Croatian father named Utiešenović and an aristocratic Venetian mother, he was given the baptismal name of George and for some reason took his mother's family name of Martinuzzi. As a young man he entered the service of the Zapolya family, with whom for a time he fought in the confused wars of the day, but at the age of twenty-five he decided to become a monk and entered the Paulician Order. John Zapolya did not forget him, however, and after he had been in the monastery for some years, Brother George (he was known universally in his own day as Frater György) was persuaded once more to work for his old master, who was by now King of half Hungary. Five years later at the age of fifty-two, he was made Bishop of Grosswardein (the modern Nagy-Varad), by which time he had also become the King's principal and closest adviser. A little later still, he was consecrated Archbishop of Esztergom and received a cardinal's red hat from the Pope.

He was a master of political intrigue, and the skill with which he managed to tread the dark and dangerous corridors of Balkan power politics for longer than any of his contemporaries, playing the Austrians off against the Turks, and one lot of domestic enemies, of whom he had many, against all other lots, was truly astonishing. But to see him simply as an archetypal machiavellian Renaissance prelate would be to do him an injustice, for it would be to ignore his genuine devotion to his own divided and bleeding country, for which he was prepared to do anything and everything, openly or if necessary covertly and unscrupulously, rather than leave it at the mercy of either the Austrians or the Turks, both of whom he loathed. When viewed superficially from the vantage point of the twentieth century, he may look totally unprincipled but, beneath his willingness to betray one side after the other with apparently amoral impartiality, there lay a determination to serve the ordinary suffering people of Hungary, and this redeems much else; and there is no doubt that he succeeded in steering the country through one of its blackest periods with consummate skill, thus proving himself to be not only a patriot but a statesman of considerable brilliance.

However, after John Zapolya's marriage to Isabella of Poland, which Martinuzzi had arranged, two events took place which changed the political face of the country: Isabella gave birth to a son, and almost immediately her husband died. His death was both sudden and unexpected, but he survived long enough to hear that he had an heir, and his last words were to beg his friends to make sure that the infant should be elected and crowned King in his place. Although this was a plain breach of the secret treaty with Ferdinand, some Hungarian nobles led by Martinuzzi obeyed the King's dying command, and the little boy was proclaimed and crowned as King Stephen. Ferdinand could hardly let such an act pass, and he invaded and laid siege to Buda; but his army was unequal to the task of capturing it and he was forced to retire. However, he left an Austrian garrison in Pesth, and this gave Martinuzzi sufficient excuse to call for help from the Sultan.

Suleiman had never had much use for either Ferdinand or Zapolya, even though for his own purposes he had supported the latter, and he had recently called them 'faithless men unworthy to wear crowns, who are deterred from breaking treaties by the fear neither of God nor of man'; but he welcomed the ambassadors of the infant King Stephen, and agreed to recognize him in return for an annual tribute of 30,000 ducats. Secretly, however, he distrusted Martinuzzi so thoroughly that he sent one of his own representatives to make sure that the child really was what he claimed to be, and it was only after this man was received by Queen Isabella with the baby at her breast that his suspicions were allayed; the Turk, it is said, fell on his knees and kissed the baby's foot, while swearing in Suleiman's name that he should rule Hungary.

It was not long, however, before it became very evident that the real ruler of Hungary was going to be Suleiman, and moreover that the country was doomed once again to be a battlefield between Turks and Austrians. All through the 1540s they fought each other on Hungarian soil, and Suleiman virtually annexed Buda and turned it into a pashalik of the Ottoman Empire. Martinuzzi did his best to preserve as much of the land as he could for the infant King by being as tactful as possible with both sides, while not letting either know that he was treating with the other; but he was treading a diplomatic tightrope, and although he did so with consummate skill in the end he slipped and fell. The only surprising thing is that he had not made a false step long before.

In 1551, in great secrecy, Martinuzzi persuaded Queen Isabella to give up some of Transylvania to Ferdinand in exchange for parts of Silesia: a scheme which suited Ferdinand, who was delighted, but enraged Suleiman, who sent an army into Transylvania to turn the Austrians out. It was late in the season, however, and the Turkish commander, Mehmed Sokollu, who was later to become Grand Vizier, contented himself with capturing the city of Lippa, placing a garrison in it, and then withdrawing with the intention of returning in the spring. Ferdinand promptly besieged Lippa, and Martinuzzi took part in the siege; but true to character as always he opened secret negotiations with the Turks inside the city in the hope of gaining Suleiman's favour if things should eventually go the Sultan's way. This time, however, he had overreached himself, for wind of his negotiations with the enemy reached Ferdinand, in whose eyes such behaviour amounted to treachery. He gave orders that whatever steps might be necessary to put an end to the cardinal's intrigues should be taken forthwith, and the commander of the Austrian army, a man named Castaldo, who neither liked nor trusted Martinuzzi, needed no further encouragement. At the head of a company of Spanish and Italian soldiers, he made his way to the old fortified Dominican monastery, where the cardinal had set up his headquarters.

On the morning of 18 December 1551 Martinuzzi's secretary, Antonio Ferraio, entered his master's room with some letters for him to sign. The cardinal, dressed only in a nightshirt and a fur-lined dressing-gown, was standing in front of a desk on which there lay an open breviary ready for his morning devotions. As he lent over the desk to sign the letters presented to him by his secretary, Ferraio stabbed him twice, once in the back and again in the neck. Calling on the Mother of God, Martinuzzi threw his assailant to the ground; but, alerted by the sound, more conspirators burst into the room with swords in their hands, and one of them struck him on the head, while others fired their muskets at him. Apparently indestructible, the old man cried out to his murderers, asking them what they were doing. At last, with sixty-three wounds in his body he fell dying to the ground with the words, 'Jesus Mary!' on his lips. His body was left contemptuously where it lay for weeks, until someone eventually had the grace to bury it at Wiessenburg in a tomb upon which was inscribed the epitaph, *Omnibus moriendum est*. He was seventy-five.

History has tended to dismiss Martinuzzi as a slippery, devious and treacherous monk; and so he was. But his aim was to reconcile and restrain those simpler and nobler souls who relied upon the sword, the bullet and the gallant cavalry charge to gain their ends, and perhaps history would not make such depressing reading if the Martinuzzis of this life had had a slightly larger hand in its governance than that exercised by those who both despised and murdered him. Such considerations do not seem to have crossed the mind of Pope Julius III, to whom Ferdinand addressed a long accusation of treason against the slaughtered cardinal in an attempt to justify his own part in ordering his assassination. Giovanni Maria del Monte had been Pope for less than two years when approached by Ferdinand, and he was much more interested in planning the decoration of his villa near the Porta del Popolo than in such minor matters as political assassinations; but since in this instance the murdered man had been a cardinal, in the intervals between attending a number of enjoyable if somewhat questionable evening parties he managed to listen to no fewer than 116 witnesses against the murdered man (and none, needless to say, for him) before pronouncing judgement. After this splendid display of impartiality, he came to the only possible conclusion, namely, that Martinuzzi had indeed been a traitor and that Ferdinand had been justified in ordering the old patriot's murder. Thus justice was seen to be done, and blessed by the Pope, and everyone was happy with the unimportant exception of the Hungarian people.

While these events were taking place in Hungary, and Barbarossa was terrorizing the coastal cities of Italy and Spain, time was creeping up on the principal actors in the international drama. Martin Luther was the first to go. He died on 18 February 1546 in his sixty-third year, leaving behind him a western world bitterly divided over religious matters and unsure which was the greater evil, the Turkish menace or the corruption of Christianity; though naturally the Catholics attributed that corruption to the Protestants, while the Protestants thought of the city of Rome as the home of Antichrist.

Less than a year later, Barbarossa followed Luther to the grave. He died of a fever in bed in his palace in Constantinople on 4 July 1546, and Islam mourned his passing with the words, 'The Chief of the sea is dead.' A generation later, Christendom paid him an unwitting tribute when Cervantes, writing of Barbarossa's time, said, 'The world was convinced that the Turks were invincible by sea.' Suleiman had the old corsair's body placed in a small, domed, grey granite tomb on the shores of the Bosphorus, where every Turkish sailor could see it as he put to sea and when he returned home again.

Half a world away, on 28 January 1547, Henry of England died, and was buried in St George's Chapel at Windsor. He had never played more than a peripheral part in the struggle against the Turks, for they were too far away to pose much of a threat to England, and he had changed sides too often to make himself particularly popular with his peers; but like Martinuzzi he had always had the well-being of his country and its unity at heart, and had been prepared to go to almost any lengths to make sure that it was not plunged back again into a civil war like that of the Wars of the Roses.

Time was also creeping up on Charles. He was plagued more and more by gout, largely as a result of his chronic intemperance at the table; but gout or no gout, he was still vigorous enough to succumb to the charms of Barbara Blomberg, who presented him at this time with an illegitimate son, the future Don John of Austria of whom mention has already been made. The Bishop of Osma, who was the Emperor's confessor, took a less than enthusiastic view of the child's birth, accusing Charles of gross self-indulgence; but if the Polish ambassador to the Emperor's court, a highly intelligent and singularly well-informed man named John Dantiscus, is to be believed, the bishop should have been the last man to cast stones at Charles for his lapse from grace, for he himself had formed a relationship with the daughters of a converted Jew, which laid him open to a similar accusation.

But if Charles was still vigorous, despite his gout, his old rival Francis I of France was shortly to die, on 30 March 1547, two months after Henry of England, at the age of fifty-three. It has often been said that he died of syphilis, and perhaps he did; but French historians tend to deny it, some saying that he died of a urinary infection, while others assert that he was carried off by pneumonia. The cause of his death is of much less importance than the achievements of his life, and however distasteful one may find some aspects of his character and policy, these were considerable. He carried the unification of France a stage further in its victory over divisive regionalism; he stood out against the very real threat of Habsburg domination of Europe; he enriched France immeasurably by his patronage of the arts; and in fact it must be admitted that with all his faults he was one of the great Renaissance princes of the sixteenth century. Without him, of all the original actors in the drama which had begun with the accession of Suleiman to the Sultanate in Constantinople a quarter of a century earlier, the only ones left were the Emperor Charles, his brother Ferdinand, and Suleiman himself; and time was having its effect on the Sultan too.

His successes in fields other than that of his struggle with western Christendom have not been described, but in fact they were remarkable. Few men can have succeeded in doing as much as Suleiman did to bring up to date the laws of the land which he ruled, while at the same time fighting successful wars on two fronts. In this respect he warrants comparison with the Emperor Justinian. Indeed, so excellent and lasting was his work in the field of Islamic legislation that his compatriots called him Suleiman el Kanuni, the law-giver, and when the Chamber of Representatives in Washington was redecorated in 1950 with two dozen medallion portraits of the world's great legislators, Suleiman took his place among them. But while these triumphs lie outside the scope of this book, they seem to have played their part in the growth of two unattractive aspects of his character, which became more and more pronounced as he grew older – his arrogance and his paranoia. As an example of his increasing haughtiness, it is enough to recall an occasion when he decided to go hunting in Asiatic Turkey; having crossed the Bosphorus, he travelled by way of Smyrna to Bursa, whose inhabitants came out on horseback to pay their respects to him as he approached their city. It was a reasonable enough thing to do, but Suleiman was furious with them for not appearing humbly on foot, and refused to speak to them. Indeed, he was so angry that he issued an order that no one but cavalry officers of high rank should ever again appear before him on horseback.

This absurd hauteur was harmless enough in itself, but in as far as it was a symptom of Suleiman's increasingly paranoid suspicion of everyone who could one day become his rival, it was by no means harmless; on the contrary it was extremely sinister, as both his family and the world were soon to discover. What made it even more ominous was that one member of his family was already exploiting it to her own ends. Since the day when Rustem Pasha, Roxelana's son-in-law, had been made Grand Vizier, her hold upon Suleiman had become very nearly absolute. With Ibrahim safely in his tomb, with Suleiman's mother also in her grave, and with Gulbehar, the mother of his eldest son, banished to Manisa, Roxelana was without a rival for the affection and confidence of the Sultan: at least, her ascendancy over him was almost unchallenged. But that little word 'almost' worried her, for she could not forget that her husband had had a son by Gulbehar before she herself had entered his life, and the mere existence of Gulbehar's offspring was a threat to her and to her children; for should he inherit the throne after Suleiman's death, almost certainly her own two sons would be put to death, and she herself would be banished to some remote corner of the Ottoman Empire to die in something very like the obscurity in which she had been born, and she had no intention of allowing that to happen. Gulbehar's son, Mustafa, had to go.

However, it was easier to decide to eliminate him than it was to do so, for Mustafa was extremely popular. Handsome, able and intelligent, he gave Suleiman's subjects every reason to hope and believe that he would make an admirable successor to his father, and they rejoiced at the prospect. But while Mustafa's popularity made Roxelana's task more difficult, paradoxically it also made it easier; for it enabled her to play on Suleiman's suspicious nature, which was only too easily aroused into a frenzy of jealousy and fear when it was suggested to him that perhaps Mustafa would not wait until his father died a natural death before grasping the throne, but might take matters into his own capable and popular hands in order to forestall nature. After all, Suleiman's own father had done something very similar and had been applauded for his action, so why should Mustafa not follow the family tradition?

Such fears were easily implanted in Suleiman's mind, and although there is no documentary proof that Roxelana was their source there is little doubt that she cultivated them. In 1553, when the Turks marched against Persia once again, her opportunity came, for Rustem Pasha was put in supreme command of the army while Suleiman, who was nearly sixty years old by this time, stayed at home in Constantinople. Rustem had not been in Persia for long before he wrote a letter to the Sultan, the contents of which must have been discussed and agreed with Roxelana before he left the capital. The army, he told Suleiman, was in restive mood, complaining of his absence and his advancing years, and calling for Mustafa to take his place. The Sultan, the soldiers were saying, was too old to lead his army any longer, and it was high time for him to make way for his son. No one but the Grand Vizier, Rustem Pasha, opposed the idea of putting Mustafa in the old Sultan's place, and he could be removed without much difficulty; then the army could chop off the Sultan's head, and Turkey would have a young and vigorous ruler once again instead of a feeble old man. Rustem ended by saying that it was common knowledge that Mustafa was a willing party to such seditious talk, and he begged Suleiman to come at once to Persia and take command.

Rustem's letter redoubled the Sultan's suspicions and threw him into a paroxysm of indecision; for it seemed to him that he had two irreconcilable duties to perform, and he did not know how to act. Every father had a duty to care for his son, and even if he had to chastise him from time to time, nothing was more important than that duty. But every sovereign had the duty to eradicate sedition with utter ruthlessness, whenever and wherever it raised its ugly head, and that duty too was paramount. So what should he do? Could it ever be right for a father to kill his son? In his perplexity, Suleiman sought the advice of the highest authority on Islamic law in the land, the Sheik ul-Islam, by putting a hypothetical case to him and asking him what should be done about it. He told the Sheik that there was a merchant living in Constantinople who had been called away on business in a distant land, and who had therefore known that he would have to be away from home for some time. So before leaving he had put one of his most trusted slaves, to whom he had shown great favour in the past, in charge of his business and his house, entrusting his wife and children to his care. But no sooner had the worthy merchant sailed away down the Bosphorus than this slave had begun to falsify the books of his master's business, steal his property, and make plans to murder his wife and children; worst of all, he had plotted to murder his master when he came home. What sentence, Suleiman asked, could lawfully be imposed on this slave? The Sheik replied that in his opinion the man deserved to be tortured to death. Suleiman thanked him, and left. He was perplexed no longer.

He left at once for Persia, and by August 1553 he had taken full command of the army there. On 21 September he ordered Mustafa to appear before him, warning him that he must come prepared to clear himself of the various accusations which were being made against him. An account of what followed was given by de Busbecq, the imperial ambassador to the Sultan's court at a slightly later date, in a letter to a friend:

Mustafa was confronted by a difficult choice: if he entered the presence of his angry and offended father, he ran an undoubted risk; if he refused, he clearly admitted that he had contemplated an act of treason. He chose the braver and more dangerous course. Leaving Amasia, he sought his father's camp, which lay not far off. Either he relied on his innocence, or else he was confident that no harm could come to him in the presence of the army. Be that as it may, he went to meet certain doom . . . On his arrival in the camp there was considerable excitement among the soldiers. He was introduced into his father's tent, where everything appeared peaceful; there were no soldiers, no body-servants or attendants, and nothing to inspire any fear of treachery. However, several mutes, strong, sturdy men were there – his destined murderers. As soon as they entered the inner tent, they made a determined attack upon him and did their best to throw a noose round him. Being a man of powerful build, he defended himself stoutly and fought not only for his life but for his throne; for there was no doubt that, if he could escape and throw himself among the Janissaries, they would be so moved with indignation that they would not only protect him but also proclaim him Sultan. Suleiman, fearing this, and being separated only by the linen tent-hangings from the scene upon which this tragedy was taking place, when he found that there was a delay in the execution of his plan, thrust his head out of the part of the tent in which he was, and directed fierce and threatening glances upon the mutes, and by menacing gestures sternly rebuked their hesitation. Thereupon the mutes in their alarm, redoubled their efforts, hurled the unhappy Mustafa to the ground, and throwing the bowstring round his neck, strangled him. Then, laying his corpse on a rug, they exposed it in front of the tent, so that the Janissaries might look upon the man, whom they had wished to make Sultan.

The sequel to the murder proved that Suleiman had not misjudged his chances of getting away with it.

When the news spread through the camp, pity and grief were general throughout the army; and no one failed to come and gaze upon the sad sight. Most prominent were the Janissaries, whose consternation and rage were such that, had they had a leader, they would have stopped at nothing; for they saw him whom they had hoped to have as their leader lying lifeless on the ground. The only course which remained was to endure with patience what they could not remedy. So, sad and silent, with their eyes full of tears, they betook themselves to their tents, where they could lament to their hearts' content the fate of their luckless favourite. First they inveighed against the Sultan as a crazy old lunatic; and then they railed against the treachery and cruelty of the young man's step-mother and the wickedness of Rustem, who together had extinguished the brightest star of the house of Othman. They passed that day in fasting, not even tasting water; nay, there were some who remained without eating for several days. Thus for some days there was general mourning in the camp; and it seemed as if there was no likelihood of any end to the grief and lamentations of the soldiers, had not Suleiman stripped Rustem (probably at his own suggestion) of his dignities and sent him back to Constantinople without any official position. Achmed Pasha, a man of greater courage than judgement, who had occupied the second place when Rustem was Chief Vizier was chosen to succeed him . . . This change soothed the grief and calmed the feelings of the soldiers, who, with the usual credulity of the vulgar, were easily led to believe that Suleiman had discovered the crimes of Rustem and the sorceries of his wife and had learned wisdom, though it was too late, and had therefore deposed Rustem and would not spare even his wife on return to Constantinople.

Achmed Pasha's precipitate promotion did him little good, though he seems to have been a conscientious man. Two years later, when Roxelana deemed it safe once again to reinstate her son-in-law in the chief seat of power as Grand Vizier, she had little difficulty in persuading her ever-distrustful husband that Achmed was guilty of plotting against him, and he was beheaded in Suleiman's hall of audience on a day in September 1555 when the Sultan was presiding over a divan there. Rustem then returned to his old office and he and Roxelana began to make plans to realize yet another of her ambitions.

Mustafa's death left Roxelana's two sons, Selim and Bayezid, as the only two contenders for the succession; Jehangir, her third son who was a hunchback and a cripple, died shortly after Mustafa's murder, some said of a broken heart. Selim, aged twenty-nine, was the older of the two and for some reason his mother's favourite. Short, obese, ugly and incompetent, it is difficult to understand how a man of Suleiman's stature could possibly have sired such an unsavoury and unattractive offspring, although it must be said in Selim's defence that growing up under the formidable and dominant shadow of a father like Suleiman could have been no easy process, and the fact that his younger brother, Bayezid, was large, handsome and talented could have made it no easier.

Selim's singular unfitness to follow his father was obvious to everyone except Roxelana, who was determined that he should succeed when the time came. Meanwhile, Bayezid, who seems to have inherited many of Suleiman's best qualities and few of his faults, took the place of Mustafa in the affections of the Janissaries, and became the soldiers' darling. This did not endear him to Suleiman whose endemic proneness to scent treachery in any possible rival for the throne was immediately aroused, and the fact that Bayezid was suspected of being mixed up in a revolt in the Balkans only made matters worse; but even so Suleiman was not blind to the truth about his two sons, for their differences were too glaring to be overlooked by anyone. He realized that everyone except his wife expected him to name Bayezid as his successor, but torn between his love for Roxelana and his duty to do what would be best for the Ottoman Empire after his death, he refused to make up his mind, postponing indefinitely the evil day of decision. Until that day should come, since the two brothers hated each other like poison, he made sure that they should not meet by giving them governorships in widely separated parts of the Empire.

Then, on 15 April 1558, Roxelana suddenly died. Suleiman was shattered, retreating from the world and wrapping himself in a cocoon of prayer, where he wept and fasted in an attempt to find solace for the bitterness of his grief though with little success. Many of his subjects, however, were both relieved and delighted by her death, for they had regarded her as a witch who for too long had been an evil influence upon the Sultan, while others hoped that her death would at least solve the problem of the succession; for with Roxelana in her tomb there would be no one to press Selim's claims over those of the eminently suitable Bayezid. But it was too late. While their father mourned, his two sons ignored their mother's death and concentrated instead on hurling insults at each other, even though at long range, while each of them busily gathered more and more adherents around him for the power struggle which was to come. This potentially fratricidal feud culminated a year later in the summer of 1559, when civil war broke out between them in Anatolia. Each was supported by part of the army but unfortunately for the Turkish people somehow or other Selim had managed to gather a more formidable force around him than had his brother Bayezid; he had probably done it by bribery, for later in life he showed himself to be a master of the art. However, in whatever way he may have persuaded so many people to fight for him, their numbers tipped the military scales in his favour, and Bayezid was badly defeated in a number of battles in Asiatic Turkey, before Suleiman could cross the Bosphorus with a sufficiently strong force to restore order there. Hearing of his approach, Bayezid wrote to his father to assure him of his affection and loyalty, and to explain that his quarrel was not with his father but only with his brother; but the letter was intercepted by one of Selim's agents, and it never reached Suleiman. Hearing nothing from his younger son, Suleiman's perennial tendency to suspect the worst was well and truly aroused; it was also sedulously cultivated by Selim, while Bayezid, receiving no reply from his father and ignorant of the fate of his letter, was forced to conclude that his protestations of loyalty had not been believed. Understandably frightened for his life, he fled to the court of the Shah of Persia, where he asked for political asylum.

His request was immediately granted. Shah Tahmasp was an amiable man by nature and he was no fool; he realized that Bayezid might become a most valuable counter in the struggle for supremacy between his country and Turkey, which had been a prime feature of Middle Eastern politics for centuries. But Bayezid's flight and his kindly reception by the Shah amounted in Suleiman's eyes to proof positive of his treason; for if he was not a traitor how could he possibly take refuge with his father's traditional enemy? So Suleiman was forced by events to do as Roxelana had always begged him to do, and to back Selim in his struggle with his brother for the succession.

There followed a long diplomatic wrangle between Suleiman and the Shah over the custody of the refugee prince; embassies went back and forth between the two, the Turks demanding either Bayezid's extradition or his execution as a traitor, and the Persians pleading the laws of Moslem hospitality in favour of continuing to give him sanctuary. The Shah's stance does not seem to have been one of high moral principle as much as one of political expediency, for at one time he tried to make a bargain with Suleiman, offering to hand over Bayezid in exchange for some land in Mesopotamia recently conquered by the Turks; but Suleiman would have none of it, and in the end the constant threat of a Turkish invasion, which lay just below the surface of these polite diplomatic exchanges, proved decisive. When the Shah was offered 400,000 pieces of gold to surrender the hapless fugitive to a small party of Turks who were sent to Persia specially to receive him, Tahmasp agreed, rather than go to war. The little party of men included Suleiman's chief executioner, and on 25 September 1561 he reached Tabriz, where Bayezid was surrendered to him. The prince was under no illusion about the nature and inevitability of his coming fate. He asked to be allowed to kiss the members of his family before he died, but he was told to 'attend to the business in hand', whereupon with no further delay the executioner threw a bowstring about his neck, and strangled him.

Four of his sons had taken refuge with him in Persia, and as soon as their father was dead, they, too, were strangled. His youngest son, aged three, who had been left behind in Bursa in the charge of a nurse when the rest of the family had fled the country, escaped the domestic holocaust in Tabriz, but he did not survive for long. Suleiman dispatched a favourite eunuch to Bursa with yet another bowstring in his pocket, and the succession was thus secured for Selim, as his mother had so passionately wanted, and the fate of Ottoman Turkey was sealed.

XIV

✠ ✠ ✠

The Unconquerable Will

What though the field be lost?
All is not lost; th' unconquerable will,
And study of revenge, immortal hate,
And courage never to submit or yield;
And what is else not to be overcome?

Milton, *Paradise Lost*

While Suleiman's family was suffering these domestic convulsions, the ruling houses of western Europe were not without troubles of their own. After the death of Henry VIII his ten-year-old son had duly succeeded him, but Edward was a sickly child and no one expected him to last for long. He survived for just over six years before dying at Greenwich on 6 July 1553, and his reign was not a happy one, for the country was locked in a vicious struggle between Catholic and Protestant, and the boy King was never more than the plaything, first of the Duke of Somerset, and then of Northumberland. What sort of King he would have made, had he lived, is a matter for conjecture; but there seems to be at least some evidence that he might have been as ruthless a protagonist of the Protestant cause as his sister Mary was later to be on behalf of the Catholics. Her accession, when he died, was followed almost at once by the execution of Northumberland, which proved to be the first of a long series of beheadings and burnings, and these brutalities, combined with her wildly unpopular marriage to Charles's son Philip of Spain, who was loathed for his Catholicism, were guaranteed to keep the fires of religious hatred burning at white heat. It is difficult to look back dispassionately on her reign, for the retrospect is coloured by the light of the fires in which such men as Thomas Cranmer and Nicholas Ridley were burned to death, and her sobriquet, Bloody Mary, has become so much an integral part of her historical image that impartiality is almost impossible; but in all probability she was not much worse than most of her contemporaries, caught up as they all were in a situation not unlike that which is still murderously familiar in Northern Ireland, and her brother Edward might well have been as bloody and divisive a ruler as she turned out to be.

In France, too, there was a very different man in control of affairs. Henry II was almost as different from his father as Selim was from Suleiman, though there the comparison ends; for where Selim was small, unpleasant and alcoholic, Henry was merely large and dull. His accession was followed by something very like a purge of the French court, for nearly all Francis's favourites were banished to their provincial estates, while the new King surrounded himself with people better suited to his own taste; but if the court changed the hard facts of *realpolitik* did not, and the rivalry between France and the Empire continued unabated.

While the governments of England and France were changing hands, that of the Empire was not, though Charles, too, was getting older and longed to be rid of the crushing burden of his imperial office and, like the Emperor Domitian before him, enjoy a few years of peace before he died. As early as 1542 he had told Lorenzo Perez, the Portuguese ambassador to Spain at the time, that he had been longing to retire ever since his expedition against Tunis in 1535. Now, over twenty years later, the deaths of Henry of England and Francis of France must have made him realize that if he was ever to accomplish his dream of ending his life in peace, he had better do something about it before death caught up with him, for it was at this time that he let it be known that he hoped that the imperial crown would pass to his son Philip, when he himself relinquished it, and not to his brother Ferdinand. Naturally enough, Ferdinand resented this, and relations between the brothers became a little strained for a while. Later, however, he and Ferdinand came to an agreement about the succession: when Charles retired or died, Ferdinand should become Emperor, while Philip would become King of the Romans and King of Spain, and would follow Ferdinand as Emperor when his uncle died. But all this was for the future, and however much Charles might long to retire, another eleven years would pass before he could take off his imperial crown for the last time, and travel to the house which he had built for himself at Yuste in Estremadura, there to make his peace with God in whatever time was left to him.

During those years, the religious troubles in Germany became no better, and the upheaval in England caused by his son Philip's marriage to Mary Tudor greatly worried Charles; and things were little better in the Mediterranean. After the death of Barbarossa the naval war there continued to be waged with undiminished vigour by a number of Turkish corsairs, of whom the most important was Dragut; he was promoted to be Commander of the Sultan's Galleys by Suleiman after a particularly daring skirmish with Andrea Doria, which roused the Sultan's admiration. In fact, it was only a minor engagement, but it was typical of many others in the naval war at this time; neither side annihilated the other, but the Turks usually came off better than their enemies, and this long series of minor defeats at sea also clouded Charles's last years. But at long last, in February 1557, he made up his mind to do what he had wanted to do for so long, and he retired to his house at Yuste.

Because the house had been built next to a monastery, people have often imagined that Charles's life in retirement was austerely monastic, but it was nothing of the sort. He had filled the house with treasures, including some superb paintings by Titian, and his garden was full of flowers, fruit and such delicacies as asparagus, of which he was inordinately fond, while pheasant, partridge and duck, some of which he shot himself, were seldom absent from his table. He knew perfectly well that over-indulgence in food and drink was his besetting sin and thoroughly bad for him; indeed, when attacked by gout, he would quote the Spanish tag, '*la gota se cura tapando la boca*' – 'the best cure for gout is to keep one's mouth closed' – but he never acted on that good advice. Perhaps he was wise not to do so, for at least he enjoyed his last few months on earth, and in fact they were destined to be very few indeed. On 21 September 1558, nineteen months after taking up residence at Yuste, he died of a fever. Don Luis Mendez Quijada, who had served him for thirty years and knew him better than most, said after his death that he was '*el hombre mas principal*' – 'the most illustrious man there ever was or ever will be'. It is a rare tribute, but if anyone has ever deserved such an epitaph, perhaps it was Charles; he was indeed a man of rare distinction. He was fifty-eight when he died.

Suleiman was sixty-three, and time had not improved his temper, nor power his tendency to megalomania. Like a spoilt child, he could not bear to be thwarted; when he failed to get his own way, though he remained outwardly calm and impassive, he neither forgot nor forgave the people responsible for his humiliation. One incident in the sporadic war, which continued to make life hideous in Hungary, was typical of others; two years before Charles's death, in the summer of 1556, the Turks besieged the comparatively minor fortress of Sziget (the modern Szigetvar with a tourist hotel inside the walls of the castle), but were forced to abandon the siege after several costly weeks and to acknowledge their failure. They had been defeated by the heroism and endurance of the defenders, as the Turkish commander –

a eunuch, whose extreme ugliness belied the nobility of his nature –
freely and generously admitted.

Suleiman was furious, however; they were not heroes but men who
had humiliated him in the face of the world, and he vowed that they
should be made to pay for their insolence; one day he would get his
revenge. Ten years later he did so. At the head of an army of 100,000
men he besieged Sziget for thirty-three days until most of the
garrison of 2,500 men had been killed, whereupon the survivors,
vastly outnumbered, broke out and died in bloody hand-to-hand
fighting with the Turks. But although the story shows Suleiman in an
unpleasant light and his Hungarian opponents in marked and heroic
contrast, it would be a mistake to draw too many conclusions from
the comparison; the war in Hungary had reduced the men on both
sides to astonishing depths of barbarism, and some of the things done
to their enemies by the Hungarians make Suleiman's rather childish
and vindictive determination to punish anyone obstinate enough to
defy his divine authority (one of his titles was 'Shadow of God on
Earth') look like a very minor and venial sin. For instance, it was at
this time that a rumour spread throughout the Hungarian and German
ranks that the Turks were in the habit before a battle of swallowing
their gold and their jewellery for safe-keeping; this encouraged the
Christian soldiers to eviscerate their prisoners in search of riches, and
having thus coped with the living to roam the battlefield slitting up the
dead and wounded and rummaging around in their bowels for hidden
treasure.

Shortly after the death of Charles, however, a peace treaty was
negotiated by de Busbecq between Ferdinand, now Emperor in
Charles's place, and Suleiman, and the war in Hungary was officially
ended. The treaty was signed in 1561, but since the Latin and Turkish
versions differed in some important respects, it did not put a complete
stop to the fighting. Warfare had become a way of life for Hungarians
and Turks alike, the country was a desolation, and border raids
continued to be made by both sides. But the treaty did one thing for
Suleiman; it freed him to concentrate upon another theatre of war, and
after years of dreary, costly, bloody and indecisive fighting on land,
he longed to follow up his series of minor victories at sea with a
crowning victory in the Mediterranean.

The most obstinate of all his enemies, the Knights of St John, whom
he had cast out of Rhodes in his first spectacular military triumph,
were now installed on the island of Malta, and that was something
which Suleiman was determined to change. He would end his career,
as he had begun it, by defeating this 'sect of the accursed Franks, worst
of the sons of error, sent by Satan . . . damnable workers of
wickedness', by once again casting them out of the island on which

they had made their home, and from which they raided the commerce and shipping of Islam with merciless efficiency.

The Knights had been homeless for eight years after being turned out of Rhodes, but in 1530 the Emperor Charles had offered them sanctuary on Malta, 'in order that they might follow peacefully the rule of their Order for the good of the Christian community, and at the same time use their forces and arms against the infidel enemies of the True Faith'. In many ways, Malta was better suited to such a godly and dual purpose than Rhodes had been; for Rhodes was situated so near to the Turkish coast that as the Ottoman power had increased over the years the Knights had become more and more vulnerable. In contrast, on Malta not only were they ideally situated to raid ships passing through the narrow sea between Sicily and Africa, but they were almost a thousand miles from Constantinople.

When Suleiman decided to attack the island they were commanded by a remarkable man of great experience, for in 1557 they had elected a new Grand Master, Jean Parisot de la Valette, who had spent a lifetime fighting the Turks. Born into a noble Provençal family in 1494, he had joined the Order at the age of twenty, and had fought under de L'Isle Adam in the battle of Rhodes. The Abbé de Brantôme, who met him shortly after the siege of Malta, described him as 'a very handsome man, tall, calm and unemotional, speaking several languages fluently – Italian, Spanish, Greek, Arabic and Turkish'. He had learned the last two after being captured in 1541, when he had been forced to spend a year as a galley slave, regaining his freedom only when an exchange of prisoners took place, and apparently surviving the appalling hardships of life in a Turkish galley both physically and psychologically unscathed. Even the tough and demanding life which every member of the Order accepted as a matter of course did not always prepare men for the sort of life endured by galley slaves, and some members of the Order were broken by it.

La Valette's ability to survive almost any hardship was a product of a number of things, chief among which were an unconquerable will, an unshakable faith and a total dedication to the Order which he served. He was a completely single-minded man, for whom the defence of the Christian faith against its enemies was the supreme purpose of his life. In the spring of 1565, when Suleiman sent the whole armed might of the Ottoman Empire against him, he was seventy, but his age did not matter; it was for this moment that he had been born.

He had ample warning of the coming storm. While Turkish sailors took fire and sword to Majorca and even passed through the Straits of Gibraltar into the Atlantic to prey on the Spanish treasure ships returning laden with riches from the Americas, Philip II, Charles's son and heir, was stung out of his lethargy into doing something to counter this naval offensive, and for the first time for years the Turks were badly defeated. It happened in Africa, where one of Barbarossa's sons, Hassan, was ordered by Suleiman to attack two of the only strong points remaining in Spanish hands in Algeria, the fortress at Oran and its twin at Mers-el-Kebir, and take them. At first, all went well, and the men of the small Spanish garrisons, greatly outnumbered, seemed doomed to surrender or be annihilated; but then, just as Hassan was about to deliver the *coup de grâce*, thirty-four heavily armed Spanish galleys, which had been sent by Philip to the aid of the defenders, arrived and took the Turks in the rear. Hassan's men were surprised and routed; twenty of his ships escaped but a number of others were captured including four large French vessels, and the Turkish troops besieging the city turned tail and fled. It was the first major reverse suffered by Suleiman's naval forces for some time, and Philip followed it up a year later in 1564 by attacking the Turkish stronghold at Velez de Gomera in Morocco almost due south of Malaga; it had been from here that the Turks had sailed westwards to slip through the Straits of Gibraltar at night to raid their enemy's shipping in the Atlantic, and it was strongly defended; but although the first Spanish force to approach the place was driven back, Philip returned to the charge, sending a much more powerful force under Don Garcia of Toledo, the Viceroy of Sicily, to attack it once again, and this time it fell almost without a struggle. Its loss determined Suleiman once and for all to make a bid for total domination of the Mediterranean sea, and it was not difficult to guess where his next blow would fall. The Knights of St John on Malta were already making preparations to withstand the greatest assault in their history.

In many ways Malta was a much more defensible island than Rhodes. It was so barren and waterless that an invading force would have to bring all its provisions with it, whereas on Rhodes the Turks had been able to live off the country; and over and above the difficulty of supplying an army there, the island's fortifications had been strengthened and modernized by men who had fought on Rhodes, and had learned the lessons of that long and bloody siege; they knew where to look for weaknesses, how to guard against mining operations by the Turkish sappers, and just how important it was going to be to have enough powder and shot, timber for repairs, medical supplies, and above all food and water to last them for the duration of the coming siege, however long that might turn out to be. In the first quarter of 1565 the island was as busy as an ant-heap, the Knights themselves working shoulder to shoulder with the islanders and with Turkish slaves repairing the fortifications and building new ones, while as the weather improved with the coming of spring those members of the Order who had been abroad began to arrive on the island in response to the Grand Master's call to arms. There were not many of them, however, for even when every available member of the Order had arrived La Valette had no more than 700 Knights and Sergeants at his disposal, though there may have been more if the Chaplains of the various *auberges* are taken into account. His numbers were made up to about 8–9,000 men by a few mercenaries and by the Maltese islanders themselves. With these he prepared to meet the largest Ottoman invasion force ever to sail down the Bosphorus against a Christian foe.

Meanwhile, of course, Constantinople too was a hive of activity as ships and men were assembled for the great expedition. Like Charles before him, Suleiman was beginning to suffer more and more frequently from gout as he grew older, but despite the pain and discomfort he visited the docks and arsenals of the Golden Horn regularly every week to see how things were progressing. Even by Turkish standards, the task of assembling something like 40,000 fighting men, an unknown but certainly large number of support troops, supernumeraries, sailors and slaves and nearly 200 ships was a formidable one. Eighty thousand cannonballs were stowed away on board the ships of the invasion fleet; 150 hundredweight of powder for the heavy guns and 250 hundredweight for the army's small arms were trundled up the gang-planks in barrels; a mass of provisions, sacks of spare clothing, blankets, tents, sails, ropes and other necessities were piled on the quays, and horses were brought in by drovers from all over European Turkey and Anatolia to await shipment with the army; they would be needed for dragging cannon up from the beaches and for transporting stores from the base camps to the men in the firing line, and in an emergency they could always be killed and eaten. But the Turks were good military organizers and despite the magnitude of the undertaking they were quite capable of resolving the logistic problems posed by the departure of such a massive expeditionary force.

The problem of who was to command it, however, proved to be much more difficult. In the end, command of the army went to a fanatical old Turk named Mustafa Pasha who, like his opponent La Valette, had fought on Rhodes as well as being a veteran of the wars in Hungary and Persia; he must have been at least seventy years old at the time (von Hammer puts him at seventy-five), but he seems to have been as vigorous as ever despite his age, and he was feared everywhere for his brutality. His family claimed descent from Mohammed's standard bearer, Khalid ben Welid, and his hatred of Christians was notorious – as indeed was his treatment of them if they were unlucky enough to fall into his hands.

Command of the navy went to a very different kind of man; Piali Pasha was not yet forty-five years old and the child of Christian parents. The story goes that he had been found as a baby abandoned by his parents near a plough in a field outside Belgrade during Suleiman's siege of that city in 1521, and had been brought up as a page in the Sultan's household; when he expressed a desire to join the Ottoman navy he was sent to sea, where he quickly distinguished himself, and it was not long before he made a name for himself as the most brilliant young sailor of his time. Finding favour, too, at court, he married one of Suleiman's grandchildren, Selim's daughter, and shortly afterwards was promoted to the rank of admiral. Both Mustafa and Piali were able men with previous experience of high command, and if they had been left alone to do their respective jobs all might have been well, though it is unlikely, for neither of them was given supreme command; but they were not left alone. Suleiman ordered them to do nothing without first securing the agreement of the corsair, Dragut, and of al-Louk Ali, a notorious Christian renegade, who had become almost as celebrated a corsair as Dragut himself. It was an understandable decision on Suleiman's part, for both men had had a great deal of experience of warfare against the Knights; they knew the central and western Mediterranean better than anyone else, and they were popular idols to the ordinary Turkish soldiers. In the event, however, their watching brief simply added to the confusion; it was bad enough that the supreme command was split between Mustafa and Piali, but the added necessity to get all major decisions ratified by Dragut and Ali made matters much worse, for no one had the power to issue the kind of quick and unquestioned commands which are nearly always necessary during the course of any military operation. Instead, the Turkish high command was condemned to squabbling and indecision.

The fleet sailed in early April, and Suleiman came down to the water's edge to see it go; it made its way by stages through the Sea of Marmara and the Dardanelles to the Aegean, where it put in to the island of Chios for water and fresh provisions. The weather was kind to it and, as it pressed steadily on, watchers on the shore took careful note of its passing and at some risk to themselves smuggled news of its progress through to the West, where it was analysed by anxious statesmen in an attempt to guess its destination, for no one yet knew for certain where the Turks were planning to attack. The two most obvious targets were Malta and La Goletta, but Corsica was a possibility, and all three places had to be adequately garrisoned until the Turkish attack was actually launched, and this meant dispersing the Christian forces in a wasteful but unavoidable way. Even so, the Grand Master on Malta was so sure that he and his island were destined to bear the brunt of the coming onslaught that in early May he assembled the Knights and warned them of what was to come; one of them, Francisco Balbi da Correggio, recorded his words. 'The battle which is about to be fought,' he told them, 'will be the great battle between the Cross and the Koran. A formidable army of infidels will soon invade our island. As for us, we are the chosen soldiers of the Cross, and if Heaven demands that we sacrifice our lives, there can be no better time to do so than now. Let us go together then, my brothers, to the altar of God, there to renew our vows and renew, too, by faith in the Holy Sacrament that contempt for death, which alone will make us invincible.'

A few days later, on Friday, 18 May, as the sun came up out of a glassy sea, watchmen on the walls of the great fortress of St Angelo were witnesses of a magnificent if frightening sight; through the dawn mist to the east of the island they could see that the sea was covered with hundreds of ships, their oars rising and falling with calm, unhurried inevitability and flashing when the sun glinted on their wet blades, as they came on in a great arc under banners bearing the crescent moon of Islam. There could no longer be any doubt as to the objective of Suleiman's armada, and the guns of Malta were fired in a prearranged signal to warn the island of the coming of the enemy, booming out and echoing and re-echoing from its rocky cliffs and stone battlements in a ragged salvo. 'At the risk of lapsing into sensationalism,' wrote the eminent French historian, Fernand Braudel, of this moment, 'I am tempted to say that Malta or rather the arrival of the Turkish fleet in Malta in May 1565, hit Europe like a hurricane.' So it did, but as the Knights of St John, roused by the thunder of the guns, tumbled out of bed and buckled on their armour, they were ready to face the storm.

At first, it looked as though Mustafa and Piali intended to land in the north of the island, for to everyone's surprise the fleet sailed slowly and majestically past Marsamuscetto, the Grand Harbour with its fortifications where the modern city of Valetta stands, and on past the bay of Marsa Scirocco on the southernmost tip of the island, where it turned northwards to anchor eventually at dusk off shore not far from the village of Mgarr. It looked as if La Valette, who had expected an immediate attack on the main fortifications on the other side of the island, had been wrong, and that the Turks meant first to capture the weakly fortified city of Mdina, in which there was only a small garrison, before turning south; but in the early hours of the next morning watchers from the shore saw the great fleet begin to weigh anchor and move slowly down the coast again. Messengers galloped off to tell the Grand Master the news, and by dawn the first Turkish ships had reached the great bay of Marsa Scirocco, where they anchored. The move to the north had been a feint, and La Valette had been right all along; the Turkish attack was going to be launched on the Borgo. Knowing for sure, at last, where Mustafa and Piali were going to strike, the Grand Master put the finishing touches to his defences; men were sent to poison all the wells within reach of the city; the last of the peasants who had not yet taken refuge there were hastily gathered in with their animals and foodstuffs; a great chain was laboriously raised from the seabed until it completely blocked the entrance to the little harbour between the peninsula of Fort St Angelo and the Borgo on the west and that of Senglea on the east; last-minute stores of food, water and ammunition were ferried across to the garrison in Fort St Elmo; some infantrymen were recalled from Mdina to join the main body in the Borgo, where the defenders were put on full alert, and the standard of St John was hoisted high above the keep of Fort St Angelo. There was nothing to do then but wait.

On Saturday 19 May the Turks began to land on the island from their anchorage in Marsa Scirocco, and by Tuesday of the next week the whole army was ashore and had occupied the southern half of the island. Apart from a minor cavalry skirmish, in which as usual the Knights were greatly outnumbered, the invaders encountered no opposition, for La Valette was not prepared to risk his men in an unequal fight with an army over three times the size of his own; but as they approached the Borgo from the south with beating drums, fifes playing, a forest of silken banners rippling in the breeze over the heads of the advancing troops, and the horsetails of Turks marking the presence of Mustafa Pasha, the Grand Master was unable to control the impetuosity and enthusiasm of some of the younger Knights, who had never known war on such a scale before; for a few it was actually their first engagement, and they rushed out to meet the enemy. Seeing them go, he sent others to support them, and although they were soon forced to retire by the superior numbers of the Turks, they fought with such furious dash and ardour that they killed several hundred of the enemy for a loss of only twenty-one of their own men before retreating into the shelter of the Borgo as the guns gave them covering fire; but although their casualties were few, La Valette knew that he could not afford to lose anyone unnecessarily if he was to hold out against Mustafa's overwhelmingly superior host, and there were no more sorties.

That night the Turkish army camped on the Corradino hills, and the Knights prepared to meet an attack on the Borgo and Senglea as soon as the Turkish artillery could be brought from Marsa Scirocco and be dragged into place; but it was not to be. An argument was taking place in the Turkish camp between Mustafa and Piali; Mustafa wanted to launch just such an attack with his main body, while detaching some troops and sending them to subdue the rest of the island and capture Mdina, but Piali was adamant that he would not leave the fleet in Marsa Scirocco for fear of a celebrated and ferocious wind, locally known as the *gregale*; this wind was greatly feared by all sailors on the seas round Malta, and shelter from it could be found only in the Grand Harbour, which was held by the Christians, or in the harbour of Marsamuscetto just to the north of Mount Sciberras, which was dominated by Fort St Elmo. Since an attack on the Grand Harbour was out of the question, Piali argued that it was essential to attack St Elmo before anything else was attempted, adding that he would not be responsible for the safety of the fleet or the landing of supplies unless his plan to make Marsamuscetto his main naval base was accepted by Mustafa. The old soldier was in no position to overrule Piali in naval matters, and so he reluctantly agreed to postpone the attack on the Borgo until Fort St Elmo had been reduced. In fact, the *gregale* never blew at that time of year, and Piali's fears were quite unnecessary.

By a stroke of luck for the Grand Master and his beleaguered companions, one of Mustafa's personal servants, who had been a silent but attentive witness of the argument between his master and Piali, was a Christian who had been captured at some time in the past, and who had pretended to accept Islam in order to save his life, but who had never ceased to be a believing Christian. With a friend who was also eager to escape from his Turkish captors, this man managed to make his way under cover of darkness to the city, where he was taken before La Valette and told his story. The Grand Master knew that, if it was true, it was of inestimable value, for the Turks would be robbed of the element of surprise while he himself still had time to reinforce the garrison of the threatened fortress before the attack could take place; and he had no reason to suppose that the man was lying. So the men in St Elmo were immediately informed that they were to be the recipients of the full force of Mustafa's first onslaught, while reinforcements were ferried across the Grand Harbour to join them, and their stores of food, water, powder, shot and cannonballs were increased.

What followed was one of those epic stories of astonishing courage, of which one is tempted to say that only members of one of the great medieval military Orders were capable; it would not be true, of course, for there have always been men in every age capable of sublime heroism, but it would certainly be true to say that no body of men has risen more often to exalted heights of valour and resolution than the Knights of the three great religious Orders – the Hospitallers, the Templars and the Teutonic Knights. Even Gibbon's somewhat scathing remark about them that they 'neglected to live, but were prepared to die for Christ' is, if ungenerous, a tribute to their courage. Although they must have known that once the weight of the Turkish artillery was brought to bear on Fort St Elmo – constructed as it was of the soft, friable stone of Malta which, though marvellous for building, was not calculated to stand up to heavy bombardment for very long – the chances of anyone getting out alive, let alone unscathed, were minimal, they fell over each other in their eagerness to volunteer for service there.

By the morning of 24 May, Mustafa had managed to drag most of his heavy cannon into place and he ordered the bombardment to begin. Understandably, the garrison of St Elmo waited anxiously for the first shot to be fired, for they knew that their fate would be determined by the success or failure of the Turkish artillery; mining could play little part in the coming battle, for Malta was a solid lump of rock into which the sappers could not burrow and tunnel as they had thirty-three years previously on Rhodes. But their artillery was known to be superior to anything on the Christian side, and in the years of campaigning in Hungary it had been improved even more. What its impact would be no one knew for certain. But they soon found out, for in the middle of the morning there was a sudden deafening roar as the Turkish gunners opened fire, followed immediately by a high-pitched whine as the first barrage of cannonballs tore through the air to crash on to their target with an impact on ears and nerves and the beating of men's hearts which it is difficult to imagine. Splinters of stone hissed viciously through the air, and clouds of dust choked the defenders, as the ground shook and shuddered under this battery of iron and granite; but when the dust cleared everyone was still alive, the fort was hardly marked, the great water cisterns had not been cracked by the impact of the cannonballs, as some people had feared might happen, and the morale of the men in St Elmo rose to new heights as they returned the enemy fire.

The artillery was soon joined by the crackle of small-arms' fire, as snipers on both sides tried to pick each other off, and although the sentries on the ramparts of St Elmo were as careful as they could be not to show themselves against the sky as targets for the Turks below them on the Marsamuscetto side, inevitably as the battle grew fiercer they suffered casualties. But so did the Turks; in fact, they suffered much greater losses than their enemies, for they looked on life as entirely expendable, if occasion demanded, and when trenches had to be dug on the exposed slopes of Mount Sciberras, or when cannon had to be dragged into new positions, or supplies had to be brought up to their forward troops, they poured men out like water. It did not matter how many were killed, for the tasks had to be done, and everyone knew that if a man died in battle against the hated Christians he would go straight to Paradise.

As the days passed, however, and St Elmo was gradually battered into a great, shapeless, crumbling mound of stone over which a cloud of yellow dust hung perpetually, as the endless stream of Turkish cannonballs slowly pulverized it, life inside the Fort became more and more precarious. Men were killed and wounded daily, but as long as a man could still stand on his feet he was expected to go on fighting, and it occurred to no one to do otherwise; minor wounds were completely disregarded, and major injuries bandaged as quickly as possible so that the wounded man could return to whatever post he was manning at the time. Only the dead stopped fighting; but each night, as darkness fell, volunteers were rowed across the harbour from the Borgo to take their places, and there was never a shortage of men eager to step into the breaches left by the day's casualties. Yet despite all this, at dawn on 29 May the garrison of St Elmo made a sortie against their enemies. They took the Turks on Sciberras completely by surprise, as they fell on them out of the darkness, their faces black with gunpowder, dust and sweat, their clothing bloody, their armour smeared with mud to prevent it from gleaming in the first light of day, and their swords already running with blood. As the Turks fled, the Christians cut them down, and for a time it looked as though the whole Turkish front on Sciberras was about to collapse as panic spread through the ranks of men snatched from sleep by the screams of the dying, the shouts of command, the crackle of small-arms' fire and the shrill notes of bugles; but at the height of the battle Mustafa, awakened in his tent by the noise of the fighting, ordered the Janissaries into action, and as had happened on innumerable occasions in the past these supremely professional soldiers turned the tide of battle. The Christians were forced back in a slow, bitterly contested rearguard action, eventually regaining the safety of the battered fort, from which a withering fire was opened by St Elmo's guns on the exposed Janissaries; but although they killed many of them, when the battle was over the Turks were even nearer to the beleaguered fort than they had been before the sortie. The Janissaries had captured one of the Christians' outposts.

Shortly after this, the corsair Dragut arrived on the island to the excitement and delight of his fellow countrymen but to the annoyance of Piali Pasha, with whom Dragut immediately took issue. Why had the whole northern half of the island and the little island of Gozo not been captured before attacking La Valette in the south? It was a cardinal error of strategy. And why waste time, men and precious ammunition on a needless and bloody attack on Fort St Elmo? Its capture was quite unnecessary, for the fleet could have stayed perfectly safely in Marsa Scirocco, while the main weight of the attack could have been directed against the Borgo and Fort St Angelo, which would have to be reduced eventually, and St Elmo could have been left severely alone. Piali defended himself hotly, but Dragut would have none of it, though he agreed reluctantly that since the attack on St Elmo had already begun, it would have to be finished and the sooner the better. It was time to launch a full-scale assault upon the battered fort.

From the moment of Dragut's arrival it became obvious that St Elmo would soon be attacked; the fire of the Turkish cannon was redoubled, thirty-six heavy guns bombarding it from the land and some of the Turkish fleet bringing its guns to bear on it from the sea. An Italian Knight inside the fort, who was later to die there, counted the number of cannonballs fired by the Turks in the course of one day, and reckoned that 'on most days an average of six thousand or seven thousand shots were fired at St Elmo', while a Spaniard, Balbi da Corregio, who witnessed the siege from the vantage point of St Michael's across the harbour, said that the fort looked like 'a volcano in eruption, spouting fire and smoke'. Dragut himself, already eighty years old but as active as a man half his age and in his element in the smoke and reek of battle, put new heart into the Turkish troops by moving among them, utterly regardless of the fire from the Christian guns of St Elmo, talking with the men, passing the time of day with them for all the world as if he had just chanced to meet them during the course of a quiet stroll through the back streets of Constantinople. He had not been called 'The Sword of Islam' for nothing, and the morale of the troops rose to new heights; with Dragut in command victory was assured.

At dawn on 3 June the long-awaited assault was launched. It began with a stroke of luck for the Turks, for the outermost defensive position known as the ravelin fell into their hands without opposition; no one knows just what happened, but it seems probable that the sentries posted there must either have fallen asleep through exhaustion or have been killed during the night. The Janissaries took immediate advantage of its capture, and as their high-pitched battle cries woke the defenders in the main fort, they streamed across the wooden bridge by which it was connected to the ravelin. Fully awake by now, the men inside St Elmo lowered the sights of their cannon until the guns were pointing down at the waves of attackers only yards away below them, and fired ball after ball into their midst with lethal effect, until the parapet on which they were crowded was covered in mangled bodies, severed limbs and a dark welter of blood; but the sight of their dead and wounded comrades served only to enrage the other members of this Turkish *corps d'élite*, and it was not long before they were massed at the foot of the main wall of the fort, where the cannon could no longer reach them. Here they set up scaling ladders and, as some of them gave covering fire, others swarmed up the ladders in an attempt to carry the wall; but the men at the top were ready and the climbers were pelted with burning hoops and attacked with flame-throwers using the celebrated Greek fire. The Janissaries wore long white robes which caught fire at a touch, and soon the foot of the wall was a confused mass of screaming men in flames; but others still came on, calling on Allah to bring death upon their infidel enemies, and still the men inside St Elmo hurled down fire and boiling tar and chunks of rock upon them, until the whole place resembled something out of Dante's *Inferno*. Eventually, the pace proved too much even for the Janissaries, and when Mustafa saw that they could not succeed he sounded the retreat. He had lost nearly 2,000 men, most of them Janissaries and thus not easily replaced, while the Christians had lost ten Knights and seventy-three other soldiers.

But although the Turks had lost the battle, they had captured the outworks of St Elmo and it was obvious that the garrison could not hold out much longer. Life inside what was left of the battered fortress was intolerable; sleep was almost impossible, the noise incessant, the atmosphere inside the place fetid with the stink of rotting bodies and bits of bodies, blood and ordure, for the exhausted soldiers had to perform their natural functions at their posts, and on top of it all many of them were wounded and weak from loss of blood. Nevertheless, La Valette took the decision at this time, if he had not already done so, that the fort must be held to the last man; for shortly after the Turkish attack on 3 June he had received news that he could expect no relief from Sicily until the end of the month, and he knew that the longer St Elmo held out and the more Turkish lives and shot were wasted on it, the better were the chances of holding the main fortifications, when eventually they were attacked. So further volunteers to replace the dead in the doomed fortress were ferried across to it each night, though only with greatly increased difficulty and risk, and the battle there went on.

Then on 18 June the Turks suffered a disaster which desperately discouraged them. Dragut was killed by a splinter of stone thrown up by a cannonball. He had walked out with Mustafa to inspect some work being done on a new gun site, and as usual he had not tried to take cover or hide himself from the enemy. In all probability a Christian gunner had spotted the two men in their distinctive clothing, and had deliberately fired at them; his cannonball had missed, but the splinter of stone struck the old man behind his right ear, and he fell to the ground with blood spurting from his ears and nose. He was carried to his tent, where, although he was not dead on arrival, it was obvious that he could not possibly survive for long. Mustafa tried to keep the news of his injury secret, but the troops soon learned that the 'Sword of Islam' had at last been struck down, and the certainty of his imminent death deeply depressed them. God no longer seemed to be fighting on their side.

But the end was drawing near for the men in St Elmo. It was impossible to reinforce them any more, for the Turks patrolled the southern shore of Mount Sciberras, and as soon as a boat was seen leaving the Borgo it was attacked with every available weapon. By the night of Friday, 22 June, the number of men capable of bearing arms in the fortress had been so greatly reduced by death and injury that those who were left knew that they would not be able to withstand the next major onslaught. There were two Chaplains among the surviving Knights and soldiers, and in the small hours of Saturday morning they said mass, and everyone received the sacrament. At dawn, the expected attack was launched after a furious bombardment, and as the guns lifted their muzzles the Janissaries came on in such dense hordes that to watchers from the battlements of St Angelo across the Grand Harbour they looked like a great white flood pouring over the rocky ruins of the fortress. The defenders fought with their usual dogged ferocity, cutting bloody paths through the oncoming hordes of Turks with their cannon and firing their arquebuses until the barrels were almost too hot to hold; for an hour they held Mustafa's army at bay, but it could not go on, and at ten in the morning the guns fell silent. St Elmo had fallen at last, and Mustafa sent a messenger at once to carry the good news to the dying Dragut in his tent; when he heard it, he closed his eyes and died. But if the old corsair was happy as he breathed his last breath, the euphoria of victory brought little happiness to Mustafa. He was too much of a realist to ignore the appalling cost of his victory, and as he stood on the ruins of the fortress, and looked across the harbour to the massive and forbidding walls of St Angelo, it is said that he exclaimed, 'My God! If so small a son has cost us so dear, what price shall we have to pay for so large a father?'

The fall of St Elmo was the beginning of the end of the battle of Malta, and it had a brutal sequel. Mustafa had the bodies of the Knights collected and stripped of their armour and clothing; they were then decapitated, and the headless trunks were nailed to wooden crosses in derisory imitation of the Crucifixion, before being thrown into the harbour where they floated gently before the wind, to be washed up at the foot of Fort St Angelo on the morning of Sunday, 24 June, as the Knights and the Maltese were returning to their posts on the battlements after mass; some of the corpses had had the sign of the cross carved into the flesh of their chests and abdomens. When the

Grand Master was told of the arrival of this grisly harvest of the sea, he gave orders that all Turkish prisoners should be beheaded, and that their corpses, too, should be thrown into the water. Their heads were to be carefully collected, and brought to the ramparts of St Angelo, where the gunners were to fire them into the Turkish lines 'to teach the Moslems a lesson in humanity', as one chronicler of the siege put it.

With St Elmo in Turkish hands, Piali could at last bring his whole fleet safely into the shelter of Marsamuscetto, from which anchorage it was much easier to supply the army on shore; but even while his ships were dropping anchor there, the fact that the Turks had not bothered to subdue the northern half of the island was once again shown to be a disastrous mistake. For at this critical juncture in the war the Christians were strengthened by the arrival of a small but immensely useful relief force consisting of forty-two Knights led by the Chevalier de Robles, twenty-five other officers – most from Italy but a few from Germany and from England – and 600 imperial Spanish infantry sent by Don Garcia of Toledo. They had landed undetected in the northern part of the island and had managed to make their way under cover, first of darkness and then of a most opportune sea mist, to within hailing distance of the walls of the Borgo, where they had identified themselves and had immediately been admitted to the city. Needless to say, their arrival raised the spirits of the defenders and infuriated the Turks when they realized what had happened.

But the jubilation of the Knights was short-lived. They were not unduly worried to see the enemy slowly but inexorably dragging his guns into position on the Corradino heights, while others were sited on the landward side of the Borgo and across Kalkara Creek, for they had expected to be surrounded after the fall of St Elmo; but a few days later something happened which worried them very much indeed. Mustafa, perhaps acting on an idea suggested to him by Dragut before he died, began to manhandle his ships across Mount Sciberras and launch them on to the waters of the Marsa, and this was a potentially disastrous development; for the western shore of Senglea was virtually unfortified. The Knights had always relied on the guns of Fort St Angelo to prevent any enemy ships from entering the Grand Harbour, and thus it had never occurred to them to build defences along the shore of French Creek, though the landward neck of the Senglea peninsula was strongly held by Fort St Michael. When La Valette saw the Turkish fleet being dragged painfully across the rocky terrain of Sciberras by teams of oxen, mules, horses and slaves he was dismayed; but fortunately their progress was exceedingly slow, and he knew that he had a few days in which to build emergency defences against this new menace. He wasted no time in mobilizing every available man to erect as strong a stockade as possible along the threatened shore line. In the event it was finished just in time, and when a combined attack by sea and land was let loose upon Senglea the Knights were ready for it. Even so, the fighting which followed was some of the fiercest and most bloody of the war, and if it had not been for a minor miracle at the last minute, Senglea would almost certainly have been captured by the Janissaries; but just when the Grand Master had begun to resign himself to its loss, the Turks were suddenly ordered to retreat, and to the utter astonishment of the exhausted defenders they turned and fled.

Senglea was saved, though no one could understand what had induced Mustafa to call off his men just when victory was within their grasp. In fact, the Turkish commander had had no choice in the matter, for at the height of the battle he had been informed that his base camp had been overrun by enemy forces, the sick and wounded were being massacred, and his stores and ammunition were being burned. In corroboration of this shattering news, he could hear a series of great explosions coming from the direction of the camp near the Marsa, and he could see a great column of brown smoke billowing up into the sky there. Imagining that at last Don Garcia of Toledo must have landed on the island with a large relief force, he returned to the camp as fast as he could to find it in ruins and strewn with corpses. A relief force had not landed, but a small force of Christian cavalry from Mdina, hearing the noise of the battle and guessing correctly that Mustafa's base camp would have been left almost undefended, had swooped down on it and destroyed it. By the time Mustafa arrived, they had gone.

It was shortly after this that the Grand Master received news that Don Garcia of Toledo was indeed hoping to come to his rescue with a relief force of 16,000 men before the end of August. Help had been promised so often, however, that he was reluctant to trust Don Garcia's word, for his scepticism about the reliability of princely promises was almost as great as his trust in God. He therefore informed the Knights that no help could be expected from outside, and that everyone must fight while he still had breath in his body, trusting only in divine Providence to bring ultimate victory; if they died in the process, the Pope had granted a plenary indulgence to all who fell fighting Islam, thus ensuring their eternal salvation, and no Christian could wish for a more glorious consummation than that. As news of his words spread, Knights and Maltese alike, together with the Spanish soldiers and the handful of men from Germany and England, resigned themselves to their fate, knowing that the only alternative to death in battle was probably to be tortured to death by the enemy, if they were captured alive. Up to this moment, it is probable that some of the Knights and many of the Maltese, remembering what had happened in Rhodes, had entertained the idea that, if the worst came to the worst, the Grand Master could arrange an honourable surrender, as de L'Isle Adam had succeeded in doing forty-three years earlier; but when they heard La Valette's words, they knew that there was to be no surrender.

For the whole of the month of August they fought with the kind of single-minded tenacity that only men who have decided to die rather than yield an inch to their enemies are capable of displaying. The heat in Malta in high summer is intense, for it is a hundred miles nearer the Equator than either Tunis or Algiers, and it is a mystery how men in armour were able to continue fighting all day when the temperature was often in the nineties or higher; yet the Knights did so day after day, and not one of them died from heat stroke as far as is known. The Turkish bombardment was heavy and incessant, and as the month went by the whole place began to stink as putrefying corpses rotted in the sun between the Turkish lines and the crumbling Christian walls. The great fortifications – Fort St Angelo, the Borgo, and Fort St Michael in Senglea – were gradually reduced to vast, craggy lumps of stone and rubble, reeking of dust and death, as St Elmo had been in its last stages. The hospital was crammed with badly wounded men; corpses lay in the streets for want of people with the time to bury them, and though there was never any threat of starvation or death from thirst, food and water had to be rationed and used only sparingly. Nevertheless, time after time, when the Turks made breaches in the wall and launched their best troops in overwhelming numbers upon the handful of hot and tired men still capable of fighting, they were thrown back after suffering terrible casualties.

The last of these great frontal attacks came on 23 August, and for a time it looked as if it was bound to succeed; inside the Borgo the last reserves of men were called upon to fight, even the wounded men being carried to the walls where they could fire at the advancing enemy, while the women and children of Malta carried ammunition, food and water to the men in the firing line. Yet, as the sun began to sink in the late afternoon, Mustafa had to call off his men; they had done everything any men could be expected to do to overcome their enemies, and they had failed. Once again, the Knights had managed to hang on, but even to a man with a faith as unshakable as that of the Grand Master, it seemed unlikely that they would be able to do so again. They, too, had done everything any men could be expected to do, and could do no more. The end, it seemed, had come.

But Mustafa had troubles of his own, of which the Knights knew nothing, though they may have guessed at some. The Turkish camp was riddled with dysentery, enteritis and a fever, possibly malaria, which had filled the place with sick and dying men; between 10,000 and 15,000 Turkish soldiers had already been killed in battle; ammunition, especially powder and cannonballs, was beginning to run out; food was short; the season was getting late, and the equinoctial gales of September were approaching too fast for Piali's liking, while, worst of all, the morale of the surviving troops had sunk almost to vanishing point. They had endured severe reverses with great courage, but again and again they had failed to break the resistance of their Christian enemies, and by the end of August they had come to believe, with the fatalism of their race, that it was simply not the will of God that they should take Malta, though God alone knew why. So the heart had gone out of them, and when they were ordered to attack once again on the first day of September, they obeyed with such a lack of dash and determination that their effort was doomed to failure almost before it began.

Meanwhile, in Sicily after months of hesitation and indecision, Don Garcia was at last preparing to come to the aid of his fellow Christians on Malta. At the time, he was bitterly blamed for taking so long about it, and the anger and impatience of the Knights and the Maltese are understandable; but it is less easy to see why so many historians have followed their example, condemning him as incompetent and even as a coward. He may have been over-cautious, but this is as understandable as the impatience of the Knights, for Don Garcia was responsible for the safety of all the Spanish possessions in the Mediterranean, and he knew that if he had thrown away the imperial fleet and a large part of the imperial army in an unsuccessful attempt to bring relief to Malta, the result would have been catastrophic. Moreover, as far as he knew Piali's fleet and Mustafa's army were greatly superior to anything he could muster, and presumably little help could be expected from the Knights themselves who were reported to be at their last gasp. His caution, therefore, was not only understandable but laudable, even if it meant that the Knights had to wait a long time for his coming; but come eventually he did, for after a false start in which the fleet from Sicily was dispersed by a sudden gale, twenty-eight galleys anchored unopposed in Melleiha Bay in the north of the island on 7 September.

Just how many disembarked from them has been the subject of dispute, but it was probably nearer to 8,000 than to 12,000, as some have suggested. Whatever the number may have been, it was small enough to alarm the Grand Master when he received news of their arrival, and he decided to try to help them by a *ruse de guerre*; summoning a Moslem galley slave to his presence, he told the man that he was to be released as an act of clemency in thanksgiving to God for the arrival of a Christian army of 16,000 crack troops, who were about to wipe out the Turkish invaders. On reaching the Turkish lines, the man was questioned, as La Valette had known that he would be, and the news that an army of 16,000 men had landed in the north of the island was immediately passed on to Mustafa. To the Turkish commander it was the last straw; he was disheartened already by the long series of reverses which his men had suffered, and he knew that they were hardly capable of fighting another battle, so badly had their morale been affected by their losses and failures. The advent of so large a force of fresh, highly trained troops left him no alternative but to abandon the siege, and he ordered an immediate evacuation of the island. La Valette's deception had been brilliantly successful.

But it was not the last episode in the battle of Malta; there was one more to come. All that night, the weary Christians could hear the rumble and creaking of the Turkish guns, as they were dismantled and dragged down to the water's edge to be embarked on the waiting ships, and in the morning the Turkish lines were empty and deserted by all but the dead. The survivors were embarking on Piali's ships in Marsamuscetto on the other side of Mount Sciberras as fast as the fleet's small boats could ferry them out to the waiting galleys and transports, some of which were already under way, and it looked as if the long-drawn-out battle for the island was finally over. But it was not.

The relief force in the north had marched inland from Melleiha Bay, and had taken up a strong defensive position on a hill to await the attack which their commander was sure that Mustafa with his superior numbers would shortly launch upon him; he had no idea that the Grand Master had tricked the Turks into believing that his force was much stronger than it actually was, and he did not know that Mustafa was embarking his troops and preparing to sail away. Meanwhile, Mustafa, surprised by the absence of the enemy, had sent some cavalry scouts to find them, and it had not been long before they had returned with the news that the newly arrived troops were not nearly so numerous as he had been led to believe. Realizing that he had been duped, Mustafa immediately stopped the evacuation of the island, and ordered his men to disembark again. Piali, who was interested only in the safety of his fleet, was furious, and the two men had a fierce argument; but Mustafa was adamant, and watchers on the heights above Marsamuscetto suddenly saw the Turkish troops streaming ashore again. A message was sent immediately to the commander of the relief force to tell him that the Turks were on their way, and when he heard that the enemy was at last approaching he drew his men up on a hill overlooking the road down which they were marching, and there he fully intended to stay until he was attacked; but when the enemy came in sight, the more enthusiastic and excitable of his troops, some of them Knights who had been trying to join their brethren for months without success, decided otherwise, and as soon as Mustafa's vanguard was within striking distance, they charged down the hill upon it without waiting for the word of command. Seeing them spur their horses into a gallop, the rest of the troops immediately followed them downhill, and the commander, bowing to the inevitable, gave the order to charge.

Then, as now, the Turks were some of the best fighting men in the world; but physically exhausted and mentally dejected by their long series of defeats, the first good news they had had for weeks had been the news that they were going to embark on the ships waiting to take them home, and it had been a miracle of discipline that they had obeyed Mustafa's order to disembark after actually finding themselves on board; even their iron discipline was not enough to induce them to withstand a sudden and violent attack by fresh troops eager for battle, and they broke and ran for the nearby shore of St Paul's Bay, where some of Piali's ships had already arrived ready to pick them up. Despite a desperate attempt by Mustafa to organize a rearguard action, in which he himself fought with conspicuous bravery, over 3,000 of his men were killed as they struggled to reach the safety of Piali's galleys once again. When at last the fighting ceased, the water of the bay was so thick with Turkish corpses that no one could go near the place for days because of the stench.

The victory of the Knights and their Maltese allies was complete, but it had been won at great cost. Of the Grand Master's original force of about 9,000 men only 600 were still capable of bearing arms at the end of the siege, and nearly all of these bore scars of battle. Of the Knights, 250 had been killed, and the majority of those who had survived had suffered terrible injuries, while 7,000 Maltese and Spanish soldiers had lost their lives. But if the Christian defenders of Malta had suffered terribly, their losses were nothing to those which they had inflicted on Suleiman's army. Mustafa had brought about 30,000 fighting men to the island with him in May, and as the summer had passed he had received large reinforcements; yet when he returned to Constantinople in October, fewer than 10,000 men were with him, and many of these were wounded. Between 20,000 and 30,000 Turks had been killed or had died of disease on Malta, and the great expedition, which was to have crowned Suleiman's old age with glory, had turned out to be the greatest disaster of his whole reign.

Suleiman.

A portrait of Roxelana in the Topkapi Palace. This is not a work taken from life but from descriptions of the lady after her death. Indeed, judging from the style of the painting, it must have been done a long time after her demise.

Khaireddin Barbarossa, corsair and admiral of the Turkish fleet. Born of Greek parents on the island of Lesbos, he became the terror of Christian shipping in the Mediterranean and adjacent seas for many years, dying eventually in his eighties.

Suleiman's son and successor, Selim II, known as the Sot from his habitual drunkenness. With his reign the slow decline in Turkish fortunes began after they had reached their highest point under Suleiman.

The Battle of Lepanto on Sunday, October 7, 1571, during which the Turkish fleet was virtually annihilated by the combined Christian fleets of Spain, Venice, the Papal States and the Knights of St John under the command of Don John of Austria. It was destined to be the last great naval

action fought with galleys, and by the end of the day the Turks had lost 30,000 men and 280 ships to Don John's losses of 8,000 men and 15 ships. Although the Turks soon built another fleet, they never again dominated the western Mediterranean as they had done before Lepanto.

A contemporary Turkish painting of Selim II the Sot following Suleiman's bier to its resting place beside the body of Roxelana alongside the Suleimaniye Mosque. It is doubtful whether Selim felt much grief over his father's death; Suleiman could not have been the easiest of parents, for he had two of his sons strangled, and there must have been times when Selim wondered whether his own turn might not come next. Perhaps that is why he drank so much.

XV

✠ ✠ ✠

The Sultan's Hour

Think, in this battered Caravanserai
Whose doorways are alternate Night and Day,
    How Sultan after Sultan with his Pomp
Abode his destin'd Hour, and went his way.

                    Fitzgerald, *Omar Khayyám*

When Suleiman heard the news of the defeat of his army on Malta, it is said that he flew into a rage. 'I cannot trust any of my officers,' he shouted in disgust, throwing the letter he had received from Mustafa on the floor and stamping on it. 'Next year I myself, Sultan Suleiman, will lead an expedition against this damnable island, and I shall not spare a single islander.' As his tantrum subsided, however, his first concern was how to save his face after such a defeat, and he sent an urgent message to Piali forbidding him to bring the fleet into Constantinople until after darkness had fallen; he did not want the people of the city to see to what a pitiful remnant the grand army, which had sailed down the Bosphorus so proudly six months previously, had been reduced. Once again it is said that, when eventually Mustafa and Piali arrived, he greeted them icily with the words, 'I see that it is only in my own hand that my sword is invincible.' After that, he refused to speak to either of them.

But six months later in the spring of 1566, it was not against Malta that Suleiman set out but against Hungary once again. Whether it was bravery, obstinacy or anger which induced him to take the field in person at the head of his army despite his advanced age, it is impossible to say – perhaps all three emotions played their part; but whatever may have moved him to do so, it was a remarkable undertaking for he was over seventy years old, and those years had not been kind to him. A Venetian, Marcantonio Donini, has left a vivid picture of him at this time:

His Majesty during many months of the year was very feeble of body, so that he lacked little of dying, being dropsical, with swollen legs, appetite gone, and face swelled and of a very bad colour. In the month of March last, he had four or five fainting fits, and he has had one since, in which his attendants doubted whether he were alive or dead, and hardly expected that he would recover from them. According to the common opinion his death must occur soon, in spite of the strong remedies resorted to by his physician, unless indeed the gladness which he feels at the death of his sons and grandsons produces a miraculous effect on his health.

The cattiness of that last remark need not detract from the rest of Donini's description of the old man at this time, for de Busbecq has left a very similar picture of him, and he too commented on his unhealthy colour:

It may be that his bad complexion arises from some lurking malady. There is a notion current that he has an incurable cancer or ulcer on his thigh. When he is anxious to impress an ambassador, who is leaving, with a favourable idea of the state of his health, he conceals the bad complexion of his face under a coat of rouge, his notion being that foreign powers will fear him more if they think that he is strong and well.

Not surprisingly in view of his age and ill health, he could no longer sit on a horse, but he did not allow that to deter him; instead he rode everywhere in a carriage. The roads were rough, and although the troops had orders to make them as smooth as possible for the passage of the Sultan, the journey must have been excruciatingly uncomfortable, for the only respite from it was at night, when he retired to his own imperial tent with such luxuries as that could provide; yet although he suffered terribly from gout, there is no record of him making any complaints. As during previous campaigns in the Balkans, the weather made the journey even worse than it would anyway have been, for though Suleiman had not left Constantinople until the first day of May it rained incessantly, killing many of the camels used by the army as pack animals, and in a flood near Belgrade the imperial tent was washed away, though fortunately at a moment when Suleiman was elsewhere. Moreover, the country through which the army moved had been fought over so often and with such devastating effect that there were neither crops nor cattle to be found; only brigands abounded everywhere, desperate men forced into a life of banditry by the dereliction of the times, who attacked the army at night or whenever they thought that they could get away with a little loot without too much risk to themselves. Suleiman was so angry at the sheer impertinence of these outlaws, who dared to pit themselves against the whole might of the Ottoman army like mosquitoes attacking a lion, that he sent out punitive parties of soldiers to bring them in to his camp from their caves and hiding places, whereupon those who had not been killed in the process were summarily hanged. For months afterwards, the army's route was marked by rotting corpses hanging from the trees as a warning to others not to incur the Sultan's wrath by becoming robbers. It probably never occurred to Suleiman that the men whom he hanged had taken to a life of robbery in the first place simply because the wars, which he himself had waged over their country, had destroyed their homes and laid waste their farms and smallholdings so completely that no other way of life had been available to them.

Ferdinand had not long outlived his brother Charles, dying in 1564 and being succeeded as Emperor not by Charles's son Philip as arranged in his brother's lifetime, but by his own son Maximilian; and the ostensible object of Suleiman's campaign in 1566 was to chastise Maximilian for various breaches of the treaty of 1561 – not only had he failed to pay the tribute which had been agreed at that time, but he had attacked various towns held by the Turkish army of occupation, whose commanders were understandably indignant. Almost certainly Suleiman also meant to get his long-awaited revenge upon the fortress of Sziget, where he had been humiliated ten years previously, and as it happened events presented him with a perfect excuse to do so. For when at last he and the army reached Semlin towards the end of June, he received news that one of his favourite commanders, Mohammed of Trikalla, had been attacked and killed by a small force under the command of a celebrated Hungarian patriot, Count Nicholas Zrinyi, who had then moved on to Sziget. Suleiman, who had just received the young King Stephen, Zapolya's son, with great pomp and ceremony, immediately changed his plans, and gave orders that the army should march at full speed upon the castle at Sziget, which was to be destroyed with every human being found inside it; above all, the insolent and insufferable Zrinyi must not be allowed to live.

Sziget was built on an island in the River Almas in marshy country, and its only means of access was by a heavily fortified and defended causeway. It was a typical marsh castle with a great central keep, formidable walls and bastions, and a triple moat to complete its watery isolation. Zrinyi was well supplied with food, and water presented no problem; he also had ample stores of powder and cannonballs and fifty-four cannon, but he had only 2,500 men with whom to defend the place against the entire might of Suleiman's army. Thus the odds against him were even worse than those against

La Valette the year before on Malta, and the chances of so small a garrison surviving an attack by so huge a host were negligible. In origin, Zrinyi was a Croat, but he had married an aristocratic Hungarian heiress, and the combination of his marriage and the fame of his exploits against the Turks, whom he detested, had earned him the acceptance and even the admiration of the normally highly exclusivist members of the Hungarian nobility. When he found himself surrounded by the whole Turkish army, he reacted with typical bravado; as Suleiman travelled down the river by yacht to view the coming battle in comfort from its decks and cabins, Zrinyi hung great sheets of scarlet cloth over the walls of the castle, and covered the keep with plates of pewter, which glinted and shone like silver in the sun, and when he saw Suleiman's yacht arrive, he ordered his men to fire his largest cannon in a mocking salute to the Sultan.

The siege began on 5 August, and lasted much longer than even the most pessimistic of the besieging Turks could possibly have predicted, for Zrinyi and his men were inspired with the same kind of determination to resist *à outrance* as the Knights had shown in the battle for Malta. At first, the Turks attacked the place furiously in the hope of a quick victory, but after a fortnight's bitter and bloody fighting Suleiman was so impressed by the courage of the defenders that in a handsome gesture more typical of him as a young man than in his old age, he offered Zrinyi generous terms if he would surrender: terms which revealed that he was still capable of greatness of spirit. Zrinyi, however, refused to surrender, whereupon Suleiman tried to suborn his men by firing arrows into the fortress with messages in Hungarian and German attached to them offering safe conduct to all those who surrendered; but he had no greater success with the common soldiers than he had had with their commander. During the last weeks of August three more attacks were made upon the place, but to Suleiman's increasing fury they were repulsed with heavy losses. A week later, however, a huge mine under one of the castle's principal bastions was fired by the Turkish sappers and a great section of the wall collapsed in ruins; the flames from the explosion were blown by the wind as far as the citadel, and this was set on fire. Zrinyi knew that he could not hold out much longer, but by some miracle of endurance he and his men held the Turks at bay for another three days of incessant attacks, as they came on again and again over the rubble of the fallen wall shouting and screaming and calling on God to come to the aid of Islam. But by 8 September the garrison had been reduced to such straits that Zrinyi knew that the next Turkish attack was bound to succeed. Rather than await the inevitable, however, he decided to make the first move, and with those of his men who had survived the siege thus far he sallied forth over the mounds of Turkish corpses and rubble in a furious charge upon the astonished Ottoman army. He had no chance at all of victory, and he and all his men were killed in less than ten minutes of hand-to-hand fighting, but before they died they killed a good many Turks too, and for Zrinyi that was victory enough.

History is full of moments of irony, great and small, and the moment of Suleiman's victory over Zrinyi and his capture of the much hated castle of Sziget was just such a moment; for the old Sultan was denied the sweetness of knowing that he had had his revenge at last. During the night of 5 September, before the battle in which Zrinyi was killed and the castle captured, Suleiman died in his tent. No one knows for sure what caused his death; perhaps he had a heart attack brought on by the strains and exertions of the campaign, or perhaps he had a stroke. It is possible, of course, that the illness which had been responsible for the decline in his health during his last few years succeeded at last in killing him; but whatever it was, he was dead before anyone could bring him the news that Sziget had at last succumbed.

The Grand Vizier at the time was a man named Mehmed Sokollu, who had been born in Bosnia as the son of an Orthodox priest; picked out in the *devshirme* as a boy for service in the Sultan's household, he had been raised as a page in the palace, where he had soon attracted attention by the number of his talents. Over the years he had gone from strength to strength, serving in various capacities as Treasurer, Grand Admiral and finally Grand Vizier; but he had held this last position for only a year at the time of Suleiman's death, and a lesser man might well have failed to rise to the occasion or even have given way to panic at the thought of the responsibility so suddenly thrust upon him. But Sokollu was equal to the challenge and, having sent an urgent message to Selim to inform him of his father's death and to encourage him to go to Constantinople as quickly as he could to claim his rightful inheritance, he made his first important decision: for the time being, he would keep the Sultan's death a secret, for he feared that news of it might demoralize the troops and even perhaps lead to riots. Some historians have alleged that he took the need for secrecy so seriously that he had Suleiman's physician strangled to ensure his silence, but this may not be true. What is certainly true is that he put it about that the Sultan was confined to his tent with an attack of gout, but that despite his indisposition he was quite capable of attending to his daily business. Sokollu then issued orders each morning as if they came from Suleiman himself; promotions and rewards were given to those who had earned them by their courage in the recent battle for Sziget; positions made vacant by death were filled, and new appointments were announced; Zrinyi's head was sent to Maximilian with the Sultan's compliments, and letters announcing his victory were sent to the Khan of the Crimean Tatars, the Shah of Persia and the Sherif of Mecca.

While all this was going on, Suleiman's entrails were removed and buried; his body was then embalmed, and placed in his litter. When Sokollu eventually gave the order in Suleiman's name for the army to begin the long march home, the litter was escorted by guards in exactly the same way as on the outward journey, as if it still contained a living Sultan. After three weeks, however, the Grand Vizier at last received the news for which he had been waiting, namely, that Selim had arrived in the capital; and he knew that the time for concealment was over. He summoned the commanders of the army to his tent that night, and broke the news to them that Suleiman was dead. As soon as it was light the next morning, the muezzins began to call the army to prayer as usual, but on this particular morning their summons was followed by the sound of the prayer for the dead being chanted round the Sultan's litter, and as the soldiers stumbled out of their tents in the grey light of dawn, they realized what had happened. They were appalled by the news of his death. For longer than most of them could remember they had been led by Suleiman, and for forty-five years, despite a few reverses, he had led them from victory to victory, during which time the Ottoman Empire had reached a pinnacle of power and prestige undreamed of even by the greatest of his predecessors. They listened without enthusiasm to the Grand Vizier exhorting them to show their love for him by their loyal obedience to his son, the glorious Sultan Selim II, who now reigned in his father's stead; but they cheered up a little when Sokollu reminded them that by tradition their new Sultan would be sure to distribute handsome gifts of money to his faithful troops as soon as they reached Constantinople. So the march was resumed, and the army which Suleiman had so often led out to war carried him home to lay him to eternal rest next to Roxelana.

When news of his death reached the capital, at first the people of the city could not believe it; for them, as for the soldiers, the Sultan had been part of the landscape of their lives for so long that they could not imagine what life would be like without him. But as his body was laid in the place prepared for it beside the mosque which he himself had built, the Suleimaniye, the reality of his death came home to them and they mourned his loss as irreparable, while the Christian world rejoiced at the passing of its greatest enemy. Both were right to do so, for his loss to Turkey was indeed irreparable, and never again would Christians have to face a man half as great as Suleiman on the throne of the Ottoman Sultans.

XVI

✠ ✠ ✠

The Last Battle

Know that tomorrow the last of many battles
We mean to fight.

Shakespeare, *Antony and Cleopatra*

Though the reign of Suleiman ended with his death, there is a sense in which the age of Suleiman did not end quite so suddenly; for although Selim the Sot, as his successor became known, was a hopelessly unworthy heir to his father, Mehmed Sokollu continued to be Grand Vizier under the new Sultan, and the true reins of government were not to be found in Selim's hands but in those of Sokollu. He was destined to exercise power for thirteen years, and during most of that time the Ottoman Empire was still ruled in the way to which it had become accustomed under Suleiman; only rarely did the drunken Selim interfere, and then it usually had disastrous consequences. Five years after Suleiman's death, in one of his frequent moments of alcoholic exuberance he asserted himself in just such a way, and the consequence of his bibulous intrusion into affairs which would have been much better left in Sokollu's capable hands was to precipitate a disaster, which did indeed bring the age of Suleiman to an end once and for all.

One of the new Sultan's boon companions was a Levantine Jew named Joseph Nasi, who had spent some time in Portugal, where he had been converted to the Christian faith; it seems, however, that his conversion was more a matter of expediency than true conviction, for as soon as he emigrated to Turkey he met a young Jewess as rich as she was beautiful, whereupon he promptly re-embraced the faith of his fathers, abjuring his newly won Christianity in order to marry the lady. With her fortune at his disposal, he set out to capture the favour of the heir to the throne, as Selim was at that time, by showering him with presents and by entertaining him in the way he enjoyed most with an endless supply of the best possible vintage wines, many of which came from Cyprus. This so delighted Selim that when he became Sultan he granted Nasi a monopoly of the wine trade. But even before this, although the Jew was old enough to be Selim's father, the two men became such inseparable companions that the rumour began to circulate in Constantinople that Nasi actually was Selim's father. Why otherwise was the young heir to the throne so entirely different from Suleiman? If the luxury-loving Jew from Portugal had somehow been surreptitiously introduced into the harem as a dashing young man in his early twenties, much would be explained; and no one was prepared to put it past Roxelana to have welcomed a change of bedfellow. It was nonsense, of course, but the fact that it became common gossip is a tribute to Nasi's success in wheedling himself so deeply into Selim's favour that, when he wanted to do so, he could exercise great power. Normally, the most powerful man in the Ottoman Empire after the reigning Sultan was his Grand Vizier, and in Selim's time Mehmed Sokollu exercised that power; but in some ways Nasi was even more powerful than Sokollu, for without being Grand Vizier he wielded much the same sort of personal influence over the Sultan as Ibrahim had exerted over Suleiman. Unlike Ibrahim, however, Nasi seldom used his power wisely or for purposes other than his own selfish ends.

Paradoxically, it was the Jew's selfishness which rendered his influence on the Sultan comparatively harmless most of the time, for usually it meant that he did not concern himself with matters of state but only with his own self-enrichment. Unfortunately, however, for some reason Nasi hated the Venetians, though no one knows why, and over the years his hatred became so obsessional that he did everything in his power to turn the Sultan against them. One day in 1570, five years after Suleiman's death, when Selim was neither sober enough to be sensible nor drunk enough to be insensible but just sufficiently inebriated to suit the Jew's purposes, Nasi suggested to him that it would be both easier and much less expensive to procure an ample supply of the best wines from Cyprus if that island was annexed to the Ottoman Empire. The Venetians had no right to be there, and it was high time that they were turned out of the place by the glorious Sultan's invincible army. The glorious Sultan was delighted by the idea and promised that, once the island was conquered, he, Nasi, should become King of it. The Jew had already been made Duke of Naxos and the twelve principal islands of the Cyclades, but the prospect of kingship raised his hopes to such an exalted point that he had the arms of Cyprus hung up in his house over the inscription: 'Joseph, King of Cyprus'.

Instead of forgetting the whole thing and despite Mehmed Sokollu's vigorous opposition, Selim sent an envoy to Venice with a long list of grievances against the Republic and a demand from the Sultan that they should either be redressed at once, or Cyprus should be ceded to Turkey in compensation for the injuries inflicted on her. Since Turkey was at peace with Venice, and most of the alleged grievances were imaginary, the Venetian senate quite rightly refused either to apologize or to relinquish the island. Justice was on their side, but Selim was more interested in the wines of Cyprus than in justice, and in March 1570, having given command of the army to a certain Lala Mustafa and that of the fleet to Piali Pasha, he overruled the objections of his Grand Vizier and ordered Lala Mustafa and Piali to throw the Venetians out of Cyprus by force. War inevitably followed.

Then, as now, the peasants of Cyprus were Greek, for Venice had acquired the island only after the sack of Constantinople, when the men of the Fourth Crusade had sat down to carve up the Byzantine Empire and to share it out amongst themselves, and the Cypriots had never liked their Venetian overlords. Knowing this, when the Turks landed in Limassol Bay on 1 August 1570, they adopted a conciliatory policy towards the local people, putting it about that it was only with the Venetians that they had a quarrel, and that they meant no harm to the Cypriots. Partly as a result of this approach, Limassol surrendered to them at once, when called upon to do so, and Lala Mustafa was as good as his word; the lives and property of the inhabitants were scrupulously protected. But when he reached Nicosia a fortnight later, it refused to surrender, and Mustafa abandoned any further pretence at benevolence; he was a brutal man and sheep's clothing did not suit his wolfish ways. The siege of Nicosia lasted seven weeks, and when at last it surrendered the survivors of the garrison were massacred and the place itself was given over to a sack, which has been compared for savagery to the sack of Constantinople. Only the young were spared, being reserved for the enjoyment of any Turk rich enough to buy one or two of them as slaves. As it turned out, however, they were rescued from this fate, so often classed as worse than death, by a noble Venetian (or possibly Greek) lady with an exalted idea of the value of chastity; she put a match to a large store of gunpowder in the hold of the galley, in which a thousand of these future purveyors of Turkish delight were about to set sail for Constantinople, thus blowing them all to smithereens but with their virginity triumphantly intact.

With the sufferings of the people of Nicosia very much in mind, the citizens of Famagusta were determined to resist to the very last rather than suffer a similar fate. They were commanded by a brave man named Marcantonio Bragadino, who defied Mustafa's command to surrender the city and inspired his fellow citizens to prodigies of valour and endurance, but after a siege of three months' duration, when they were reduced to eating their half-starved horses, donkeys and dogs, they had little alternative but to ask for terms of surrender. So, on the morning of 1 August 1571, they ran up a white flag above the citadel, and hostages were exchanged between the two sides to ensure the safety of those engaged in the coming peace talks. On the Christian side these were conducted by two leading citizens of Famagusta, who were welcomed by one of Mustafa's sons with the utmost courtesy and taken to the tent of the commander of the Janissaries, who complimented them upon the outstanding bravery of those who had defended the city for so long. Thus all seemed set fair for an honourable agreement, and indeed by the end of the day the Venetians had agreed to capitulate on the understanding that they were to be allowed to leave the city with their arms, their belongings, five cannon and three horses belonging to the three Venetian commanders, and then proceed by ship to Crete in vessels supplied for them by the Turks; the inhabitants were also to be allowed to leave with their possessions, if they wished to do so, while the safety of those who chose to stay was guaranteed. Meanwhile, the Turks would retire to a distance of three miles from the city.

They were remarkably generous terms, worthy of Suleiman at his greatest and not unlike those granted to de L'Isle Adam at the end of the siege of Rhodes, and at first they were strictly observed by the Turks. In fact, when some of the Venetian soldiers approached the Turkish camp out of sheer curiosity, they were welcomed in a most friendly way and with every sign of respect for their courage throughout the siege. Three days later, the evacuation of Famagusta was complete, and Bragadino sent a messenger to Lala Mustafa to say that he hoped to have the honour of presenting the keys of the city to him that evening. Mustafa replied that it would give him the greatest pleasure to meet the brave commanders of the men, who had proved themselves to be such worthy opponents, and that he would await their visit with impatience. So, three hours after sunset, Bragadino presented himself and a number of other high-ranking Venetians at the Turkish camp, and they were led with due ceremony into the presence of Lala Mustafa, who greeted them all with impeccable civility. The last act in the drama of the callous invasion of Cyprus seemed about to bring one of the most dishonourable incidents in Turkish history to a close on an unexpectedly honourable note. It did not do so.

What happened next is clear, though why it happened is not. Lala

Mustafa inquired of Bragadino what guarantee he could give for the safe return of the Turkish galleys which were taking the garrison to Crete, and when the Venetian commander replied that such a guarantee had not been part of the terms of surrender, the Turk demanded a hostage instead. Bragadino, perhaps more abruptly than was tactful, refused, and within seconds a fierce row had broken out between the two men. Lala Mustafa now threw off all pretence of amiability, and ordered the guard to strangle the Venetians with the exception of Bragadino, who was forced to watch as a bowstring was tightened around the necks of his friends until all of them fell dead. Utterly horrified, he was held fast, while a soldier cut off his nose and ears; bleeding profusely, he was then dragged from the Turkish commander's tent, and thrown into a cell. A messenger was ordered to take ship and catch up with the vessels on their way to Crete with instructions to them to return to Cyprus at once, and when they reached the island the Christians on board were sent to the slave market for sale.

It is impossible to tell whether all this was the result of a deliberate deception by Lala Mustafa, who had never had any intention of honouring the terms of surrender signed by Bragadino, or whether he genuinely lost his temper because of the Venetian's haughty refusal to leave a hostage to guarantee the safe return of the Turkish ships after they had delivered their human cargo in Crete. He was a notoriously violent man, from whom no one would normally have expected to receive the kind of honourable treatment and generous terms of surrender granted to the garrison of Famagusta, and this lends credence to the idea that he deliberately deceived them. On the other hand, why should he have bothered to do so, when he had them in his power anyway? It seems more probable that for once he was genuinely moved by the courage of his Venetian enemies, and that this induced him to act with untypical generosity, but that his benevolence gave way to a more customary homicidal mood when he felt himself to be insulted by Bragadino. If that is the true explanation, then Bragadino was forced to pay an appalling price for his moment of thoughtless incivility. After ten days in chains, he was publicly tortured, while Lala Mustafa looked on laughing. Eventually he was flayed alive, and his skin was stuffed with straw; it was then promenaded around the town on the back of a cow before being sent to Constantinople as a present to Selim together with the rotting heads of the other Venetian nobles who had been strangled.

This unprovoked attack on Cyprus by the Turks proved too much for the Christian powers to swallow, as Mehmed Sokollu had feared might be the case. Pius V, who was Pope at the time, was not the man to sit idly by as Christians were maltreated by the Turks. As a young man, he had been appointed Inquisitor in Como, where his treatment of anyone suspected of the slightest taint of heresy had been so savage that he had had to be recalled, and a consuming and icy hatred of all heretics and infidels was the driving force of his ministry for the rest of his life. No one can pretend that he was an appealing man, but he was exceedingly able, and on his inexorable way to the papacy he collected successively a bishopric, a cardinal's hat and the office of Grand Inquisitor. Once firmly seated on St Peter's throne, he intensified the bloody persecution of heretics, greeting the news of the massacre of St Bartholomew's Day with grim satisfaction, while wasting no sympathy on the slaughtered Huguenots for whom he considered death too good a fate. In this and other similar ways, he demonstrated the Christian zeal for which he became both famous and much feared, and in virtue of which he was later canonized. But before that well-deserved seal of God's approval could be set upon his saintly, if bloodstained, career, he did the one thing from which Europe and his fellow Christians actually derived some positive benefit: he formed a Holy League to counter any further aggression upon which the Sultan Selim might decide to embark in another of his moments of alcoholic euphoria, and to chastise him for his invasion of Cyprus.

In the summer of 1571 a triple alliance was formed between Spain, Venice and the papacy. As usual, France stood aloof from fear of doing anything which might be to the advantage of Spain; indeed, she went further, and tried to prevent the formation of any such league against her ally, Turkey, but failed to do so. Venice, too, was afraid of doing anything to increase the power of Spain at the expense of Italy, while the Spaniards had little love for the Venetians, who had been so keen to protect their eastern trade that for years they had acted almost like vassals of the Ottoman Sultans. However, when these mutual suspicions had been overcome a number of other Italian states agreed to act in concert with the Holy League, and the Knights of Malta offered their services to the allies if they should be needed in any future campaign against the Turks, and especially in any naval campaign, for which they were both well situated in their island fortress and well equipped with ships; and in fact it was at sea that the alliance was destined to carry the war to the enemy.

The combined fleets of the contracting parties formed a formidable force by any standards, but it was obvious to everyone that its effectiveness would depend upon the quality of its commander; for like all allied forces, the various national contingents of which it was composed could only be welded together by the man at the top. Eventually, supreme command was given to Don John of Austria, the bastard son of the Emperor Charles by Barbara Blomberg, who had caught his fancy a quarter of a century previously. The product of this somewhat improbable union had grown up to be a fine young man, and although he was only twenty-four years old his appointment proved to be an inspired choice, for Don John had precisely the gift of leadership which was needed to unite and enthuse the polyglot armada over which he was set. It consisted of 200 galleys and six huge heavily armed galleasses from Venice, and it was manned by 30,000 fighting troops from almost every European country except France. As it assembled, news arrived that the Ottoman fleet was ravaging the Dalmatian coast, and it was there that Don John decided to seek battle, as soon as the Christian fleet was ready to set sail from Messina, where the various contingents had been gathered together.

He weighed anchor on 25 September 1571 and set sail eastwards in the direction of Corfu, which the Turks were once again besieging, but on reaching the island he was told that they had already raised the siege and sailed away southwards. News was also received at this time of the fall of Famagusta and of the treatment received by Bragadino and his men at the hands of Lala Mustafa, and this did little to lessen the hatred which every Christian felt for the Turks; anger mounted throughout the fleet and the men vowed that when at last they met the enemy they would exact vengeance for the crimes committed in Cyprus. In fact, they were to get the opportunity to do so sooner than they could have guessed, for the Turkish fleet had anchored in the Gulf of Patras, and as Don John's ships sailed south in search of them they were spotted by the Turks as they sailed between the Ionian islands of Cephalonia and Ithaca. It was Sunday, 7 October 1571.

While mass was being said on board the Christian ships an argument was taking place on the Turkish flagship, where the admiral in supreme command, Muhsinzade Ali Pasha, was listening to the advice of some of his senior officers, who considered that he should stay on the defensive, remaining where he was, allowing the Christian ships to come into the narrow waters of the Gulf, if they dared; but one of his deputy commanders, the celebrated corsair Uluj Ali, the Dey of Algiers, poured scorn on such timidity. They were not at sea to behave like nurse-maids, he said, but to destroy the infidels and to capture their fleet for the Sultan, and Muhsinzade Ali Pasha agreed with him. Orders were therefore given for the fleet to weigh anchor and sail out to engage the Christian armada. In numbers, Ali Pasha was slightly superior to Don John; he had 273 ships under his command, but they were of lighter build than the Christian galleys, and they were also outgunned by Don John's ships, all of which were armed with heavier cannon and carried a larger number of arquebusiers aboard than did the Turkish vessels. But as the Turkish fleet sailed out of the sheltered waters of the Gulf of Patras, leaving the little coastal town of Lepanto (the modern Naupactos) behind them, to form a long line abreast in the open waters of the Ionian sea, it had one inestimable advantage over its enemy: a well-earned reputation for invincibility, which endowed its crews with supreme self-confidence, and which struck fear into the hearts of Don John's men before ever a shot had been fired by either side.

The battle which was about to begin was destined to be the last great naval battle to be fought by galleys, and as each side manoeuvred into position they must have presented an observer on the shore with a remarkable sight, the sea covered with a forest of ships' masts, their many coloured triangular lateen sails poised as elegantly as sea birds against the blue of the Greek sky. The Turkish fleet was divided into three squadrons facing their Christian enemies; as supreme commander, Ali Pasha took up his position in the centre of the line, his ship, the *Sultana*, marked by a sacred banner from Mecca embroidered with verses from the Koran; on his starboard side between him and the coast was the Bey of Alexandria, Mehmed Chuluk, who was universally known as Scirocco, while on his port side to seaward Uluj Ali was in command. Opposite Ali Pasha, Don John of Austria also took command of the centre or 'battle' in his flagship, *La Real*, flying the papal banner with a figure of Christ crucified on it, while to seaward of him facing Scirocco the Proveditore Agostino Barbarigo, a Venetian, was in command of the ships from Venice, and to landward Gian Andrea Doria, a nephew of the man who had served the Emperor Charles for so long, commanded the Genoese squadron opposite Uluj Ali. In front of the Christian fleet, evenly spaced in a line and looking like ponderous great floating forts, Don John had stationed the galleasses where they would be able to rake Turkish ships with their broadsides as they passed between them; and he kept a squadron in reserve behind the main fleet under the command of the Marquess of Santa Cruz. Somewhere in the Christian fleet a young Spaniard named Cervantes, whose left hand would be shattered by a Turkish bullet during the course of the day, was preparing himself for the coming battle; somewhere else an equally young Englishman named Richard Grenville, who was to win immortal fame later in the century off the Azores in his ship *Revenge*, was doing the same thing, and so were 30,000 other Christians and a similar number of soldiers of the Prophet.

For a time the two fleets confronted each other in silence except for the noise of the wind in the rigging and the waves curling and breaking on the ships' sides. Autumn in Greece, though cooler than summer, is often as fair a time as any earlier in the year, and on this particular Sunday in early October the sun shone in a cloudless sky over the deeper blue of the Ionian Sea. The feelings of the men as they waited for the guns to open fire can only be imagined, but probably a sense of awe at the enormity of that which was about to happen was uppermost in the minds of most of them, as it was in that of Cervantes. It was, he said after the battle, 'the most memorable and lofty occasion which past centuries have beheld; nor do those to come hope to see the like'. The first sign that a watcher on the shore would have had that the battle was about to begin was a puff of white smoke followed by the thud of a cannon shot from Ali Pasha's flagship. It was more of a salute and a challenge than a shot fired in anger, for the round had been blank; but Don John replied with a cannonball, which whistled through the rigging of the Turkish ships before falling harmlessly in the sea, and immediately the two fleets were galvanized into furious activity: orders were shouted at the galley slaves, whips cracked, and everywhere the huge banks of oars creaked and groaned as they began to rise and fall in heavy rhythmic sweeps and the galleys moved slowly into action. The battle of Lepanto had begun.

The great galleasses in front of the Christian line had little effect on the Turkish advance, though they broke their line for a time and inflicted some damage and a few casualties; but Ali Pasha's men knew their business, and they passed between these Christian outposts with the minimum of fuss and re-formed in line abreast at once. Scirocco, in command of the Turkish right, was the first to make contact with the enemy, attacking Barbarigo's Venetian squadron and at the same time trying to outflank the Christian galleys by passing between them and the shore; but as the guns thundered and the arquebusiers on both sides tried to pick off their enemies with small-arms' fire, galleys ramming and grappling each other in hand-to-hand fighting, the superior discipline of the men of Venice and the better build of the ships of St Mark began to tell, and it was not long before many of Scirocco's ships had either been sunk or driven on to the shore. Some of the Turkish crews tried to escape inland but few succeeded, for the Venetians, wild with excitement, chased them and cut them down. Scirocco himself was wounded as his galley was rammed, falling into the sea where he might have been left to drown or to cling to a piece of wreckage until rescued, if the splendour of his clothing had not marked him as a man of importance; spotted by a group of Venetians, however, he was pulled out of the water, and his head was struck off. The fighting near the shore was so confused and bloody that no one knew which way the battle there was going; at the height of it Barbarigo, too, his galley attacked from all sides, was hit by an arrow and mortally wounded, though he did not die until a few days later.

Meanwhile in the centre a furious duel developed between Don

John of Austria and Ali Pasha, whose ships rammed each other with such violence that the beaked prow of the *Sultana* became jammed in the rigging of *La Real*. Don John had held the fire of his bow guns until just before colliding with his enemy, and they had inflicted great damage as they had raked the *Sultana*'s deck, ploughing through the soldiers massed on it in readiness to board their enemy at the moment of impact, so that when the two ships did collide the deck of the Turkish flagship was already littered with corpses and screaming men. As supporting vessels of both sides came to the aid of their commanders, a great knot of entangled ships, locked together and unable to move or manoeuvre, became a confused battlefield over which boarding parties from both sides scrambled, while arquebusiers perched in the jungle of rigging fired at each other and at the struggling mass of men below them on the ships' decks. For two hours the fighting raged without either side gaining much advantage over the other; but the Christian artillery was superior to the Turkish guns, and Ali Pasha's ships were not so easily defended from boarding parties as the Christian galleys, so that most of the hand-to-hand fighting took place on Turkish decks and gradually the battle began to go against them. The *Sultana* itself was fiercely defended by 300 Janissaries, and more than once boarding parties from *La Real* were forced to retreat after inflicting heavy casualties on the defenders; but eventually Don John led an attack in person with such dash that his men captured half the ship's bridge before the Turks could recover. But recover they did, and Ali Pasha, not to be outdone by his Christian rival, led a furious counter-attack against the boarders, which seemed to be on the point of success when the Ottoman commander fell, mortally wounded by a bullet. A Spanish soldier immediately cut off his head (to Don John's horrified disgust, it was said), and someone hoisted it to the top of the mast of *La Real*, where it could be seen by half the Turkish fleet. Enraged by the sight, the Turks fought back with such fury that for a time the tide of battle turned once again against the Christians. Don John, realizing that the crisis of the day was fast approaching, summoned his reserve squadron under the Marquess of Santa Cruz to his aid, and the arrival of these fresh troops was decisive; within minutes the *Sultana* was captured, and although the Turks tried desperately to recapture it they failed, and the battle in the centre was as good as won by the Christians. Everywhere triumphant and excited Spaniards were setting free the galley slaves in captured enemy ships, arming them with pikes and swords and anything which could be used as a weapon and letting them loose upon their former masters, whom they slaughtered with relish and savage enjoyment, venting the hatred accumulated over months and sometimes years of crushing servitude and brutal ill treatment; and as the Turkish centre collapsed, the news spread throughout the fleet that Scirocco's squadron to landward had been annihilated by Barbarigo's Venetians, every single Turkish ship having been either captured, sunk or driven ashore.

But out to sea Gian Andrea Doria had fared less well. His opponent, Uluj Ali, was an accomplished naval tactician who had learned his trade during a lifetime of warfare at sea as a corsair, and as the battle began he made a move to outflank his adversary. Doria immediately ordered his galleys to row out to sea southwards in order to frustrate the Turkish manoeuvre, and when they did so Uluj Ali saw his opportunity and slipped through the gap opened up in the Christian line to attack Don John's ships in the rear. He was prevented from doing so by the Maltese galleys of the Knights of St John, upon whom his Algerines turned with a ferocity born of long years of rivalry and hatred; the Knights, outnumbered by their enemies, fought with their customary bravery, but they were badly mauled and their flagship was captured together with the Grand Prior of Malta and the Spanish governor of Messina, who, for some reason, was promptly decapitated by Uluj Ali in person. The Knights would have fared much worse, however, if the battle elsewhere had not gone so badly for the other Turkish squadrons, for they were virtually at the mercy of Uluj Ali when he decided to make his escape while the going was still good; and despite a belated attempt by Doria to intercept him, he succeeded in doing so. At the head of forty galleys with every sail they possessed set to catch a most opportune offshore evening breeze, he sailed through the centre of Doria's ships almost as though he was taking part in a regatta at home in the Bay of Algiers. For Doria it was an inglorious end to the battle in which he and he alone had signally failed to play the part allotted to him; his failure to engage Uluj Ali, compounded as it was by his failure to prevent his escape, was the one thing to mar the completeness of the Christian victory.

When news of the defeat of the Turks at Lepanto reached the capitals of Europe, the Christian world exulted; for years people had become accustomed to hearing of Turkish victories on land and even more frequently at sea, and at first they could hardly believe that their terrible enemies had suffered a defeat of such catastrophic magnitude as that inflicted on them by the combined fleets of the Holy League. Of the Turks, 30,000 had been killed or drowned, while 280 of their ships had been either destroyed or captured and 15,000 Christian galley slaves had been set free. It was almost too good to be true. Pope Pius V let it be known that he had received news of the victory by divine communication at the moment of Ali Pasha's death, and that he had immediately fallen on his knees in an ecstasy of thankfulness; when a more mundane messenger from Don John of Austria arrived in due course, he greeted him with the words from the fourth Gospel: 'There was a man sent from God, whose name was John,' and everyone was delighted by the aptness of the quotation. Venice greeted the first ships to return to the city, as they sailed into the lagoon trailing captured Turkish flags in the sea behind them, with rapture; salvoes of guns were fired in St Mark's Square as the crews were fêted. Spain, too, was swept by a great tide of excitement and rejoicing, and in England a peal of bells from the tower of St Martin-in-the-Fields in London rang out to mark the 'overthrow of the Turk', while bonfires were lit in towns and villages throughout the land and sermons preached on the manifold mercies of God. Even in France, for so long a partner in the 'impious alliance' with infidel Turkey, the King grudgingly ordered a *Te Deum* to be sung for the defeat of his ally, Selim the Sot. Of course, there had been losses on the Christian side too; Don John had lost fifteen galleys and 8,000 men, but in the heady atmosphere of rejoicing by the living only those who had been bereaved remembered the dead. Lepanto, everyone agreed, was the greatest Christian victory over Islam that the world had ever seen.

But was it? With impressive unanimity, historians have followed one another in declaring that it was nothing of the sort; for Uluj Ali succeeded in reaching Constantinople with the forty ships which had escaped with him after the battle, supplemented by forty-three others collected from various ports *en route*, and the loss of the vessels which did not survive the battle of Lepanto was very soon made good with new ships. At first, the Turks were appalled by the losses in both men and ships inflicted on them; Selim was so furious that he ordered a massacre of all Spaniards and Venetians in his dominions; but as tempers cooled, the Grand Vizier Sokollu persuaded the Sultan to countermand his homicidal decree and instead to order every shipwright and gunsmith in the Ottoman Empire to set to work to repair the damage done to the Ottoman fleet. As a result, within a few months another Turkish fleet almost as numerous as that lost at Lepanto was ready to sail down the Bosphorus once again to challenge the Christian nations of the West for mastery of the Mediterranean, thus rendering the victory at Lepanto null and void. All this is true, but it overlooks one thing. Years later, as Cervantes looked back on that Sunday in early October 1571, when his left hand had been shattered by a Turkish bullet, he described it in *Don Quixote* as 'that day so fortunate for Christendom, when all nations were undeceived of their error in believing that the Turks were invincible'. The Turks may have been able to make good the losses suffered by their fleet within a few months of the battle of Lepanto, but they could never repair the damage done to their reputation for invincibility or destroy the effects of their crushing defeat on Christian morale. Fernand Braudel has written, to quote him once again:

If, instead of considering what happened after Lepanto, we turn our attention to what had gone before, the victory can be seen as the end of a period of profound depression, the end of a genuine inferiority complex on the part of Christendom and a no less real Turkish supremacy. The Christian victory had halted progress towards a future which promised to be very bleak indeed. With Don John's fleet destroyed, who knows, Naples and Sicily might have been attacked, the Algerines might have tried to revive the flames of Granada or carried them into Valencia. Before joining Voltaire in his ironic comment on Lepanto, we should do well to measure the immediate impact of the victory – which was breath-taking.

It was indeed, for the tide of Turkish expansion had been running strongly ever since Mehmed the Conqueror, at the age of twenty-three, had ridden into Constantinople on horseback and claimed the throne of the Byzantine Emperors as his own by right of conquest, and the lands of western Christendom had been the principal sufferers. Indeed, pressure on Christendom was older than that, for ever since the two centuries of aggressive Christian expansion eastwards by the Crusaders had ended with the last Frankish citizens of Outremer being thrown out of Acre in the spring of 1291, the tide of history had been running against Christendom, and the forces of militant Islam had been carried further and further westwards. During the reign of Suleiman they reached their high watermark, as they washed up around the walls of Vienna and broke on the fortifications of Malta; before these two bastions of the Christian West, the Ottoman army was decisively defeated. At Lepanto, the Turkish fleet suffered the same fate, and it never again achieved the domination of the sea, which it had enjoyed for so long.

As for Suleiman himself, what is one to say? It is virtually impossible to sum up the achievements of such a man in a few words, or adequately to take his measure in a couple of paragraphs. That he was a great man and a great prince is certain; but was he greater than his ancestors, greater than Osman, and greater than Mehmed the Conqueror of Constantinople? It is like asking whether Michelangelo was greater than Giotto or Giotto greater than Cimabue. The fact is that they were very different as people, and they lived in different times, inherited different problems, and were given different opportunities, while all of them were remarkable human beings. It is almost as difficult to compare Suleiman with his contemporaries, especially with the Emperor Charles V, although there is little doubt that he himself did not find it at all difficult to do so, for modesty was not his most conspicuous virtue. He can hardly be blamed for that, however, for the first half of the sixteenth century was not a time distinguished by the bashfulness of its princes, and Suleiman was a child of his time. Indeed, despite the deep religious and cultural gulf which separated him from the Renaissance princes of western Europe, he was remarkably like them in some ways. He shared their taste for magnificence, even perhaps for the kind of ostentatious splendour which a purist might condemn as vulgar display; he shared, too, their egotism, their ruthlessness, and the tendency towards megalomania which seems to have been common to many of them; and he certainly shared some, if not all, of their least amiable characteristics, murdering his sons and old friends like Ibrahim with a cold savagery in astonishing contrast to the generosity and magnanimity of which he was capable on other occasions. But he lived in an age in which such deeds were committed by most men in positions of great power, whether they happened to be kings or popes, and few people blamed them. Suleiman, who openly admitted that his ambition was to be 'Lord of the Age', and whose jealousy and intolerance of rivals became more and more pathological as he grew older, probably exercised more real power more absolutely than any of his contemporaries, and if there is any truth in Lord Acton's celebrated *dictum* about absolute power, perhaps one of the greatest tributes one can pay to Suleiman is to say that it is surprising that the power he wielded during his long and illustrious life did not corrupt him more than it did. Moreover, it must never be forgotten that while the spotlight of history has tended to focus upon the drama of his assault upon western Christendom, his greatest achievements were probably domestic; for not only was he an outstanding jurist, but he was also one of the most highly respected and best-loved rulers in the annals of Ottoman Turkey. His achievements as a jurist have already been noticed, while as a ruler he presided over the fortunes of the vast Ottoman Empire for forty-six years, when it was at the zenith of its power and glory, and in the process won the loyalty and genuine affection of millions of his subjects; and that in itself is a tribute to his stature.

After his death, the Empire ruled by his descendants from Constantinople was destined to endure for a long time, so firmly had Suleiman built upon the foundations laid down by his forefathers, and it was not his fault that the tide of history had at last turned against the Turks in Europe's favour; but in fact it had done so, and once Suleiman was in his grave the Ottoman Empire entered a long period of gradual but inexorable decline, while western Europe, forged out of Christendom under the hammer of the Turks, went from strength to strength as her people spilled out over the whole world in three centuries of astonishing expansion. Perhaps the creation of this aggressive latter-day Europe was not the least of Suleiman's many achievements, even if he was only partly and unwittingly responsible for it and would have been horrified by such an untoward result of his lifelong struggle for pre-eminence. But even a man as great as Suleiman is not exempt from the irony of history.

Select Bibliography

To make a comprehensive list of books dealing with the men and events of the first half of the sixteenth century, even a list limited to books concerned only with the Turkish assault upon Europe, would be a massive undertaking. It would also be wholly inappropriate here. However, since there may be some people who would like to delve more deeply into the history of the period than has been attempted in this book, a few works have been singled out from the many available and are briefly described below.

General

BRAUDEL, FERNAND. *The Mediterranean and the Mediterranean World in the Age of Philip II*, 2 vols, trans. Siân Reynolds, London, 1973. Although this work refers specifically to the age of Philip II, it is equally descriptive of his father's time, giving the social, cultural and economic background to life in the Mediterranean countries in the sixteenth century more fully than any other work and in fascinating detail. As a history it is *sui generis*.

HAMMER-PURGSTALL, J. F. VON. *Geschichte des Osmanischen Reiches*, 10 vols, Pesth, 1827–35. (French trans. by B. Hellert, *Histoire de l'Empire Ottomane*, 18 vols, Paris, 1835–46.) Despite its age this is still an indispensable work, not least because it includes so many extracts from Suleiman's diary. It is not available in English.

CREASY, E. S. *History of the Ottoman Turks*, 1878 and KINROSS, LORD. *The Ottoman Centuries*, London, 1977. Two one-volume histories of the Ottoman Turks, one rather out-of-date and one rather dull, covering the rise and fall of Turkish fortunes from the founding of the Ottoman state down to modern times.

INALCIK, HALIL. *The Ottoman Empire*, London, 1973. A study by the Turkish Professor of History in the University of Ankara of the social, economic and cultural life of Ottoman Turkey.

LEWIS, RAPHAELA. *Everyday Life in Ottoman Turkey*, London, 1971. A less specialized social history of the Ottoman Turks than Professor Inalcik's work.

LYBYER, A. H. *The Government of the Ottoman Empire in the time of Suleiman the Magnificent*, Cambridge, Mass., 1913. The political organization of Suleiman's Empire and the machinery of government.

VAMBÉRY, A. *Hungary in Ancient, Medieval and Modern Times*, London, 1887. Old-fashioned but a mine of information on a subject about which few people seem to have written in English.

BUSBECQ, OGIER GHISELIN DE. *Letters*, Oxford, 1927. An invaluable contemporary account of life at Suleiman's court and in Ottoman Turkey during his reign by the imperial ambassador to Constantinople from 1554 to 1562.

Biographies

MERRIMAN, R. B. *Suleiman the Magnificent*, Cambridge, Mass., 1944. An American life of Suleiman and the only readily available biography of him in English.

TYLER, ROYALL. *The Emperor Charles V*, London, 1956. One of many biographies of Charles, but by far the best. The author paints a picture both of the man and his age which is as enjoyable to read as it is scholarly.

TERRASSE, CHARLES, *François Ier, le roi et le règne*, 2 vols, Paris, 1945. The best of many available lives of Francis I and better than any in English.

BRADFORD, ERNLE. *The Sultan's Admiral, Life of Barbarossa*, London, 1969. A good account of the naval warfare of the day and its principal Turkish exponent.

Military History

BROCKMAN, ERIC. *The Two Sieges of Rhodes, 1480–1522* (London, 1969). A detailed account of the battle.

TAUER, F. *Histoire de la campagne du Sultan Suleiman Ier contre Belgrade en 1521*, Prague, 1924.

PAVET DE COURTELLE, M. *Histoire de la campagne de Mohács par Kemal Pasha Zadeh*, Paris, 1859.

BRADFORD, ERNLE. *The Great Siege*, London, 1961. A detailed account of the siege of Malta.

KHALIFEH, HAJJI. *The History of the Maritime Wars of the Turks*, trans. by James Mitchell, London, 1831.

The above are five books which may be of interest to those wishing to read more about the wars of Suleiman's time. Bradford's account of the siege of Malta and Brockman's history of the battle for Rhodes both make highly enjoyable reading as well as being informative.

Index